Alexander Schellinger, Philipp Steinberg (eds.)
The Future of the Eurozone

Political Science | Volume 51

ALEXANDER SCHELLINGER, PHILIPP STEINBERG (EDS.)

The Future of the Eurozone
How to Keep Europe Together:
A Progressive Perspective from Germany

[transcript]

This publication is based on a study conducted at the Friedrich-Ebert-Stiftung, International Political Analysis.

We want to especially thank Dr. Dominika Biegon at the Friedrich-Ebert-Stiftung whose expertise on European social and economic policy has greatly benefited this project.

Bibliographic information published by the Deutsche Nationalbibliothek
The Deutsche Nationalbibliothek lists this publication in the Deutsche Nationalbibliografie; detailed bibliographic data are available in the Internet at http://dnb.d-nb.de

© 2017 transcript Verlag, Bielefeld

All rights reserved. No part of this book may be reprinted or reproduced or utilized in any form or by any electronic, mechanical, or other means, now known or hereafter invented, including photocopying and recording, or in any information storage or retrieval system, without permission in writing from the publisher.

Cover layout: Kordula Röckenhaus, Bielefeld
Proofread by James Turner
Translated by James Turner, Meredith Dale, Paul Hockenos
Printed and bound in Great Britain by Marston Book Services Ltd, Oxfordshire
Print-ISBN 978-3-8376-4081-6
PDF-ISBN 978-3-8394-4081-0
EPUB-ISBN 978-3-7328-4081-6

Contents

1. Introduction: The future of the Eurozone
   Alexander Schellinger and Philipp Steinberg | 7

PART I: CHALLENGES

2. Has the Euro robbed Europe of democracy?
   Christian Beck | 19

3. The flaws in the design of the Economic and Monetary Union
   Henrik Enderlein | 37

4. The social dimension of the Eurozone
   Michael Dauderstädt | 51

PART II: POLITICS, POWER, IDEAS

5. Germany's own special path?
   Fundamental economic principles underlying German policy
   Mark Schieritz | 69

6. Which reform path for the Eurozone?
   A mapping of political actors and their influence in the German debate
   Björn Hacker and Cédric M. Koch | 81

7. The legal framework for reform projects and the role of the German Federal Constitutional Court
   Franz C. Mayer | 101

PART III: REFORM OPTIONS

8. Rethinking economic policy – a better fiscal framework for the Eurozone
   Jeromin Zettelmeyer | 123

9. An institutional framework for a reformed Eurozone
   Daniela Schwarzer | 145

10. Developing the social dimension
    Peter Becker | 161

11. Plan B – retreat from integration?
    Possibilities, risks and costs
    Armin Steinbach | 175

12. Three scenarios for the Eurozone – and conclusions
    Alexander Schellinger and Philipp Steinberg | 189

Authors | 197

1. Introduction: The future of the Eurozone

Alexander Schellinger and Philipp Steinberg

The British vote to leave the EU ("Brexit") in June 2016 plunged the Community into its deepest crisis since the signing of the Treaties of Rome in 1957. The Union is set to lose a Member State for the first time in its history. This is the fourth shock to rock the foundations of the European project within just a few years, following the Euro crisis, the war in Ukraine and the refugee crisis. Anti-European forces are gaining ground across Europe and elsewhere. Doubts about the Union are growing, along with a belief that fundamental problems can better be resolved by the nation-state.

Yet the EU has a track record of using crises as opportunities to break deadlocks and bridge political rifts. The chances for major reform are not so slim, despite the state of the EU and the Eurozone, which many regard as troubled. In fact, pending reforms could be bundled into a European package including the Eurozone, with the Brexit negotiations acting as a catalyst. The Fiscal Compact must anyway be reviewed by 2017 and the debate over adapting and restructuring the Multiannual Financial Framework has already begun. In this volume we lay out proposals for reform of the Eurozone and of the EU as a whole, along the way reprising the relevant European debates. We proceed in three steps:

We begin by analysing the Eurozone's problems in their political, economic and social dimensions. We move on to investigate the factors shaping European decision-making and reform proposals. Finally, we present reforms that offer effective solutions to the Euro crisis in political, economic and social terms. For all the proposals we make, we outline the legal framework and requirements and, given the difficulties in finding unanimity on Treaty amendments, indicate measures below that threshold wherever possible.

The challenges faced by the Union of 28 or 27 Member States are of such complexity that it would appear sensible to concentrate on the smaller Eurozone, the nineteen Member States that use the Euro as their currency. Nevertheless, many of the observations and solutions we describe can also be applied to the EU as a whole. Although the institutions of the Eurozone and EU overlap in significant respects and are indeed in certain respects identical, the Eurozone has developed a political dynamic and depth of integration of its own warranting separate analysis.

While this volume offers a perspective from Germany, we aim to develop solutions as a contribution to the European debate. We concentrate on Germany not only because we have been able to follow developments here very closely in recent years and because Germany has assumed a central role in the Eurozone and the EU, but also because we believe that understanding the specifics of the discussion in Germany is of great importance for further reforms.

ANALYTICAL FRAMEWORK AND CONTENT

We are well aware of the political context and the obstacles to change within the Eurozone (and even more so in the EU as a whole). This led us to examine the conditions for reforms. We consider three strands or processes: Problems, politics and policies.[1] "Problems" in this context mean strong and sustained pressure in a particular area (such as the Brexit negotiations with the United Kingdom, high unemployment or a financial crisis). "Politics" stands for the positions and interests of political actors, with public debates and elections playing a central role. Successful "policies" are reform proposals that offer answers to policy problems and are taken up by politicians. These processes make up the building block of this volume: In part one we examine the problems of the Eurozone. In part two our authors examine the politically relevant actors in Germany. And in part three we lay out reform proposals, taking into account the problems of the Eurozone and the political situation as a whole.

We begin in part one by examining the problems from the political, economic and social perspective. In Chapter 2 Christian Beck examines the institutional problems of the Eurozone, including those created by the Brexit vote. Henrik Enderlein outlines the economic challenges of the Eurozone as a monetary union in Chapter 3, paying particular attention to the persistent divergence between the Member States, the single monetary policy of the European Central Bank and the difficulties of fiscal policy coordination. In Chapter 4 Michael Dauderstädt takes up the social challenges faced by the Eurozone, including unemployment, income distribution and poverty, and examines the effects of the Economic and Monetary Union (EMU) on these.

In part two, we move on to analyse the central actors in the German political discourse. Mark Schieritz traces the economic policy debate in Chapter 5 and shows why its trajectory in Germany differs from most other countries. In Chapter 6 Björn Hacker and Cédric M. Koch identify the decisive political actors in government, parties and civil society and outline their positions – and contradictions – on Europe. On the basis of those positions, they formulate a series of conditions for successful reforms. In Chapter 7 Franz C. Mayer relates the development of European law in recent years, analyses the role of the German Federal Constitutional Court and describes how the central proposals presented in this volume would be implemented legally.

In the final part we present specific reform proposals. In Chapter 8 Jeromin Zettelmeyer proposes a Eurozone budget and greater budgetary flexibility for Member States to increase growth and employment, along with the creation of a debt restructuring mechanism. In the context of the Brexit vote, Daniela Schwarzer proposes institutional reforms of the Eurozone (Chapter 9). In Chapter 10 Peter Becker presents ideas on minimum social standards and a European short-time work allowance to address the social challenges, while in Chapter 11 Armin Steinbach explores the costs and risks of reversing integration and shows how that would not solve the problems. In the last Chapter we draw together the findings and venture an outlook on possible future developments.

THE DEBATE THUS FAR

Ever since the outbreak of the Euro crisis analysts have pointed to the structural problems of the Economic and Monetary Union (EMU). One central argument is that the Member States lost their economic flexibility without creating new compensating mechanisms at the Eurozone level.[2] The members of the Eurozone have relinquished macroeconomic policy instruments (for example the ability to adjust national exchange rates), while strict budgetary rules at the Eurozone level constrain their fiscal options. Moreover, many economists criticise the anti-cyclical configuration of the Eurozone's monetary and economic policies. The charge was for a long time directed especially at the European Central Bank and its focus on price stability and strict budgetary rules, and naturally above all at the bailout programmes for the crisis-stricken countries of southern Europe and Ireland. While these analyses have done a great deal to illuminate the relationship between monetary and economic policy between the Member States and the EMU as a whole,[3] their worst fears – the collapse or break-up of the Eurozone – have thus far proved unfounded. One reason for this may be that since the outbreak of the crisis the statute of the European Central Bank and the new fiscal rules have been interpreted much less restrictively than many may have expected; quite the opposite in fact: New ways were found to exploit the flexibility that was included in the framework.

This brings us to the political questions of the Eurozone. Whereas economists have largely concentrated on the mechanisms by which EMU functions, political scientists and legal scholars tend to concentrate on its political and social institutions. One strand, for example, uses the tools of political economy to examine how national economic models interact in the Eurozone (in particular, concerning differences in wage formation systems).[4] Institutional analysis focus on both the power relation between Member States and the European institutions (in particular, Germany's new role) and the role of inter-governmental agreements and informal coordination processes in the EU's legal system. Yet another set of literature analyses the central decision-making actors and institutions at the European level. Here there is often criticism of democratic deficits in Member-State-driven (intergovernmental) agreements and the role of national governments vis-à-vis parliaments. On the whole, these contributions highlight the political, social and legal fundamentals of the Eurozone.[5]

Our hope is that this volume succeeds in bringing together both debates and perspectives. While work on the functioning of the EMU has generated innovative and sophisticated reform proposals that have found their way into the political process, these economic analyses generally concentrate on very complex technical issues while neglecting important political/institutional aspects. In political science literature the problem is reversed: Here central political problems are spotlighted but – with a handful of notable exceptions – rarely followed up with concrete reform proposals.[6] In this volume we seek to develop reform proposals that find answers to both the technical and the political challenges facing the Eurozone. Only if both perspectives can be brought together and if we entertain a broad and well-informed public debate does the Eurozone (and the EU) have a future.

OUR ARGUMENT

On the basis of the contributions presented in this volume, our argument is made up of three building blocks:

1. We argue that the Eurozone crisis is not primarily – still less exclusively – an economic crisis, but also a political and social crisis. It is clear to us that what the EU and the Eurozone are experiencing is above all a fundamental political crisis in the sense of the inefficiency of European decisions and the dominance of the executives in a time of growing populism in most Member States. Worse still is the EU's apparent or actual failure to fulfil its promise of prosperity. Economic and social divergence are increasing steadily both within and especially between the Member States. We do not believe that resolving the crisis – understood as a currency crisis – will be enough to lastingly consolidate the Eurozone and the EU.
2. The outcomes of the reform process will depend both on interests, for example of national governments, and on ideas and institutions, for example in the sense of economic beliefs and the possibilities and limits of

European Treaties. This needs to be taken into account when analysing past political decisions – and when developing new reform proposals. Unlike other political commentators, we do not believe that the outcomes of the crisis management of recent years can be attributed exclusively to either national interests (related for example to debtor and creditor roles) or sets of ideologies (such as German "ordo-liberalism"). Because the political system of the EU and the Eurozone is characterised by a multitude of actors with veto rights, the status quo is especially hard to change and the need for compromise is exceptionally great. We therefore want to develop ideas that promote political coalitions over and above opposing interests, and not only abide by the rules of existing institutions but also contribute to their development.
3. We also argue that the Eurozone needs to be strengthened as a political, economic and social union. The Eurozone can only endure as a political union if it has an effective and democratic decision-making process. As an economic entity the Eurozone requires significantly better coordination of national economic, financial and budgetary policies for its stability and growth. Next to coordination of national policies, instruments need to be developed at the Eurozone level to implement policies across the union as a whole. As a social entity the Eurozone must improve social equality within and between its Member States. European integration has progressed too far for the social question to be resolvable within the national context alone. We are convinced that this will also be expedient for the EU as a whole.

Our proposals will also encounter scepticism. But we are firmly convinced that an economically successful, democratic and socially just Eurozone is the best – and perhaps also the only – answer to the growing dangers of populism and Euroscepticism demonstrated perhaps most clearly by the Brexit vote. It is our belief that the Eurozone is not in fact facing a binary choice between a European federal state or club of nation-states. Europe will continue to pursue a third way.

THE CHALLENGES

The problems exposed in the course of the financial and Euro crisis underline the urgency of reforming the EMU. The need is diminished neither by the measures named above nor by better crisis management for example through the European Stability Mechanism. The underlying problem is excessive economic and social divergence combined with a lack of instruments suitable for reducing it. The main mechanism by which EU Member States have in the past been able to stimulate competitiveness and growth at least for a time – namely by devaluing their national currency – is no longer available. Instead they must conduct a real devaluation, in particular by reducing unit labour costs.

Useful mechanisms – such as the macroeconomic imbalance procedure – that take account of the entire Eurozone (and EU) remain limited, because instruments for cushioning symmetrical and asymmetrical shocks are lacking. The Stability and Growth Pact is configured to prevent excessive national deficits, which means that the policies it produces can be either too loose (in an upturn) or too strict (in a downturn). At the same time there are no supra-national balancing mechanisms, for example in the form of "automatic stabilisers", to provide for Eurozone-wide growth and convergence programmes. The constraints on national budget policies have been tightened and monitoring stepped up, but without creating instruments to boost growth and employment. The European Central Bank is alone in seeking to compensate this design fault through its monetary policy; indeed, it is the only actor with relevant powers. But it cannot succeed on its own, even if we are willing to accept the impacts on savings.

The Euro crisis has strengthened inter-governmentalism, creating an even more complex system that hampers effective and democratic decision-making. During the Euro crisis, inter-governmental solutions often represented the only possible option. The existing instruments were too weak and the disagreements between national governments too large. But the great flaw of European policy over the past five years has been to neglect to move towards an effective and democratic decision-making process at the supranational level. Instead of utilising inter-governmentalism as a means to an end, it became an end itself.

The existing coordination instruments amount to little more than ritualised recommendations and reports; only in the monitoring of national budgets are there more robust rights of intervention (and yet budgetary coordination between Eurozone states still leaves a great deal to be desired). The limits to European rules and laws are fundamentally political in nature. Even with strengthened budgetary coordination instruments such as the Fiscal Compact, Six-Pack and Two-Pack, it is inevitable that European rules will be bent and broken in the context of national elections and national responsibilities.[7] Even more problematic than the inadequate observance and application of rules is the underlying assumption of the rules-driven approach in the EMU (in particular, in budgetary policy). While institutionalized rules can enhance the stability and sustainability of political action, they cannot and must not substitute political decision-making. Indeed, the focus on a purely rule-dominated economic policy is one of the causes of the Eurozone's economic problems. The belief that ever stricter budgetary rules would represent a sufficient economic policy instrument for the Eurozone if they were only obeyed fails to account for the multidimensional challenges of a growth- and employment-driven economic policy.

The dynamic of European integration has largely been economic in nature. But the Single Market and the EMU can also curtail and threaten social policy achievements at the national level. The Eurozone's lack of policy instruments influences the especially tangible fields of social and employment policy and threatens the existence of the Eurozone as the core of the EU. Historically, social and employment policy are secondary in the EU/Eurozone.[8] This constitutional subsidiarity has been further exacerbated by economic integration in the course of the Euro crisis. Without macroeconomic instruments offering greater flexibility of adjustment, internal devaluations will continue to be conducted primarily through wages (and prices). This can lead to falling incomes and excessive austerity, as demonstrated by the painful adjustment programmes in the crisis states. But unemployment, inequality and poverty are also rising or are persistently high in other Member States, while the EU's social dimension still remains in its infancy. In almost all areas – from employment policy through labour law to labour relations – recent years have witnessed stagnation at best.

We are convinced that it is necessary to challenge some of the fundamental principles of the Maastricht regime. Strengthening the Eurozone will demand more than minor reforms of existing rules that are largely restricted to budgetary matters. Observing the rules is necessary and important. But that will not repair the underlying mistakes. The objective must be to create economic policy instruments to improve the viability of the Economic and Monetary Union and to stop and reverse the economic and social divergence processes. In a common currency area – even if it is not an optimal currency area and is not going to become one any time soon – fiscal instruments at Eurozone level will need to at least supplement the existing national ones. So for us the questions of governance and of economic and social policy are central.

Towards a sustainable economic governance

The greater the convergence of the EU economies, the smaller the costs of cushioning imbalances. Existing supply-side mechanisms (such as rules for national budgets) need to be supplemented with demand-side instruments to reduce existing asymmetries.

In the form of a common fiscal capacity (in the sense of own resources for the Eurozone, for example in the form of a Eurozone budget – as proposed by the President of France, Emmanuel Macron) a convergence instrument should be established to reduce structural differences within the Eurozone.

This could be a special instrument to increase growth and convergence in the Eurozone, similar to the EU's structural funds. Such a mechanism would be funded either through new Eurozone resources (such as a proportion of the revenues from a financial transaction tax or a small share of national corporation taxes), a new Eurozone tax or direct contributions from the Eurozone states.

Such a convergence instrument would be activated politically and could be supplemented with an automatic stabilisation mechanism – in other words a macroeconomic instrument – to counteract the effects of economic downturn (analogous to the effect of national unemployment insurance systems). Given the expected difficulty of establishing a European unemployment insurance system (even as a supplement to national social insurance systems), the introduction of smaller, more limited mechanisms such as a European short-time work allowance scheme should be considered.

These Eurozone instruments should also encourage growth- and employment-boosting policies by granting some fiscal flexibility to Member States. These mechanisms must ensure that the enlarged policy space does not serve to expand consumption without increasing sustainable investment. First of all, this requires effective governance within the Eurozone. The Commission needs to be empowered not only to apply a set of rules but also to weigh up complex economic choices.

Secondly, an institutionalised debt restructuring mechanism could be introduced in the Eurozone, to be activated when pre-defined thresholds were crossed. Such a mechanism could fulfil a dual function:

- It would ensure that the no-bailout clause (exclusion of community liability for debts of individual Member States) was observed, and avoid wasting funds bailing out insolvent Member States. Even before it was used, such a mechanism – depending on its details – would also send a message to the markets on refinancing costs.
- It would save Member States from having to implement excessive internal devaluations (especially lowering social spending, wages and salaries) which are very difficult to carry through in a democratic society.

Such an ambitious set of economic instruments would need to be accompanied by new and improved institutional structures to enhance the efficiency of decision-making processes and democratic accountability. Collective (central) coordination would need to be reinforced, for example through a Eurozone finance minister, but with democratic control by a Eurozone chamber in the European Parliament. The objective here would be to expand policy space and political responsibility: If enhanced powers are to be used at the Eurozone level there must be democratic accountability.

THE SOCIAL DIMENSION

Under the given conditions, the social dimension of the Eurozone can and must be developed, too. Alongside economic aspects, the EMU also requires social and employment convergence, for example through coordinated national reforms of labour market and social policies. A European short-time work allowance scheme could serve as an automatic stabiliser. Resembling a European unemployment insurance system, it would offer support at the level of individual actors and could therefore be especially effective. Additionally, legally binding European frameworks provisions and minimum standards could be defined: For example, a floor for national minimum benefits, reintegration of long-term unemployed, or national minimum wages. Coordination between the social partners at Eurozone level should be improved through closer integration in the European Semester, expansion of European co-determination and the establishment of European coordination instruments between national social partners. To us it is clear that the Eurozone can only survive in the long term if next to financial and economic actors, trade unions are included in the decision-making process, if the hard economic requirements are balanced by binding social policy measures and if workers' representation at EU level continues to improve.

NOTES

1 | We base our framework on the findings of the classical policy research after John W. Kingdon: Kingdon, John W. (2003 [1984]): Agendas, Alternatives and Public Policies. New York: Longman.
2 | The Theory of Optimum Currency Areas forms an important starting point. It demonstrates that in a monetary union shocks can no longer be cushioned by depreciating national currencies. With internal flexibility through labour mobility being comparatively weak in the Economic and Monetary Union, the European Central Bank adjusting its interest rate for the currency area as a whole and the absence of other fiscal mechanisms, economic shocks cannot be cushioned across the economy as a whole. See Scharpf, Fritz W. (2011): Monetary Union, Fiscal Crisis and the Preemption of Democracy, Max-Planck-Institut für Gesellschaftsforschung Discussion Paper 11/11.
3 | See for example Enderlein, Henrik/Bofinger, Peter et al. (2012): Completing the Euro: A Road Map towards Fiscal Union in Europe: Report of the "Tommaso Padoa-Schioppa Group", http://www.institutdelors.eu/media/completingtheeuroreportpadoa-schioppa groupnejune2012.pdf?pdf=ok (accessed 12 May 2016).
4 | Iversen, Torben/Soskice, David et al. (2016): The Eurozone and Political Economic Institutions, Annual Review of Political Science, vol. 19.
5 | See the excellently edited volume Matthijs, Matthias/Blyth, Mark (eds.) (2015): The Future of the Euro. New York: Oxford University Press.

6 | See for example Bogdandy, Armin von/Calliess, Christian et al. (2013): Aufbruch in die Euro-Union, http://glienickergruppe.eu/de/aufbruch-in-die-eurounion/ (accessed 12 May 2016).

7 | The Six-Pack and Two-Pack are secondary EU law instruments to improve fiscal coordination by strengthening the deficit procedure and coordinating national budget planning. The Fiscal Compact requires budget rules ("debt brakes") to be included in each Member State's national constitution.

8 | On the history of the EU's social dimension see Schellinger, Alexander (2016): EU Labor Market Policy: Ideas, Thought Communities and Policy Change. Basingstoke: Palgrave Macmillan.

Part I: Challenges

2. Has the Euro robbed Europe of democracy?

Christian Beck

THE RULES OF THE EUROZONE AND WHY THEY DO NOT WORK

The project of Europe is currently cause for concern. European governments are not prepared to formulate a common policy to overcome the social divide in Europe, to remedy the Euro's instability, to avert the threat of climate collapse, to solve the refugee crisis, or to combat terrorism. The impression that the European institutions are systematically overburdened makes it possible for populists to paint a picture of the European common project that is worse than it really is. They gush about national sovereignty as if it is really a viable solution.

Yet, they offer nothing but pseudo-solutions. Right-wing populists, but also "left-wing" parties with nationalist arguments, say that the EU, and especially the Euro, jeopardize democracy. And in fact, the billions in loans to Greece in exchange for its tightening the purse strings was rejected by the Greek population and, in surveys, by the majority of Germans, too – yet it happened anyway. Nevertheless, voters enabled the governing parties in both Athens and Berlin to continue to remain in office after these decisions. This means that the citizens of both countries want to keep the Euro. The anti-EU rhetoric of the major mainstream parties, however, is picked up and carried forward by the others.

France's former president Nicolas Sarkozy speaks of wanting to "take back 50 per cent of the EU's powers" – though without stating which ones. Italy's conservative opposition argues the same way. The divided conservatives led the United Kingdom into a referendum on the EU. In order to understand political and institutional problems, we need to take a closer look.

European rules, national decisions: How the Economic and Monetary Union is supposed to work

Economic and Monetary Union (EMU) – on this politicians from many parties and countries agree took away immeasurable decision-making leeway from the democracies of the Member States. The pressure exerted by European institutions on national policies is contrary to the impression of a merely technical project that politicians created when the Euro was introduced. A Stability and Growth Pact had been agreed upon, but not political union. The deal was that political decisions about government spending and tax revenue remain with the Member States and their parliaments, and be approved between governments (an intergovernmental decision). Social policies should become more alike through agreement on goals and a bit of "group pressure", but without binding obligation (the so-called "open method of coordination").

Economic and Monetary Union reduces the costs of trade with foreign countries and can thus promote trade and the economy. However, with the loss of control of interest rates, individual states also lose an important instrument for stabilising their economies and are therefore dependent on common action in the event of crises. The EMU resembles an eight-person boat rowing that can be faster than a one-person boat, yet such an advantage can only be achieved if everyone rows in synch. However, even in the 1992 Treaty of Maastricht there were no provisions for solidarity in the event of financial crisis. Rules against debt and inflation should prevent this from being necessary at all. The Maastricht criteria, as well as the Stability and Growth Pact, focused on government debt and inflation. But the dangers posed by financial markets were off-limits.

On the way to the decision as to which countries clear the hurdle of the Maastricht criteria, there was indeed a process of convergence. After the introduction of the Euro, there was a boom in southern Europe, which gave reason to hope for further convergence. Real estate bubbles and squandered investments in southern Europe, on the one hand, and a stagnation of real, inflation-adjusted wages in Germany, on the other hand, led to imbalances in productivity. These imbalances were initially ignored by euphoric investors. When the banking crisis broke out, however, many investors then panicked, and tried to get hold of capital in the form of German federal bonds – and in doing so fuelled the crisis further. Since then, companies in Germany have benefited from very low credit rates. The massive reduction in real wages in southern Europe, on the other hand, has not changed much in terms of its scandalously high unemployment.

Stability Pact: How the rules bend to the pressure of reality

Since the crisis, the approach to reform has been to strengthen the Stability and Growth Pact. The core rules of the pact are the three per cent limit for an annual budget deficit and the 60 per cent limit for the total debt of a country relative to its annual GDP. The figures are examined by the European Commission, which can also propose sanctions, but they must be imposed by the Council of Finance Ministers. Yet, this never took place although Greece, Germany, and France all broke the pact. In 2002 and 2003, Germany and France, applying political pressure, were able to prevent the pact from being invoked against them.

In the meantime, the launch of the "six-pack" and "two-pack" reforms were supposed to make the quasi-automatic sanctions stiffer. The voting rules for sanctions were also changed. In this way, political influence is kept as limited as possible. If the Commission proposes sanctions, it is no longer necessary to take an active decision, but it happens "automatically" if the Council of Ministers of Finance does not expressly declare the opposite. So far, there has been no real test of it.

However, the new harshness of the rules also led to a shift in political influence. In the past, sanctions were hindered, and now the forecast of economic data is a battlefield. The European Commission is in a predicament when it comes to forecasting economic development for the Member States: There can be adverse consequences if it enforces the rules, and if it does not apply them this weakens the rules further. If the Commission were to force all Member States to implement austerity policies, deflation could occur. Then prices fall and normal economic expectations are destroyed, which can lead to a long recession. An example of this is Japan, which has been in a recession for more than a decade. However, if the Commission allows Member States to apply the new rules in a half-hearted manner, the revised requirements lose credibility.[1]

If the economy of a country is already in a poor condition, a reduction in government spending can lessen demand. When the German government cut spending during the crisis at the beginning of the 2000s, demand in the booming countries of Southern Europe helped offset this. For the current German government, however, a balanced federal budget ("black zero") is more important than massive investment in infrastructure, education, and so on. Yet, in Germany, austerity policies have a lot of public support against the backdrop of the problems associated with the other Euro countries' debt. In the EMU, there are no hard-and-fast rules that would force the German government to adopt a different policy. And so far, the EU has none of its own financial resources to invest on a relevant scale. As long as the Commission lacks the economic policy instruments to address the side-effects of enforcement, it will probably shrink from applying the rules.

**European recommendations to sovereign parliaments:
How Europe can only make itself unpopular**

As a substitute for the lack of common EU instruments in economic policy, the Euro countries under the leadership of the European Commission should at the very least organize themselves better. Because this worked so poorly before the crisis, the so-called European semester was introduced in 2011 for a better coordination of economic policy. Budgetary problems are not to be subjected to sanctioned post facto, but rather prevented in advance. In spring, the Commission analyses the economic situation of the Union. The governments of the Member States draw up their budgets and then send them to the Commission. The latter analyses them and gives the individual countries so-called country-specific recommendations, which the Member States are then to take into account in their budgetary decisions.

The recommendations are, of course, impacted by the conservative-liberal majority in the European Commission, the Council of Finance Ministers, and the European Parliament. That is why many countries have been told to reduce government expenditure and protection provisions for employees. On the other hand, there is hardly any talk of more taxes on the wealthy. For Germany, the Commission regularly recommends the abolition of the splitting of income between spouses for purposes of taxation, the conversion of mini-jobs into permanent positions, the raising of wages in accordance with productivity, tax reductions for low-income groups, and increasing expenditures on social security and education. This advances not only national goals, but also the previously described overall European logic of an anti-cyclical fiscal policy.

Saving in the south, spending more in the north. Such a compromise policy sounds logical for Keynesian economics, yet it raises a challenge for real power politics. Tax policy and government spending have redistributive effects. Such policy requires a democratic mandate for good reasons. Since the beginning of parliamentarism, decisions on the budget have been a central parliamentary right and are therefore particularly safeguarded. In Germany, the constitutional court emphasized this in its judgment on the Lisbon Treaty: Decisions on the nature and amount of taxes levied on citizens as well as essential expenditures of the state must be taken by the Bundestag as long as the overrepresentation of small countries in the European Parliament does not correspond to the standards of the Basic Law, Germany's constitution.

The implementation of an all-European strategy is up to national parliaments. The country-specific recommendations of the European Commission cannot bind parliaments. The public procedure is supposed to convince national publics and thus put pressure on the parliaments. But this works worse from year to year. Of the Commission's 140 recommendations for reform forwarded in 2012, the Member States only implemented or made significant progress on 17 of them in 2013.[2] Of the 528 recommendations from 2014, only seven were fully implemented in 2015 – and not one in Germany.[3]

The European Commission submits the recommendations to the Council, and they are adopted there. But with this approach, none of the politicians involved can really put their own stamp on the recommendations. They are often interpreted as school grades for national policies. In the national arena, the recommendations face friendly disinterest or rejection, such as, for example, the demand for the deregulation of labour markets in France, which President

François Hollande rejected as interference in national sovereignty. Politicians have no incentive to defend the European interest as a whole to their national publics. They are elected by a national mandate, which in France does not, for example, foresee the deregulation of labour markets.

The Commission itself often finds it difficult to have its arguments heard in national public spheres. Sometimes, the opposition uses EU-criticism to attack national governments. However, more often, the country-specific recommendations are exploited by governments to criticize their neighbours. In the country concerned, however, this only increases the population's solidarity with the government and prevents a rethinking. Politicians can use unpopular demands to pose themselves as defenders of national sovereignty. This is how the blame game is played, in which Brussels is responsible for all things bad. National governments want to be responsible only for good deeds and successes. Because it is so popular to stand up to Brussels, the country-specific recommendations ultimately become a delegitimation machine for European policy.[4]

Contractual Partnerships: Self-commitment as a solution?

Due to lack of success of voluntary recommendations, the reform debate has continued. Recent proposals aim to achieve an even stronger commitment. Accordingly, the Member States and the European Commission are to conclude "contractual partnerships" in which States are committed to certain reforms, such as with regard to pensions and the labour market. In return, a new budgetary pot would be set up to provide these countries with financial support for reforms.

Even according to liberal economic theories, the dismantling of protective rules for employees does not pay off immediately, but only after a few years. Payments could help to replace these costs and be an incentive. One thought is that the obligation should also be enforceable by the European Court of Justice. This idea appeared in the Bundestag election platform of the CDU/CSU as a "pact for competitiveness". It is now also included in the coalition agreement with the SPD in the guise of "contractual reform agreements". The European Council supports the idea in principle. Specifically, however, it has not been passed yet. Even the ultimate source of the financing for the support payments is wide open.

One advantage of contractual partnerships would be that agreements between governments of the Member States would still apply even if a change of government happened in the meantime. In the summer of 2012, the newly elected Syriza government, for example, no longer wanted to implement the pledges that the previous government had agreed upon with the European Council. This advantage, however, is at the same time the main disadvantage:

Those responsible for economic policy can no longer be voted out of office. Of course, the contracts would have to be ratified by national parliaments or even by referendum. But in terms of proper democratic control, course corrections must also be possible. Otherwise, a one-time majority in a country could determine economic policy for years to come without the population subsequently being able to change it.[5]

The crisis-forged Troika and the Euro group: Transparency and democratic control are missing where the real power is

While in normal times European rules and institutions remain weak, the short-term solutions created in the heat of crises have real power but lack checks and balances. The rules created in crisis times only apply to those countries that had to pay for billions in emergency credit with painful reform commitments. Instead of external devaluation, which is not possible any longer within the EMU, internal devaluation had to be applied by cuts in wages, pensions, privatisations and the like. The power and liquidity of these states depend directly on the loans. In controlling this flow, EU institutions do have real power. Yet, to organise emergency liquidity, common EU institutions tend to be bypassed. Institutions have been formed as emergency solutions. A troika of the EU Commission, the European Central Bank and the International Monetary Fund (IMF) was formed. The main decisions when programmes are duly followed and loan tranches are handed out are made by the Eurogroup at meetings of finance ministers of Euro countries.

Such programmes have addressed areas of economic and social policy, such as wages and pensions, in which EU institutions are prohibited from enacting EU legislation. Economically, these reforms are still being analysed in detail (see Chapter 3). But, politically, too, the quickly enacted emergency measures have led to – in the long term unacceptable – informal institutions.

Still today the Euro group is an informal meeting, usually getting together before the official meeting of EU finance ministers. Its legal basis, Protocol 14 to the EU Treaties, merely provides for the group's existence and the election of a chairman.[6] Despite its wide-ranging decision-making powers, the Euro group has neither rules of procedure, nor does it issue complete protocols, nor is it accountable to any other EU institution, even though in its final declarations it regularly issues work orders to the European Commission. In particular, it is impossible for citizens to assign personal responsibility to those who have proposed and defended the idea to lower wages and pensions, or to privatize state wealth and who have opposed or failed with alternative proposals. Thus, there is not just the conflict between countries that want to save more and those that want to save less. The voters also need clarity as to who has influenced the burdens that have been imposed on the affected societies in what way. If the governments of crisis-ridden countries act in the interest of the richest and to the detriment of the economically weakest, they should not be able to hide behind the governments of other countries. These emergency rules are not acceptable as a new standard.

Rodrik's Trilemma: Democracy, nation-state, and globalisation can never be realised at the same time

The policy laid down in terms of loans for the crisis countries show what the contractual partnerships would mean for all EU Member States. The contractual partnerships would be the most extreme form of intergovernmental policy coordination. They clearly reveal a basic conflict between democracy, nation-states, and globalisation. The developmental economist Dani Rodrik has described this as a trilemma:

"you begin to understand what I will call the fundamental political trilemma of the world economy: We cannot simultaneously pursue democracy, national determination, and economic globalization. If we want to push globalization further, we have to give up the national state or democratic politics. If we want to maintain and deepen democracy, we have to choose between the nation-state and international economic integration. And if we want to keep the nation-state and self-determination, we have to choose between deepening democracy and deepening globalization."[7]

As citizens in a democratic nation-state, we expect our state to guarantee everyone the same rights of participation so that the state can legitimately weigh in on social issues. But how much democratic control do we really exercise over the world we live in? Our lives do not stop at the border of our nation-state. We buy cars, apples, and stock shares from other countries; compete with products from elsewhere; pollute rivers that flow elsewhere and air that blows elsewhere; go abroad to study; perhaps fall in love with someone from somewhere else; marry, move there. Most complex products are now mainly supplied by suppliers scattered across the EU: The result of an intensive European division of labour. "Made in Europe" now hits the nail on the head more accurately than "Made in Germany, France, or Italy".

European environmental policy began when acid rain – caused by emissions from Swedish factories – suddenly poisoned German and French forests. European environmental regulations reduced emissions; filters and nature reserves are now mandatory by EU law. The EU has slowed the dying off of forests considerably and saved the Sunday stroll in the woods for the time being. The successes of political cooperation are thus decisive for our quality of life.

As long as societies were largely secluded, it was sufficient to have democracy within states. Cross-border issues were limited; they could be left to foreign ministries and technocrats. However, the more numerous and relevant problems become, the more inefficient it is to let them be negotiated by government representatives who are accountable only to their own population. The problem is that these representatives do not consider the overall interest, but only the interests of their own country. Luxembourg's tax policy creates a few well-paid jobs there. But overall, tax competition creates huge injustices with disadvantages for almost everybody except for a few very wealthy people. In such a system, free riders can act in their own self-interest at the expense of almost everyone else.

A second problem is that democracy is restricted when solutions are negotiated between government representatives. I, as a citizen, cannot influence, do not control, let alone vote out of office most of the people at the table. In a dominant state, this is less noticeable: The smaller the country, all the more so. Citizens can give their representatives very narrow mandates in negotiations; they can even approve or reject an outcome with a referendum. But the more representatives are bound to democratic mandates at home, the more difficult it is to find a solution at the negotiating table in the first place. And so the two disadvantages of solving interstate problems are complementary: The more negotiations are based on democratic foundations, the more ineffective they become. The more freedom given to technocrats, the further their decisions are removed from citizens.[8]

Populists come to the conclusion that we should renounce globalisation and/or European integration in order to protect democracy. At the very least, everything negative (or negatively perceived) should be stopped at the border: People seeking protection, international crime, food and toys laced with poison. But how realistic is this? Do we give up Facebook, Google and iPhones if these companies do not comply with our tax laws? Is it enough to fight climate change by planting a few new trees in Germany while others make quick money by ignoring the environment?

But what if we admit that we cannot turn our backs on globalisation? What if we want to continue to enjoy globalisation's advantages? Or that as a single country we can no longer do anything against tightly intertwined banks and financial markets? Then we have to try to make democracy as good as possible – despite the problems. Then it is better if we, together with other Europeans, choose a common parliament whose rules banks cannot easily circumvent. Then it is better to hammer out data-protection standards in the European Parliament, which Facebook in Ireland also has to respect. If most Germans preferred national security over international quality, they would still use StudiVZ.[9]

Negotiating with multinational corporations on an equal basis is not something that 80 million Germans can do; but a continental market with 500 million inhabitants who are among the richest in the world can do so. However, this form of equality and respect can only be achieved together. Members of the European Parliament, who established European data-protection standards, were for the most part not Germans, and this would also have been the case if the negotiations were purely intergovernmental. But they represent European parties that want to compete and be elected everywhere in Europe. MEPs of different countries who are, however, members of the same party close ranks since they depend on the success of their European party also in other Member States if they want – over the long term – to turn their ideas into policies. In contrast to intergovernmental negotiations, every participant in the negotiation process must above all be completely transparent and act in full view of the public. If negotiations between the finance ministers in the EU Council were as transparent as the work of the European Parliament, a financial transaction tax would probably already exist. Instead, the finance ministers use the non-public nature of their negotiations to hide behind one another. Everyone wanted to reach an agreement, they say, but the others did not allow it. Of course, finance ministers have to reflect the will of their parliaments. But the other finance ministers who are allegedly to blame are then unfortunately not available to question national ministers' political alibis. The final vote in the Council is public, but there is no accountability before compromise and unanimity are achieved. Negotiations on exceptions worth billions, negotiators blocking compromises – all of this happens behind closed doors. If it is to the detriment of financial stability and citizens, there will be no financial transaction tax, no one wants to be responsible. The Bundestag cannot even examine whether the federal government is acting the way that the Bundestag stipulated.

Excursion on tax policy: Where the trilemma will be particularly expensive

Tax policy is a particularly good place to see the effects of different methods of governing Europe. Tax competition with weak coordination of national policy in the alleged "national" interest has reduced tax revenues in Europe by one-third in 20 years. These tax cuts, however, did not end up in the pockets of very many EU citizens, but rather in the pockets of the very wealthy. Multinational corporations have also been able to construct elaborate tax vehicles with huge departments specialising in such things in order to save on taxes. But because Starbucks pays almost no taxes, the traditional café next door pays more.

The governments of many states have not been victims, but rather perpetrators in the process. Luxembourg Leaks, Panama Leaks: Bold whistleblowers like Antoine Deltour and "John Doe" have uncovered the complicity of states and companies. States deliberately build loopholes in order to attract capital away from one another and to prop up financial industries. Luxembourg has benefited from many very well-paid jobs. In the Netherlands too, some banks and lawyers have been enabled to profit from the bustling activity of the tax-dumping supplier industry. But as a whole, EU countries have lost many more billions in taxation, while at the same time giving companies dominating markets unjust advantages over small and medium-sized companies, thereby destroying markets – and walking roughshod over many citizens' sense of fairness.

While the EU Council puts on the brakes, the European Parliament takes up the scandal, establishing an investigation committee. The European Commission demands back unjust financial benefits from companies. Step by step, the EP urges Member States to adopt better common rules. More transparency on ownership of companies in the future is supposed to prevent fraud by means of offshore companies. An exchange of information between states and fiscal authorities is to eliminate the advantages that complicated financial constructs enjoy, but that ordinary consumers do not. The fight regularly threatens to get lost in detail. But the pressure of a parliament and its committees which can all be followed live on the Internet makes it much more difficult for lobbyists for special interests to push decisions in their favour.

Why is the Eurozone not moving forward?

The Member States are the masters of the Treaties – and want to remain so

Dani Rodrik's trilemma is clear: If we do not give up European integration and globalisation, and still want to keep democracy, democracy has to become European. But because of the way the EU is built, this sounds easier than it is. The EU was built by the Member States, not by citizens. It is based on the principle that the EU is only responsible for what is expressly allowed in the Treaties. Everything else the Union is forbidden to do.

So if new problems arise, the European Parliament together with the Council cannot simply fix them. This is only possible in those cases in which the Treaties explicitly foresee EU competence. Otherwise, loose coordination between the Member States remains the only way. Amendments to the Treaty would be an alternative, but this is an extremely complex procedure. For, unlike the amendment of national constitutions, not even a two-thirds majority suffices. The EU Treaties must be ratified unanimously by all Member States. Whenever something is changed, everyone has their own list of desires regarding what also should be changed upon the opportunity and is able to blackmail the others.

Regarding crucial Eurozone issues, the EU has more competencies than it currently uses. The problem is, however, that on tax policy the Member States do not decide in the Council by majority, but rather by unanimity. Thus, there can only be progress if every single state agrees.

It is easy to make decisions in parliaments because they simply vote until a proposal receives the necessary majority. But between states it is usually not acceptable if some countries are completely overruled – and then still have to accept the solution. In intergovernmental cooperation, therefore, a solution is usually sought until it can be decided unanimously or almost unanimously. This takes longer because almost everyone can say "no" and prevent a solution with a veto. Enlargement has brought in ever more countries, and thus more veto players, into the EU Council.

One particularly difficult, but also important, example is the adoption of the EU budget. In order to enable all of the representatives in the EP and the Council to reach a compromise on the basis of European general interest, the EU budget has to be adopted by a majority of the EP and Council following a public debate. The heads of state and government may not interfere in the passage of EU legislation. In actual fact, however, they provide detailed orders on how the EU budgets are to look in the next few years behind closed doors in the European Council.[10] In this manner, citizens are cheated out of their right to a transparent process.[11] This promotes compartmentalized, nationalist thinking. The EU budget is mainly fed by contributions from the Member States. That is why governments try to get as much from the EU budget as they pay into it. A waste of money is acceptable as long as it serves national symbolism. Were these procedures public, as is supposed to be the case, they could be controlled by media and civil society to prevent waste. But they are not.

If the EU spent money derived from its own taxes instead of contributions by national governments, the latter would lose the incentive to waste money to improve bargaining power. In the U.S., a set corporate tax rate goes to the federal budget, and a greater balance to the federal states.

Countries with and without the Euro: A reason to split the EP?

The Euro is the currency of the EU, according to the Treaties. 338 out of 508 million Europeans – two-thirds – already do business with it. Except for Great Britain and Denmark, all governments have pledged to eventually introduce it. Only 14 per cent of EU citizens live in countries which do not have any prospect of introducing the Euro. After Brexit it would be even less. In addition to the 19 Euro countries, is is mainly Eastern European countries that do not yet meet all of the Maastricht criteria for the Euro's introduction, although they are coming ever closer to them. In Poland and Sweden, any adoption of the Euro has been completely rejected. The Baltic states have introduced the Euro despite the political crisis, with Lithuania being the last of the three to do so in 2015.

The question facing European democracy is which parliament should represent the interests of the citizens in matters involving the EMU when all citizens are not equally affected by it. The idea of granting more rights to European institutions, of deciding on questions of monetary, economic and financial policy, and not just giving advice, is directly related to this question. This is because practically everyone agrees: If the European level is to have more decision-making power, it must also be democratically legitimized and controlled. However, opinions then differ as to the best form for this to happen.

Joschka Fischer and others call for a "Euro chamber", namely a separate parliament that would only deal with EMU issues. It is argued that it should be composed of representatives who are sent by national parliaments.[12] This is how the European Parliament functioned when it was still called the "Common Assembly" [of the European Coal and Steel Community] before it was elected directly in 1979 for the first time. One particularly popular proposal in France is that a separate monetary parliament be composed of seconded national and European parliamentarians, probably in equal parts.

A third proposal is not intended to establish a new parliament, but proposes for the European Parliament to be divided into nominees from Euro countries and non-Euro countries. This could then happen in the form of a huge committee within the Parliament. The first two proposals build on the undoubtedly higher level of awareness that national politicians have. Fischer above all wants to recruit persons from national parliaments who are familiar from radio and television for his Eurozone parliament, namely the leaders of the political groups in national parliaments and the budgetary speakers. If European politicians do not make it into television talk shows, he wants to bring national politicians from television talk shows into a parallel new European parliament.

A national solution to a European problem, however, would be associated with the same difficulty as with the governments: National parliamentarians are also obligated only to their own national public spheres. Like lids that are too small, they never fit the European pot. As long as their re-election and their influence are essentially dependent on national questions, their incentives will hardly change. According to the proposal made by Joschka Fischer, there would be politicians deciding European questions who would finally generate attention in television and media. Yet problems would remain, just like the ones plaguing European elections: Discussion would focus on a national perspective and centre around national problems, even though such problems are highly interconnected in Europe and can only be solved at a European level.

How, then, should the quandary be resolved that the electorate voting the members of the European Parliament and those affected by the EMU are not fully congruent? EU institutions are already providing an answer in their current form: The parliament represents common European interest, the Council represents the interests of individual States depending on the level of concern. In the Parliament, MEPs represent the interests of all EU citizens. The 14 per cent accounted for by the British and Danes also benefit from a stable Eurozone as their main trading partner. Poles and many other non-Euro countries want to have the prospect of joining a properly functioning Euro. Only those representatives from the countries affected then vote on those issues in the Council.

How can the EU best further develop? Dividing European democracy into Euro and non-Euro countries would destroy many development possibilities. The fact that European MPs represent all EU citizens is an important basis for progress. A parallel parliament would eliminate the growing clarity of the division of labour: Political groups forming the majority in the European Parliament and supporting the Commission and a minority working as opposition. Clarity instead of blurred roles in a parallel parliament is imperative in order to allow European elections to have an impact on European policies.

Top candidates and transnational electoral lists: When does a chancellor want to become president of the Commission?

What can the European institutional system of the Commission, the Parliament, and Council of Ministers learn from federalism in Germany? After all, the currency union from Kiel to Munich has existed for much longer than that between Lisbon and Helsinki. Why did Bavaria never follow through with its threats to leave in light of the transfer union institutionalized between the federal government and the federal states (*Länderfinanzausgleich*)? Along with economic and cultural factors, this also has to do with the integrated political system. Local politicians want to be regional (*Länder*) politicians and *Länder*-level state premiers want to become chancellors. But why does the Chancellor not appear to want to become President of the Commission? Why do national politicians not want to enter the European Parliament?

European-level parties are only amalgamations of national parties. Their impact on European policy remains limited. In terms of the development of the Eurozone, there have been no meaningful initiatives from the parties; there has been no majority-building across the member parties. The European People's Party (EPP), the European Socialists (PES) and the Liberals (ALDE) meet before the meetings of the European Council. But at the European level, financial and social policymakers from the different parties practically never come together. This is because perhaps the most important function of parties, namely the staffing of official posts, is now only performed by the national parties. This goes for European elections as well.

This changed a little in the last elections when, for the first time ever, parties ran joint top candidates. The most important thing: A top candidate must persuade people in both Greece and Germany, and cannot play electorates off against each another with impunity. If this method were to be adopted, candidates for the top office would probably also devise more coherent programmes and set up a party apparatus for the election campaign. Only then would national fiscal policymakers have an incentive to devise good fiscal policies for the European level, and also be concerned about who are the respective shadow finance ministers of parties' top candidates.

Transnational nominees for European Parliament elections would change this even more.[13] This is because if EU citizens were to vote directly for top candidates, the clout wielded by heads of parties and government politicians in their backroom negotiations would dissipate. Some members of parliament would then compete against each another in a common electoral district, namely the entire EU. German voters would count the same as Maltese voters. And in this way, the concerns of Germany's Federal Constitutional Court regarding unequal representation in the European Parliament would be reduced or even completely mitigated. Such a principle, however, presupposes that – just like in the Bundestag – all members of parliament are committed to all voters, not just a section of them. Therefore, such progress will only be achieved if the unity of the European Parliament is preserved and a parallel parliament is avoided.

The history of the United States testifies that from very different party systems at the federal state level, a federal, all-continental party system can emerge quickly if the growing relevance of a higher level makes it necessary. The New Deal of the 1930s under President Franklin Delano Roosevelt fundamentally changed financial relations between the federal states and Washington. Roosevelt's federal programmes ensured that the federal government redistributed more money than did the federal states. And indeed, the American party system also changed: While before many states had their own political parties which did not operate anywhere else, the centre of the discussion shifted to the federal level: Republicans and Democrats coordinated their actions nationwide.[14]

TAXATION AND LABOUR MARKETS INSTEAD OF ENVIRONMENTAL AND PRODUCT STANDARDS: THE MORE CORE ISSUES, THE MORE DISPUTES

For a long time, European integration meant above all the opening up of closed national markets. Companies had to abide by ever more European product, environmental, and labour standards. But they often also benefited from the fact that there was only one EU rule instead of many regulations in the Member

States. Since the financial crisis – with the establishment of the banking union, the introduction of EU financial supervisors and an initial tax policy beyond the existing range of customs duties and value-added tax – EU laws and auditors also regulate core issues involving statehood and intervene in wealth-distribution issues. Powerful, well-heeled interests have thus come into conflict with the goal of stronger European integration, which would lead not to more market freedom, but rather to more European market control. European integration thus came to reproduce the American antagonism between democratic and republican ideas. Left-wing Democrats in the U.S. want more federal rules for social welfare, while right-wing Republicans want fewer rules at the federal level and more economic freedom for the federal states and individuals.

CONCLUSION: GIVE CITIZENS THE CHOICE ON WHICH EUROPE THEY WANT INSTEAD OF THE OSTENSIBLE CHOICE OF BEING ANTI-EUROPEANS

Millions of people with low incomes, and meanwhile the middle class as well, are globally under pressure from globalization. Europe is not at the core of this, but it does not use its possibilities to turn it around and is therefore vulnerable to anti-European attacks. The political institutions of the Eurozone do not work because democracy has not kept pace with the economy. While monetary policy is mutualised, budgetary policy is subject to strict European rules. In a closely interwoven economy social transfers and democratic rules are only possible in tandem. Democracy, on the other hand, is supposed to function primarily nationally and is weakly coordinated at the European level. Thus, the real alternatives that common European action could offer are not put up for vote by citizens, who are accordingly disappointed by the EU and turn their backs on it. There is a need for greater transparency and clear responsibilities in order to ensure that there are fewer European free riders and no more games of hide-and-seek with responsibility. In the Euro group and the Council of the EU as well, voters need to know who is promoting joint action and who is blocking it. To establish clearer responsibilities, it would be helpful to build a centre of political responsibility: The more Member States allow the European Commission to become a European government, the clearer the separation of powers will be. A limited number of politicians could really decide on European matters and, in return, would then be accountable to parliamentarians and, finally, voters.

A real choice between people, however, must also be a choice between programmes; that would make populism unattractive. Wherever elections offer real choices between distinguishable political propositions, more people will cast their votes and fewer will find populists interested. Also, if European elections make it possible for voters to choose whether they want this or that type of Europe, hardly anyone will ever want to decide on Europe with just a "yes" or a "no" vote. If the Member States were to allow this, it would finally be possible to decide whether multinational corporations should be transparent and pay taxes, or whether tax competition should prevail. It would be possible to vote on whether a slightly higher tax on companies and wealth should be invested in structurally weak regions. The example of the U.S. in the 1920s and 1930s makes it clear that if decision-making governing large sums of money takes place at the federal, continental level, parties will adapt. Top candidates with pan-European programmes would offer a choice between genuine policy options. This would yank the carpet from beneath the feet of political quacks and populist charlatans because in the dispute over genuine political alternatives, it would be easier to see that in the age of globalisation national sovereignty can neither create jobs nor provide justice. A European democracy, even one with flaws, but operating at the same level as transnational corporations and banks, is better than a national democracy that looks nice but has no influence.

Decisions deciding the future of Europe will be taken within existing institutions, however. So EU citizens will determine the future of Europe less through the 2019 European elections, and more in France and then in Germany in 2017, and finally in Italy in 2018 as well as in the many other elections for national governments. [15] These governments will form the European Council, the Council of Ministers, and the Euro group. Decisions will be made on whether the great pro-European parties offer a positive vision for a democratic and social Europe – or just mimic the populists. The shock victory of the populist "Leave" campaign in the British referendum could translate into a political opportunity for a reform breakthrough. Pure win-win solutions do not exist in today's Europe. Governments have to accept short-term costs in order to display strength through their joint actions and those of the entire EU. Even the IMF urgently recommends the reconciliation of interests between Euro countries: Billions of Euros for European investment in left-behind regions in return for more common economic policy. Federal government bonds are currently available at zero interest rate, billions in taxes from large corporations can finally be released once action has been taken against tax dumping. In other words, the time to invest in this effort is ideal. The backdrop to upcoming elections, on the other hand, is gloomy: In France, the National Front has been boosted in polls by Brexit, in Italy the Five Star Movement is getting stronger. This could actually cause the Euro to collapse. Political parties in Germany must therefore carefully weigh out the efforts and costs of more investment, transparency, and democracy on the one hand, and the potential costs of populist, anti-European governments in France or Italy on the other. Right after the Brexit vote, the majority of the German population expressed a preference for a closer union (49 per cent) instead of greater independence for Member States (37 per cent).[16]

Notes

1 | Giegold, Sven (2015): Herbstprognose der Kommission: In den Regelbruch getrieben (5.11.2015); www.sven-giegold.de/2015/herbstprognose-der-kommission-in-den-regelbruch-getrieben/ (last accessed 21/6/2016).
2 | Giegold, Sven (2013): Europäisches Semester: Europaparlament schafft Transparenz durch Tabellen (31.5.2013); www.sven-giegold.de/2013/europaisches-semester-europaparlament-schafft-transparenz-durch-tabellen/ (last accessed 21/6/2016).
3 | Giegold, Sven (2015): Europäisches Semester: EU-Mitgliedsländer blamieren sich bei Koordinierung der Wirtschaftspolitik (27.5.2015); www.sven-giegold.de/2015/europaeisches-semester-eu-mitgliedslaender-blamieren-sich-bei-koordinierung-der-wirtschaftspolitik/ (last accessed 21/6/2016).
4 | Müller, Manuel (2013): Länderspezifische Empfehlungen, oder: Wie mache ich mich unbeliebt? (5.6.2013); www.foederalist.eu/2013/06/landerspezifische-empfehlungen-oder-wie.html (last accessed 21/6/2016).
5 | Müller, Manuel (2013): Vertragspartnerschaften als »goldene Zwangsjacke«: Wie in der Eurozone die Demokratie erodiert und welche Alternative es gäbe (27.11.2013); www.foederalist.eu/2013/11/vertragspartnerschaften-als-goldene.html (last accessed 21/6/2016).
6 | Protokoll (Nr. 14), betreffend die Euro-Gruppe; www.europarl.europa.eu/brussels/website/media/Basis/InternePolitikfelder/WWU/Pdf/Protokoll_14_Eurogruppe.pdf (last accessed 21/6/2016).
7 | Braunberger, Gerald (2011): Rodriks unmögliches Dreieck: Nationalstaat, Demokratie und Globalisierung sind zu viel (28.3.2011); Article on Rodrik, Dani (2011): Das Globalisierungs-Paradox. München: Beck; www.faz.net/aktuell/feuille ton/wirtschaft/rodriks-unmoegliches-dreieck-1612995.html (last accessed 21/06/2016).
8 | Müller, Manuel: Warum Föderalismus? (without date); www.foederalist.eu/p/warum-foderalismus.html (last accessed 21/6/2016).
9 | Sicherheit im VZ: Datenschutz (no date); www.studivz.net/l/security/24 (last accessed 21/6/2016).
10 | Europäischer Rat (2013): Tagung vom 7./8. Februar 2013, Schlussfolgerungen (mehrjähriger Finanzrahmen) (EUCO 37/13); https://www.consilium.europa.eu/uedocs/cms_data/docs/pressdata/de/ec/135379.pdf (last accessed 21/6/2016).
11 | Crowe, Richard (2016): The European Council and the Multiannual Financial Framework, in: Cambridge Yearbook of European Legal Studies, Vol. 17, p. 1.
12 | Hildebrandt, Tina/Wefing, Heinrich (2011): Joschka Fischer: "Vergesst diese EU", in: DIE ZEIT Nr. 46/2011; www.zeit.de/2011/46/Interview-Fischer/komplettansicht (last accessed 21/06/2016).
13 | The Council's legal service even admits this in internal documents. They can be found at: www.sven-giegold.de/2016/baerendienst-fuer-die-europaeische-demokratie-bundesregierung-will-eu-spitzenkandidaten-verhindern/ (last accessed 21/6/2016).

14 | Chhibber, Pradeep/Kollman, Ken (1998): Party Aggregation and the Number of Parties in India and the United States, in: American Political Science Review, Vol. 92, No. 2.
15 | Deutscher Bundestag: Wahltermine der Mitgliedsländer der Europäischen Union; https://www.bundestag.de/bundestag/wahlen/wahltermine-eu (last accessed 21/6/2016).
16 | Forschungsgruppe Wahlen: Politbarometer Juli 2016 (Mainz, 8.7.2016); www.forschungsgruppe.de/Umfragen/Politbarometer/Archiv/Politbarometer_2016/Juli_I_2016/ (last accessed 21/6/2016).

3. The flaws in the design of the Economic and Monetary Union

Henrik Enderlein

A full two decades after its conception and around a decade after its actual implementation, the common currency area still has significant design flaws. The crisis in the Euro area since spring 2010 has shown this clearly; but opinions diverge on exactly what these design flaws are because functional deficits are due to both economic and political factors. There are three interpretations of the crisis:

1. The first interpretation highlights the fact that the basic conception of the Maastricht Treaty as a "rule-based community" could have worked. Its implementation, in particular with regard to stability criteria, deviated too much from the original framework, which then led to the crisis. This interpretation identifies the major structural defect in the fact that policy violations, especially in the case of debt level, were not effectively sanctioned. As a result, the entire framework for control was gradually eroded.
2. The second interpretation argues that a common currency must fail in a geographical area that has neither a high degree of political integration nor does it meet the criteria of an optimal monetary space. There are two subcategories of this interpretation:
    - On the one hand, the focus is on the lack of a single currency's legitimacy, which in principle makes it impossible to compensate for the functional flaws of a monetary union which is not an optimal monetary area. Since a monetary union cannot exist without a political union in the long term, and a political union in the present context does not appear realistic, the project of Economic and Monetary Union (EMU) is doomed to failure.
    - On the other hand, there are the fundamental economic difficulties of reconciling an economic space of such high structural heterogeneity as the Euro area with a single currency – irrespective of political structures. It is economically impossible to keep a currency union of such different countries stable in the long term. Thus, for example, a split

into a North Euro and a South Euro or a return to national currencies would be appropriate.
3. This interpretation also points to the structural divergences and the insufficient degree of political integration. However, it argues that the common currency can be maintained through additional political, institutional, legal, or economic measures. The challenges are not so fundamental as to jeopardize the possibility of a properly functioning single currency.

This Chapter focuses on the economic challenges and describes why the Euro as an incomplete monetary union has always had to deal with divergences and instability. This is the basis for possible solutions that are considered in detail in the third part of this compendium (see, in particular, the Chapters by Daniela Schwarzer, Jeromin Zettelmeyer and Peter Becker).

AN INCOMPLETE MONETARY UNION

Open economies which are closely linked through trade relations will always have to decide what is more important to them: Fixed exchange rates with their trading partners or monetary policy geared to the national economic cycle. The dilemma only vanishes when economic cycles of trade partners are very similar or when there are strong adjustment mechanisms, such as a common budget or labour mobility. Then common monetary policy can have a stabilising effect on all of the countries involved – despite fixed exchange rates. In economic literature, these basic requirements are described in connection with a monetary union as the 'criteria of the optimal monetary space'. There has been broad agreement among economists that the Euro area never met these criteria. That is why economists were sceptical about whether the Economic and Monetary Union could succeed. However, many accepted the political arguments, which favoured EMU and the Euro as a political project within the framework of European integration logic.

The Economic and Monetary Union therefore occupies a certain position in the long and functionally defined chain of integration steps. At the beginning of European integration, military conflicts were made more difficult by means of a closer exchange between European nations. In the economic sphere, this exchange encompassed the four freedoms – free movement of people, goods, services, and capital – which were implemented in the Single Market. No country was to enjoy competitive advantages through implicit trade barriers, discrimination or subsidies.

It is a given that such an internal market is incompatible with exchange rate fluctuations because short-term competitive advantages can always be achieved through devaluations. Therefore, the project of a single currency was the functionally conclusive answer to the Single Market. The community currency is therefore not an end in and of itself, but the consistent continuation of a coherent integration logic.

However, the question of how to implement the common currency remained unresolved for a long time. Even as far back as the early 1990s, all the parties involved were aware that the European States were not an optimal currency space – and would probably not constitute one in the foreseeable future.

Thus, in the discussion over the Maastricht Treaty in the late 1980s and early 1990s, there were two divergent, but equally coherent, approaches up for discussion:

- The French approach called for a common currency which had to be backed up by powerful economic governance so that a common, homogeneous and, in an economic sense, "optimal monetary space" could be created in the medium term.
- On the other side was the German position, which demanded that the homogenous and integrated economic space become a reality *before* the common currency be instituted.
- What happened in Europe with this debate is well known: A compromise. The common currency was introduced. However, no institutional framework was created to ensure the realization of a homogeneous economic space. Such an institutional framework at the European level would have made it possible to intervene in national economic policies if they were considered to be inappropriate.

The consequence of this basic compromise was clearly visible in the first decade of the Euro. There are two basic problem areas, which can then be broken down into more detailed functional deficits:

- *Problem 1:* The Euro remained a heterogeneous currency area in the first decade until the beginning of the major recession in 2008. The hope of many macroeconomists was that by dint of EMU member countries' economies would converge. But this did not happen. This applied to both real convergence (the convergence of living standards) and cyclical convergence (the convergence of economic fluctuations).
- *Problem 2:* The Eurozone, even today, has no effective alternative adaptation mechanisms that could counteract real or cyclical divergences. In other heterogeneous monetary unions, such as the U.S., there is a common budget, common tax levied at the federal level, common unemployment and social insurance, labour mobility, and deeply integrated financial markets that enable cyclical adjustments through capital flows. These elements, when used correctly, can keep stable a monetary union plagued by structural divergences.

The following sections describe the functional deficiencies associated with these problem areas and show what would be necessary to remedy them.

A LACK OF CYCLICAL CONVERGENCE

The Euro did not lead to greater convergence in the Euro area, but rather strengthened differences (divergences). This can be seen in both real and cyclical convergence. Both forms of convergence are central to a monetary union.

Cyclical convergence refers to the convergence of economic cycles. Economic cycles are fluctuations in overall economic activity. Usually, they have a strong impact on the inflation rate. During an upturn, inflation rises, while in a recession it falls. When countries go simultaneously through upturns and downturns, economic cycles are synchronized. Cyclical convergence is important for the functioning of the common currency because the European Central Bank (ECB) establishes a uniform interest rate based on the weighted average of inflation rates in the Euro area. Its mission is to ensure that inflation remains below 2 per cent. During an upturn, it raises the interest rate to avoid overheating. During a downturn, the ECB cuts interest rates in order to boost the economy and kick-start economic activity.

In the early years of EMU, the core grew more slowly than the periphery. In the mid-2000s, synchronisation improved somewhat, and then in 2009 all of the Euro countries finally slid into a deep crisis. As a result, the core countries recovered more rapidly, while the peripheral countries remained in recession. Since then, both groups of countries have recorded similarly low growth rates.

The empirical literature on the convergence of economic cycles shows that EMU did not significantly contribute to greater convergence (see also Chapter 4). The countries that had similar per capita incomes up to the 1970s display similar economic cycles over the decades. This core group of relatively similar countries consists of Germany, France, Belgium, and the Netherlands. The other group is more diverse and does not display a common trend. Some countries have caught up, others have not.

Even after the crisis, the picture did not change. There is strong interdependence between some countries in the Eurozone due to common factors that explain half of the deviations in national GDP: German and French economic cycles were similar, while Spain remained on another trajectory after the crisis.

This lack of convergence of economic cycles has two important implications:

1. It appears that management of EMU, including the Maastricht criteria and the Stability and Growth Pact, was unable to bring about convergence.

2. It is likely that the monetary policy of the ECB causes even more divergence by reinforcing upturns and recessions.

As for economic cycles, the EMU failed to create the requisites of an optimal monetary space.

The "One-Size-Fits-None" Problem of the ECB

With perfectly coordinated economic cycles, the ECB can pursue a monetary policy which is equally suited to all Euro area economies and has a stabilising effect. If, however, there is no cyclical convergence, the interest rate will be too low for countries in an upturn and too high for countries in a downturn. This exacerbates booms and depressions.

The simple conclusion that structural and cyclical divergences within the Eurozone countries are very large has the following consequences: If growth and inflation rates in the Eurozone countries are different, the uniform interest rate set by the ECB will increase these divergences.

Since the beginning of EMU, there have been substantial differences between the respective national growth and inflation rates of the Member States. These divergences are undoubtedly a result of different national economic policies and institutions. Common monetary policy has only reinforced this.

Since the ECB's decisions on interest rates are not based on the economic developments of individual Member States, but rather on the Eurozone as a whole, its monetary policy is at the same time too restrictive for one country and too loose for other countries. In Member States with an inflation rate above the Eurozone average, the common nominal interest rate has led to low real interest rates, stimulating higher investment rates and consumption. This has accelerated growth beyond the production potential and thus had an inflationary effect, especially on the prices of fixed assets such as the real estate market. Ireland and Spain in the pre-crisis years are examples of such developments. In countries with an inflation rate below the Eurozone average, the opposite was true: Real interest rates were too high, while investment and consumption rates were too low. The best example was Germany until about 2008.

The ECB's monetary policy did more to aggravate these divergences than it did to prevent them. Instead of a one-size-fits-all solution, the ECB's monetary policy turned into a solution that did not fit any country: One-size-fits-none. This triggered disadvantageous and even self-reinforcing, pro-cyclical effects in the Member States. This was despite the fact that the ECB did exactly what was required of it: It set its monetary policy at the Eurozone average. The consequence was that it made the right monetary policy for a country that does not exist.

How is more cyclical convergence achieved?

This problem of the ECB is the result of a self-reinforcing real interest channel. The higher the key interest rates, the lower the growth dynamics and deflation; the higher the real interest rate, the lower the growth dynamics and inflation. Or the other way around: The lower the key rate (which can even slip into the negative, as happened in Ireland in the early 2000s), the higher are growth and inflation.

Of course, EMU is not the only heterogeneous currency area in which such divergences can be found. But the Euro area lacks adaptation mechanisms to deal with the divergences. There are several different mechanisms that could take over this role: The real exchange rate, national adjustments, and financial compensation mechanisms.

The real exchange rate

Normally, in a country experiencing significantly higher growth than the rest of the Eurozone, inflation is also higher. If the real exchange rate channel works, countries with high inflation will ultimately lose competitiveness: In a fully integrated economic area, higher costs will lead to less competitive products and services. A drop in demand will then bring growth and inflation back to the average of the Euro area. This is referred to as real exchange rate adjustment. However, this adjustment requires that the various regions are so closely linked economically that the real exchange rate channel can function.

However, the Eurozone has proved to be an only partially integrated economic area. While capital has moved freely, there have still been numerous obstacles in trade in goods and services. Therefore, some sectors have not been able to compete against foreign goods. This has resulted in a split into regions with high growth and high inflation – countries like Spain and Ireland – and regions with low growth and low inflation like Germany. The competitiveness of the first group deteriorated because of rising prices and wages, but their growth did not slow down. Increased domestic demand compensated for declining exports.

Before the start of Economic and Monetary Union, most theoretical analyses assumed that the real exchange rate effect would largely determine the real interest rate, leading to a high degree of internal stability in the Euro area. This is based on the assumption that domestic prices (and thus also real interest rates) necessarily converge in a monetary union in view of the free movement of goods and services in the Single Market. If similar goods are produced in Germany and Spain, but local inflation in Spain is well above the German level, Spanish goods in Germany will increasingly lose their competitiveness. As a consequence, economic activity in Spain declines, but increases in Germany.

This means that in the medium term growth will fall and an increase in prices will occur – whereas the opposite will take place in Germany.

However, a core problem of EMU was (and still partly is) the insufficiently integrated Single Market. Indeed, many goods or services are not in direct competition with goods from other countries in the Euro area. In the service sector, which accounts for about three quarters of value added in the Euro area, cross-border trade only accounts for about 20 per cent. In fact, much of the economic performance of a country is geared to 'spatially fixed factors', such as real estate or heavy machinery, which is not directly affected by price competition. Regional economic adjustments, which are based on real exchange rate differences, therefore take a very long time.

While the EU has certainly created a Single Market on paper, it is still far from a truly integrated economic area. This functional deficit would have to be overcome by an even more integrated market for goods and services. Whether the countries of the Eurozone are ready for further market deepening is, however, questionable. Indeed, political barriers to the reduction of barriers in the service sector are high.

National adjustment

A second way to deal with imbalances in the EMU is to use economic policy instruments remaining in the national area for stabilisation: Mainly in financial policy, wage policy, national tax policies, but also in national banking and financial market regulation, which, however, can be triggered directly by European coordination. During the first ten years of EMU, however, national authorities neglected to use these instruments effectively – especially in high-growth countries, where economic overheating and speculative bubbles were clearly visible. In Spain and Ireland, for example, growth cycles were out of control and led to dangerous price bubbles, particularly in the real estate sector, but also to rapidly rising government revenues (Ireland and Spain did not violate the Stability and Growth Pact before the crisis).

A determined, European-wide, coordinated anticyclical budget policy could have synchronised national economic cycles. For this reason, the architects of the Euro had planned in instruments for economic policy coordination. But their tools proved blunt: The European Treaties provided recommendations on the principles of economic policy and obliged the Member States to treat their economic policy as "a matter of common concern" (Article 121 of the Treaty on the Functioning of the EU). But in the years up to the crisis, these instruments proved ineffective. When in 2001 the Commission complained to the Irish Republic because it cut taxes despite an overheating economy, the Irish government simply did not react. And the warning from the European Commission faded away without there being any consequences.

The other main instrument, the Stability and Growth Pact, is supposed to limit public deficits. However, it did not coordinate budgetary policy adequately, as it concentrated asymmetrically on the deficit side, but was unable to exert pressure on countries experiencing an upswing. Furthermore, in 2003 the European Commission was not even able to impose the deficit rules on core Member States, such as France and Germany – because France and Germany vehemently resisted it.

The interaction of inadequate market integration and weak economic policy coordination has rendered the synchronisation of economic cycles impossible. The uniform interest rate of the ECB increased the impact. Ultimately, the lack of convergence led to intolerable macroeconomic imbalances. The loss of competitiveness in the GIIPS countries (Greece, Italy, Ireland, Portugal and Spain) against countries with low inflation in the Euro area has been reflected in GIIPS countries' current account deficits and growing private debt.

In Greece, this was only aggravated by excessive public spending. This situation could be maintained for some time through favourable loans granted by optimistic creditors, but high public and private debt made GIIPS countries vulnerable to interruptions of capital inflow. When the crisis broke out in 2008, severely restricting foreign financing, it had devastating consequences for the Eurozone.

The costs which arose from the subsequent chain reaction are well known. It would be too easy to argue that the Euro crisis was only caused by a lack of cyclical convergence and the resulting credit imbalances. There is no doubt, however, that they played a central role. Even today heterogeneous growth rates in the economies of the Eurozone hinder crisis management. The ECB has little political support for a strong anticyclical monetary policy as long as some parts of the Euro area are in crisis and others are growing.

A monetary union which enables its members almost unrestricted national economic policy autonomy therefore simply cannot succeed. Anyone wishing to remedy this deficit must limit the autonomy of national economic policy, which is very difficult to achieve within the framework of the current Treaty.

Financial compensation mechanisms

The third way to deal with the economic challenges of EMU is to introduce financial compensation mechanisms between the Member States. These compensation mechanisms can be implemented through the tax system, through a common unemployment insurance scheme, through a common social insurance system (see Chapter 10 by Peter Becker) or through an effective and highly integrated capital and financial market, which leads to high yields in one part of the Economic and Monetary Union that can be transferred to other parts of the Union.

It is logical that in the many discussions about the future of the Eurozone observers have put forward different instruments that would have a dampening effect on the divergent economic cycles in the Euro area. Various proposals, such as a Eurozone budget (see Chapter 8 by Jeromin Zettelmeyer), an EU unemployment insurance or the capital market union in Europe, must always be viewed against the backdrop of the fact that they create automatic compensation mechanisms for the Euro area.

However, the fact that such proposals often meet with scepticism should not surprise us. Economic historians can tell how fiscal federations were created with the aim of counteracting the inherent economic challenges of a monetary union. At the same time, they describe how the resulting redistribution often ended with the collapse of formerly politically integrated territories. The triangle of conflicting priorities between stabilisation through transfers and a related "moral hazard" problem is clearly evident. And the German debate over the "transfer union" reflects this triangle very precisely.

The promise of the Maastricht Treaty that the "common currency" would smooth out economic cycles – the "optimal currency space" would not have to be the starting point of monetary integration, but could produce it with time – has not come true. However, what is necessary in terms of further steps in integration to smooth out economic cycles is highly controversial.

A CONTINUATION OF THE CURRENCY UNION IS THE ONLY WAY

In the face of these major economic challenges, Euro critics will now quickly demand immediate termination of the project (see Chapter 11 by Armin Steinbach). I hold this to be irresponsible. The Euro guarantees competition, which is particularly important for Germany in the European internal market because competitive devaluations are ruled out. The Euro strengthens the position of Europe in the world market because it has become a world reserve currency. The Euro is also the political guarantee underscoring that we are serious about the European project.

The exclusion of individual countries is also dangerous. Not only because politically and legally it remains completely unclear how it could happen. But also because a currency union that contains an exit option is nothing but a system of fixed exchange rates. Imagine the crisis from 2010 to 2012 against the backdrop of an exit option. The consequences would have been devastating. Would the financial markets and the private investors have left their money in the crisis countries if an exit had been possible? Would Ireland and Portugal have carried out their politically difficult, but economically urgent, structural reforms if they had had the possibility to exit? The impossibility of exit protected the Euro during the crisis.

THE GENERAL OVERHAUL: A SELECTIVE DEEPENING OF THE MONETARY UNION

Demolition or reconstruction would result in immense costs. A general overhaul is therefore the wiser approach. What Europe needs is a selective deepening of EMU (see the proposals by Peter Becker, Jeromin Zettelmeyer and Daniela Schwarzer as well as future scenarios in Chapter 12 by Alexander Schellinger and Philipp Steinberg). Outlined below are four areas.

Complete the Internal Market

The Euro area lives in the illusion of being an integrated market. But it is not. There is a lack of cros-sborder trade, especially in the service sector. And as long as services are embedded in the nation-state – obscure rules permit scarcely any mobility and trade from one country to another – the divergences between countries will remain. The Euro area must become a genuine Single Market, with common regulation of capital movements and the digital sector as well as a marked increase in labour mobility. In these fields, however, very little is happening. This shows that the main causes of the divergences in the Eurozone are still misunderstood.

Complete the banking union

Although there is now uniform supervision and processing, stability is not yet guaranteed. A migration of deposits could trigger the next crisis in EMU. If the question is asked in Italy about whether the Euro can survive, one will hear that it is only a matter of time before savers transfer their deposits to German accounts. This flight of deposits is the biggest threat to the Euro area. Capital controls in Cyprus and Greece show that a Euro does not have the same value in all countries. In this context, separate deposit-guarantee systems pose a danger. In view of remaining risks in many countries, it is understandable that many actors in Germany are sceptical about a European deposit guarantee system. But these concerns are short-sighted. Those who rule out a common system, which can also be achieved while pursuing reinsurance, fall into the trap of time incongruence: The long-term costs of a collapse of the EMU or even a hasty overnight rescue could exceed today's risks.

Rework crisis instruments and politicise it

The European Stability Mechanism is far from being a genuine European currency fund that creates real risk-sharing between countries, but also calls for a gradual transfer of sovereign rights. The fact that the ESM currently contains only pro-rata liability is consistent with the fact that national sovereignty in the crisis countries is almost completely intact. But the balance between the sharing of sovereignty and that of risk-sharing has still not been found. In a monetary union, sovereignty ends when solvency ends. This sentence is still being transposed via the chaotic ad hoc transmission of sovereign rights in a "Memorandum of Understanding" by a faceless Troika which operates largely outside of democratic control. But this transmission of sovereignty is neither transparent nor democratically anchored. Come the next political crisis, this Troika approach could lead to political instability much earlier than we could possibly expect. What is urgently needed is a democratically controlled European Monetary Fund headed by a European finance minister. He or she would oversee European rules, but would also have political room to manoeuvre in a crisis and would act as the face of the Troika. In serious cases, such a finance minister should also have a veto right over national budgets.

Improve democratic control

Everywhere in the Economic and Monetary Union, the Euro is battling a legitimacy deficit – but its origins differ from country to country. In the crisis countries, "Monetary Union" often stands for de facto occupation and budget austerity; in Germany it can stand for the loss of power to the ECB and expensive rescue packages. Both perspectives show that the national viewpoint is dominant. The view on the Euro area as a whole does not play a role. The latter plays no role at all. It is necessary to eliminate such legitimation deficiencies: Preferably through a joint chamber of national parliaments and the European Parliament, which controls the European Monetary Fund. As far as the legitimation structures are concerned, Europe should also meet the requirements of a genuine multi-level governing system.

I consider these four measures to be a kind of minimal package that would make the Euro viable in the long term. Less integration is not an option. More integration does not have to take place.

Conclusion

Until 2010, Currency Union perpetuated indirect redistribution in the Euro area; the ECB's "one size fits none" policy has, in combination with the different national economic policies, exacerbated heterogeneity in the Euro area. After 2010, the crisis led to a second wave of redistribution, triggered mainly by the correction of the skewed pre-2010 economic policy. This second wave was interpreted very differently in the EU: In the crisis countries as a dictate of the countries from the north, in Germany as a loss of power. Both perspectives illustrate that the national viewpoint dominates; the entirety of the Eurozone as such does not come into the picture.

This Chapter has described the main economic challenges in the Economic and Monetary Union and presented a kind of criteria catalogue for a minimal package that could make the Euro viable in the long term. But even this minimal package is currently on the back burner.

And thus, three core questions remain unanswered which are essential for a general overhaul of the Euro:

1. How should the Eurozone deal with countries that refuse further integration and the urgently necessary transfer of sovereignty? As described above, an exit clause would be very dangerous. It would fundamentally alter the character of the Euro area. At the same time, however, the irreversibility of Eurozone membership also creates a certain possibility for blackmail which, if we are honest, posed a real problem in negotiations with Greece. In order to avoid this, the Euro area must find ways to completely remove a country from the solidarity system of the EMU. "Leave alone instead of lock out" should be the maxim. This means, however, that benefits such as the ECB's liquidity aid must not become a rescue line that cannot be let go of. It is an anachronism that such aid is today given by national central banks and not by the ECB.
2. Must a country that can no longer service its debt leave the EMU? Not necessarily. An orderly state insolvency without leaving the Economic and Monetary Union is possible if there is a clear framework for such. But so far, only few actors in Europe are confident enough to propose a mechanism for enabling orderly insolvency in the Euro area. It is probably also because the largely risk-free treatment of government bonds in bank balance sheets would be passé and banks would have to underwrite state bonds with equity. Nothing would be more logical than a double step, including both an insolvency regime and risk mechanism to back it up. In Chapter 8, Jeromin Zettelmeyer introduces a possible mechanism for doing just that.
3. Do we need a Europe of different speeds? This question, which is up for discussion once again in the aftermath of the departure of Great Britain, can be cleverly answered once the dust from the referendum has settled. Europe will have to be structured in two rings. An inner ring, the "Euro union", would be inside the present Treaty; an external ring, the "internal market union," outside of the Treaty. The new status of Great Britain could be pioneering for the future relationship between the EU and Turkey, Norway, Switzerland, perhaps even Hungary, and maybe one day Ukraine.

Clearly, EMU has to be reformed. As outlined in this Chapter, the economic challenges constitute the core of the problem. But if one looks more closely at the economic challenges, one will soon find that there is more to do than tinker.

The specific structure of the Economic and Monetary Union is inherently a political issue – this collection of essays attests to that. Addressing the economic challenges must ultimately be open to risk-sharing and the displacement of sovereignty without simultaneously undoing the overall project's democratic anchoring. This undertaking is political, just as the Euro was a political project from the outset.

4. The social dimension of the Eurozone

Michael Dauderstädt

Social development in the Eurozone is a source of concern (see Table 1). However, there are significant differences between countries as well as in development in the period before and after the crisis, as the following section shows. National policies and structures as well as European and global factors have contributed to this development. Economic and Monetary Union (EMU), as shown in the previous section, has a clear responsibility for development in countries that were subject to the conditions of support programmes from 2010 on (GIIPS: Greece, Ireland, Italy, Portugal, Spain and Cyprus).

THE SOCIAL DEVELOPMENT IN THE EUROZONE: FUNDAMENTALLY DIVERSE AND ALARMING

Unemployment is above 10 per cent (2015), the poverty rate is at 23.5 per cent (2014), the rate of material deprivation (i.e. people who lack vitally necessary basics) is 7.4 per cent (2014) and inequality (S80/S20 ratio – the ratio of the income of the richest fifth of the population to the poorest fifth) is at 5.2 or at a Gini[1] coefficient of 0.31. The wage rate is slightly over 56 per cent. At the same time, expenditures on social protection amounted to almost 30 per cent of GDP in 2013.[2] Compare these figures with the average of the EU as a whole: The Eurozone is performing worse in terms of unemployment, but better in terms of poverty and deprivation. This is due to the fact that the Eurozone comprises predominantly richer EU countries, but has a lower rate of growth. Compared to Sweden or Denmark, however, the Eurozone is a social disaster area. This is especially true for the programme countries Greece, Ireland, Portugal, Spain and Cyprus, where social development has been catastrophic since 2010.

The current figures for the Eurozone do not represent the nadir of development everywhere (see Table 1). Unemployment and deprivation had reached their maximum levels in 2013 and 2012, respectively, at twelve per cent and 7.8 per cent, respectively, but the 2014 rate holds the sad record for the poverty

Table 1: Social indicators of the Eurozone

	2000	2001	2002	2003	2004	2005	2006	2007	2008	2009	2010	2011	2012	2013	2014	2015
Unemployment	8,9	8,3	8,6	9,1	9,3	9,1	8,4	7,5	7,6	9,6	10,2	10,2	11,4	12,0	11,6	10,9
Wage share	56,6	56,3	56,3	56,3	55,6	55,3	54,8	54,3	55,2	57,1	56,3	56,1	56,5	56,4	56,6	56,2
Nominal cost per unit of labour	82,4	83,9	86,1	88,2	88,9	90,3	91,2	92,7	96,2	100,6	100,0	100,6	102,4	103,6	104,7	105,4
Social protection expenditure rate	26,7	26,7	27,3	27,7	27,6	27,6	27,3	26,8	27,5	30,4	30,3	30				
Poverty rate						22,0	22,1	21,9	21,7	21,6	22,0	22,9	23,3	23,1	23,5	
Deprivation						6,3	6,0	5,6	5,9	6,0	6,1	6,9	7,8	7,5	7,4	
Gini						29,4	29,4	30,0	30,5	30,3	30,3	30,6	30,4	30,7	31,0	
S80/S20-ratio						4,7	4,7	4,8	4,9	4,9	4,9	5	5	5	5,2	

Source: Eurostat

Remarks: Unemployment in per cent, wage rate in per cent, nominal unit labour costs as index (2010 = 100), social protection expenditure rate, poverty rate and deprivation in per cent, Gini and S80/S20 ratios dimensionless. Data availability varies from indicator to indicator as well as the actual country composition of the Eurozone.

rate and inequality. Prior to the global crisis (2008/09), it looked much better: Unemployment in 2007 was 7.5 per cent, the poverty rate was 21.6 per cent, the deprivation rate was 5.6 per cent, and inequality was at 4.7 per cent, while social spending amounted to only 25.9 per cent of GDP. The wage rate has fallen from around 56.6 per cent in 2000 to almost 54.2 per cent in 2007. In the great recession, it rose briefly to 57 per cent, but since then it has slid back. Nominal unit labour costs rose (2010 = 100) from 82 in 2000 to 105 in 2015.

Increasing inequality in the Eurozone (visible in the increase in both the Gini coefficient and the S80/S20 ratio) only reflects the development of inequality within EU Member States. Thanks to more rapid growth in the poorer countries (particularly in Eastern Europe, but also in the southern periphery up to the crisis), EU-wide inequality had decreased before 2009. Since 2010, however, it has hovered at the same level.

However, this average data for the entire Eurozone conceals very divergent developments in different countries. This is particularly true of wages and labour costs. When one looks at the countries of the Eurozone, one can identify regional variations based on relevant differences in social development: The special case of Germany; other rich countries (France, the Netherlands, Belgium, Luxembourg, Italy, Austria, Finland); the programme countries (Greece, Ireland, Portugal, Spain and Cyprus); as well as the relatively poor eastern periphery (Slovenia, Slovakia, Baltic states, Malta).

Special case of Germany: From unemployment to inequality

Germany started in the EMU with perceived competitive weakness and a social crisis, aptly symbolised in the title of Hans-Werner Sinn's 2003 book "Can Germany Still be Saved?". High unemployment, weak growth, and a desultory government financial situation were the main features in this gloomy picture. An ageing and declining population were seen as additional long-term problems. Unemployment reached a peak of 11.2 per cent in 2005. Despite continued high export surpluses, competitiveness was considered to be at risk, which many experts (among them Sinn) blamed on high wages, rigid labour markets, a hostile tax system and an overly generous and misguided welfare state. Others, such as the German economists Peter Bofinger and Fritz Scharpf, also placed the blame on the ECB, whose interest rates were too high for the stagnating German economy. Opinions differed over the question as to whether Germany had entered EMU with an overvalued exchange rate between the German mark and Euro.

Germany was a country of net immigration, albeit with a sharply declining balance: From about 220,000 in 2002 to 22,000 in 2006. In the first half of the 2000s, income distribution was relatively egalitarian with a Gini of about 0.26 and an S80/S20 ratio of less than four. Only about 40 per cent of the unemployed were poor. In 2005, 4.6 per cent of the population suffered from deprivation and 18.4 per cent from poverty. The wage share was around 58 per cent.

Between 2003 and 2005, the federal government adopted a series of reforms (Agenda 2010, Hartz laws) in the fields of tax policy, labour market policy and social legislation to reduce unemployment, shore up government finances and achieve long-term sustainability. An important lever in both objectives was the reduction of non-wage labour costs, which was also intended to be achieved by reforms in the fields of health and pension insurance ("retirement at 67").

Developments after 2006 were distorted by massive shocks in the global financial market crisis (2007/08) and the great recession (2009). However, many indicators display relatively continuous development between 2006 and 2014, only interrupted by a short V-shaped intermission in 2009. The most noticeable development has been the unemployment rate, which fell from 11.2 per cent (2005) to 4.6 per cent (2015). Similarly, employment grew by about two million people. Unemployment fell by the same number. However, the number of hours worked rose significantly more slowly than employment, only reaching the approximate level of 1993 in 2015, with four million more people employed in 2015 than in 1993. In particular, average working time decreased until 2010, as full-time jobs were replaced by precarious part-time jobs. The demographic trend also contributed to an ease in pressure on the labour market. The net migration balance was low until 2011 (even negative in 2008) and the active population (between the ages of 15 and 64) declined in number by more than two million between 2003 and 2014. In 2010, however, immigration began to pick up again.

The development of wages has reflected conditions in the labour market. High unemployment, stricter rules for what jobs long-term unemployed workers must accept (one-Euro and 400-Euro jobs) and conditions surrounding access by the unemployed to, and liberalization of, the labour market (for example, looser restrictions on temporary agency work) put pressure on wages. Trade unions and works councils went along with a policy of wage dispersion. The ratio of poor persons among the unemployed rose from 40 per cent (2003) to 70 per cent (2010) and is still by far the highest in the EU. Real wages fell between 2001 and 2009. A large low-wage sector was created, which in 2010 included 23 per cent of employees. The wage share fell from 58.8 per cent to 53.7 per cent between 2000 and 2007. Accordingly, real labour unit costs fell, further improving the price competitiveness of the exporting country. More importantly, nominal unit labour costs remained virtually unchanged between 1999 and 2008, and rose only slightly afterwards. Only from around 2011 onwards did wages increase over a longer time period, also supported by the introduction of a statutory minimum wage.

Income distribution has deteriorated significantly. The S80/S20 ratio increased from 3.8 (2005) to 5.1 (2014). The poverty risk also rose from 18.4 (2004) to 20.6 (2014). The Gini of disposable income grew from 0.25 to over 0.3; the Gini of the market income surged from 0.4 to over 0.5. Both statistics declined over the past few years. Inequality of disposable incomes and market incomes differ relatively significantly from each another. This suggests that redistribution through taxes and transfers has a significant corrective effect on very uneven market distribution.

Social spending initially rose, reaching a peak of 29.8 per cent of GDP in 2003. It then fell slightly – probably also because of the reforms – reaching a relatively low level of 26.8 per cent of GDP in 2007. In the crisis of 2009, it again rose above the level of 2003 (to more than 30 per cent of GDP), but then declined again.

The social (and economic) development of Germany is a special case. This went in a very different direction than in the rest of the Eurozone, especially compared to the crisis countries (GIPS). After a prolonged critical phase at the beginning of EMU, the situation stabilised and finally improved, which was reflected internally in the labour market and government finances, but also externally in growing export surpluses. In terms of wage development, Germany remained well below the EMU average. The price that society had to pay for it was high: A steep increase in inequality, which could serve as a breeding ground for radicalism.

The rich middle of the Eurozone: Slow recovery from the crisis

Development in the richer Eurozone countries of France, Italy, Belgium, the Netherlands, Luxembourg, Austria and Finland – regardless of their differences (Luxembourg is an extremely rich, special case) – is very close to the average of EMU, which of course is also strongly influenced by these major economies. Unemployment was usually lower than in Germany before the crisis, but subsequently rose sharply. Above all, in France and Italy, it was over ten per cent in recent years. All countries have relatively high levels of net immigration, led by Italy (3.8 million between 2002 and 2013). The wage share rose slightly in France and Italy, but remained relatively stable at 53 to 55 per cent. Real wages grew by between five and ten per cent between 2001 and 2009. In the case of nominal unit costs, which are more important to competitiveness, increases registered between 1999 and 2015 were 25.4 for France and 31.1 for Italy, slightly higher than the Eurozone average of 23.9 (which was also pulled down by Germany). Until 2008, these grew by 15.2 and 20.7 points, respectively, thus more significantly than in Germany (1.2), whereas after 2009 these rates were lower (6.9 in France, 5.5 in Italy) than in Germany (9.0). Overall, their growth rates were on average about two per cent per year, meeting the European Central Bank's inflation target.

Inequality, measured by the S80/S20 ratio or the Gini Index, remained relatively unchanged in these countries. Although in Italy it was above the German level and above the EMU average, it was below the German level in the other countries. Social expenditures (as a share of GDP) rose above all after the crisis (unlike in Germany). These were relatively high in France in the long term (about 33 per cent), while in Italy they were relatively low (under 30 per cent). Also, poverty rates remained relatively stable and were mostly below the German figures. France's poverty rate rose from under 19 per cent in the first post-crisis years, but fell again to 18.1 per cent in 2013. Only Italy and Belgium tended to have higher rates; Italy, with figures almost 30 per cent, registered much higher levels than the Eurozone average.

Until the crisis, this "core group" could be seen as a virtual anchor of stability for the Eurozone; indeed, its wage development was based on the economic policy objectives of EMU. However, recovery after the recession was slow, a development which goes hand in hand with wage restraint, rising social spending and higher unemployment.

The new Member States: Poorer and more ambitious

The smaller countries of Slovenia, Slovakia, Estonia, Latvia, Lithuania, Malta and Cyprus (to be examined in the next section), which joined the EU in 2004, inevitably became members of the Eurozone relatively late (between 2007 and 2015). The Baltic countries even decided to join the EU after the outbreak of the "Euro crisis" (Estonia 2011, Latvia 2014, Lithuania 2015). But even before this they were subject to the Maastricht Treaty and had fixed exchange rates linked to the Euro.

All of the new countries are poorer than the Eurozone average. With the exception of more prosperous Slovenia and Malta, the new Member States still had double-digit unemployment rates at the beginning of the century. However, these fell sharply (to 4 to 7 per cent) until the financial crisis hit in 2009, during which they rose sharply, with the exception of Slovenia, which slipped into crisis three years later. The recovery that began in 2011 was slow. The Baltic countries have high net emigration, in contrast to Slovenia and Slovakia.

Nominal unit labour costs rose massively. Between 1999 and 2015, these grew by 23 per cent on average. In Estonia, nominal unit labour costs rose 66 per cent, 53 per cent in Latvia, 46 per cent in Lithuania, and 56 per cent in Slovakia. Only Slovenia remained at roughly the EMU average. Most catching up took place before the crisis, slowing down for just one to two years. Real wages grew by about 75 per cent between 2001 and 2009 in Estonia and Latvia, by approximately 55 per cent in Lithuania, 30 per cent in Slovakia, and roughly ten per cent in Slovenia and Malta.

Inequality soared in the Baltic countries (Gini significantly above 0.3, S80/S20 ratios above five, even over six in Lithuania and Latvia), while in Slovenia, Slovakia, and Malta it was below the EMU average. In Latvia, Lithuania and Slovakia, the decline in poverty is clearly visible, whereas in Slovenia and Malta it rose after the crisis. Apart from Slovenia, the level of expenditure on social protection was – as is typical of poorer countries – well below the EMU average. These rose in the recession, but then gradually fell again.

The new Member States can be broadly divided into two groups. The Baltic states and Slovakia are poorer, their development more uneven and more dynamic, especially with regard to wages. Slovenia and Malta are somewhat richer and more social, but also more moderate in wage growth.

The programme countries: Busted dreams

Ireland and the peripheral southern countries of Greece, Spain, Portugal and Cyprus have a very different EU integration history. Ireland rose to become the second-richest EU country in the 1990s (measured in terms of GDP/per capita), while the other countries continued to be among the "EU middle class": Richer than the post-communist countries, but poorer than the north-western Member States. What they all had in common was the sovereign debt crisis, triggered by the banking crisis, the great recession, and attempts to save banks and stimulate the economy again. It led to all of these countries requiring aid, which the EU (together with the International Monetary Fund) provided to them, albeit subject to conditions. In order to better assess social development in these countries, it is necessary to distinguish between the pre-crisis period up until 2008/09 and the phase dominated by austerity policy from 2010 onwards.

Booming labour market until the crisis

Labour markets developed positively in the first years of EMU membership. Above all Spain, but also Greece, were able to significantly reduce their historically high unemployment rates to about eight per cent. In Ireland, Portugal, and Cyprus, unemployment was already much lower in 2000 and remained largely unchanged; only Portugal had an increasing unemployment rate from 2002 onwards. This labour market development is all the more remarkable because Spain, but also the other countries, had high immigration surpluses. Between 2002 and 2008 alone, four (!) million people (about ten per cent of the population of 2002) migrated to Spain. Ireland accounted for 370,000 (almost 10 per cent), Portugal (270,000 immigrants) (2.7 per cent) and 70,000 (about 8 per cent) in Cyprus. There is no equivalent data for Greece, but the balance is expected to be around 200,000 (two per cent), with a high estimated volume of illegal immigration.

Wage developments reflected the positive labour market situation: Real wages grew by over 20 per cent in Ireland between 2001 and 2009, about 15 per cent in Greece and Cyprus, almost ten per cent in Spain and by only five per cent in Portugal. Nominal unit labour costs grew strongly until 2008. With an index of 100 for 2010, these costs increased by 32 points in Ireland between 1999 and 2008, 23 in Greece and Cyprus, 27 in Spain and 20 in Portugal. By way of comparison: The EMU average was almost 15 points, with the increase for Germany only being one point. The development of the wage share (corresponding to real unit labour costs) was mixed: In Spain, Portugal and Ireland, it declined, in Greece it rose by about five percentage points, and in Cyprus it only fluctuated slightly. These increases in wages have hardly slowed export growth, but have contributed to the deficit in the current account, which has been interpreted as a loss of competitiveness.

In this phase up to 2008, income distribution only changed slightly measured in terms of the Gini coefficient or the S80/S20 ratio. Inequality in all countries except Cyprus was above the EMU average. It only fell slightly in 2005 in Ireland and Portugal, which had the highest inequality in the EU from 1999 to 2001. Poverty rates were also above average, especially in Greece, but fell by around five percentage points by 2009. The decline in other countries was weaker by two to three percentage points.

Expenditures on social policy (as a share of GDP) in all peripheral countries was below the EMU average of around 26 per cent. The gap in social spending was particularly high in Ireland and Cyprus (each 15 per cent), while Spain spent nearly 20 per cent, Greece and Portugal 22 to 23 per cent of GDP.

Until the crisis, the social situation in the periphery can be roughly summarised as follows: Strong growth in jobs with high immigration levels, accompanied by rising unit labour costs and decreasing poverty. The growth model focused on the non-tradable goods and services sector, with real estate bubbles in Spain and Ireland. Societies had relatively great inequality and poverty with relatively weakly developed social states.

Into the abyss of austerity

This picture changed completely with the financial market crisis, the great recession, the subsequent sovereign debt panic and the implementation of austerity measures and reforms required by creditors. Credit-financed growth, especially in the real estate sector, collapsed.

The labour market situation deteriorated dramatically. The unemployment rate rose from the single-digit range to more than 26 per cent in Spain and Greece, 16 per cent in Portugal and Cyprus, and 14 per cent in Ireland. A slight improvement was registered from 2013 onwards, most clearly in Ireland. This was also due to the changed direction of migration: Immigration countries became emigration countries. From Spain, a total of 460,000 people emigrated between 2010 and 2013, 145,000 from Greece, 138,000 from Ireland and 79,000 from Portugal. Only Cyprus had net immigration by 2013.

Creditors insisted upon reforms in the wage-setting system and wage reductions in the public sector and a minimum wage. The real value of the latter fell by 30 per cent in Greece.

The development of wages followed the development of the labour market and policy towards declining real wages, a falling wage share and a decline in nominal unit labour costs. While the latter increased by 4.7 points in EMU between 2009 and 2015, and by nine points in Germany (2010 = 100), it fell by nearly 16 in Ireland, almost 14 in Greece, and about six points in Spain, Portugal, and Cyprus.

Inequality increased. The Gini coefficient rose mainly in Cyprus and Spain; with regard to the S80/S20 ratio, growing inequality was even more evident: By 2014, it rose to 6.8 in Spain (from 5.6 in 2008), in Greece to 6.5 (from 5.6 in 2010), in Ireland to 4.7 (from 4.2 in 2009), in Cyprus to 5.4 (from 4.3 in 2008) and in Portugal to 6.2 (from 5.6 in 2010). The poverty rate in Ireland, Greece and Spain rose perceptively by about five percentage points, in Cyprus by four and in Portugal by two and a half points.

Social policy could hardly mitigate these developments as budgets were increasingly scaled back. Nevertheless, between 2007 and 2012/13, the share of social spending in relation to GDP increased everywhere: In Greece from 23.7 per cent to 31.6 per cent, in Spain from 20.3 per cent to 25.7 per cent, in Ireland from 17.3 per cent to 23 per cent (2010: 24.5 per cent), in Portugal from 23 per cent to 27.6 per cent, and in Cyprus from 16.6 to 22.3 per cent. This increase is also due to the decline in GDP, which serves as the denominator in these social protection rates. Between 2010 and 2012, actual nominal expenditures (i.e. cumulative values), which grew by 3.5 per cent on average in the Eurozone, fell by 6.6 per cent in Greece, 0.1 per cent in Spain, 1 per cent in Ireland, 2 per cent and 4.2 per cent in Portugal.

Overall, the periphery mirrored a social catastrophe that was worst in Greece and the most fleeting in Ireland. Unemployment and poverty increased and social safety nets decreased as declining social budgets faced increasing numbers of people in need. However, in the last three years, a slow recovery has been evident, especially in Spain and Ireland. Countries whose dynamic growth had once attracted people became countries of net emigration, with thekir inhabitants having to seek their fortune abroad, often in Germany.

A differentiated picture of the Eurozone

The social development of the Eurozone therefore contrasted greatly between the centre, on the one hand, and the periphery, on the other. While in Germany – after an internal devaluation with growing inequality – a relatively stable post-crisis phase with low unemployment took hold, the other rich countries in Western Europe only overcame their crises slowly. In the east, the new Member States halfway succeeded in recovering their pre-crisis momentum (exception: Slovenia). But the programme countries – those implementing austerity measures – lost most of the social progress they had made during the first years of EMU membership.

HOMEMADE AND EXTERNAL CAUSES OF SOCIAL DEVELOPMENTS

Differing social development in the individual countries of the Eurozone results from a complex interrelationship between their national structures and policies, on the one hand, and external conditions and influences resulting from their integration into EMU, the EU, and the global economy on the other.

National factors

There are different types of welfare states and variants of capitalism, which have been explored by Fritz Scarp, Goats Espying-Andersen, Peter Hall and many other scholars. Industrial relations and trade union structures influence wage developments in the respective country. Strong, unified trade unions in Germany and the Netherlands are able to enforce wage restraint in the interest of job security and competitiveness. But such trade-offs in countries with politically fragmented, competing trade unions (France, Italy, Spain, Portugal) are much more difficult to achieve. While in north-western and southern Europe, wage-setting is mostly taken for entire sectors, company-specific agreements are the dominant form in Eastern Europe and Ireland. Training and innovation systems differ from one country to another. While very specific knowledge is taught in Germany in the dual training system, in other countries this is left to companies.

In the welfare states, Central European countries are marked by their "Bismarckian" social systems, which operate according to an insurance principle linked to dependent employment. In other countries, there is usually a more universal or weak social state, as can be seen from the different social protection quotas discussed above. Significantly, the Scandinavian and Anglo-Saxon welfare states (they are cited as specific types in the literature) have refused to join EMU (exception: Ireland) because they felt that their models were threatened by membership.

From a less sociological perspective, for example, countries are classified by the World Economic Forum according to their competitiveness or by the World Bank according to their business-friendliness ("doing business"). Among other things that play a role: The intensity of regulation of product and labour markets, wage-setting systems, protection against dismissal, regulation of business start-ups, efficiency and transparency of the tax administration, and education systems. In general, southern European countries fare relatively poorly in these assessments. Northern and central European countries are very well placed, while Eastern European countries are scattered between them, with the Baltic states coming off better than the rest.

The economies of the individual Eurozone countries have different patterns of specialisation characterising regional and sectoral composition of their foreign trade sectors. Even the importance of foreign trade and the sector of non-tradable goods and services differ considerably from country to country. Germany's economy is, for its size, extremely international, whereas for Greece, for example, the share of exports is very low.

External shocks and the impact of the currency union

These internal structures are subject to external "shocks", which they are unevenly equipped to cope with. This includes the opening up of markets to Eastern Europe and emerging markets (mainly China), which is based on EU foreign trade policy. Individual Member States only have an indirect influence on this. This affects countries with competing supply structures (southern periphery) more than Germany, which with its export profile benefits from global growth.

The free movement of workers within the EU facilitates inward and outward migration, although intra-EU migration is often less important than immigration from third countries. Migrant workers and competitive offers – through freedom to provide services – from low-wage Member States exert pressure on wages, working conditions and prices (and income) in some service sectors (e.g. logistics). EU law also restricts national policy options, for example in the area of industrial policy or the expansion of public supply that potentially competes with private supply.

These external influences have equally affected all EU countries. For members of the Eurozone, there are once again tighter constraints on national economic and social policies and the handling of specific shocks. Above all, large fluctuations in the external value of the Euro, which can be seen in the Euro-dollar exchange rate, affect national economies differently. The marked appreciation of the Euro after 2000 (around 50 per cent) has worsened price competitiveness in markets in third countries and cheapened imports. The latter has, on the one hand, improved purchasing power (through relatively low prices of oil imports, for example); on the other hand, however, local production has been put under pressure by greater competition.

Within the Eurozone, on the other hand, nominal "exchange rates" were inevitably stable. It was therefore no longer possible to compensate for different rates of inflation and wage increases through appreciation or depreciation of respective currencies. To the extent that prices, wages, and profits have developed along different trajectories, there have been real appreciations and depreciations. Germany actually depreciated, while the periphery in the south and east, in real terms, appreciated. The centre around France stayed relatively neutral.

Another effect of the EMU has been the integration of capital markets. The most important factor, the interest rate, has only varied slightly between EMU members. Capital movements and cross-border investments have increased. In particular, the dynamic regions of the periphery have experienced strong inflows. Their banking systems have expanded the allocation of credit in light of good growth and optimistic growth expectations, thus increasing automatically purchasing power and without risk of exchange rate fluctuations (in the Eurozone). On the other hand, low interest rates offered households and companies incentives to take on debt, which in light of growing income seemed unproblematic. In part, these also compensated for falling income from transfers from abroad, especially from Europe. Rising purchasing power and spending has not only increased imports, but also demand for domestic supply, especially non-tradable goods and services. The increase in employment has also led to higher wages. This has resulted in a positive feedback effect from purchasing power, production and employment.

The most decided external interventions in the social development of EMU Member States, as a condition for aid, have been made in the context of the adjustment programmes imposed on the highly indebted countries of Greece, Spain, Portugal, Ireland and Cyprus. Minimum wages and wages in the public sector have been frozen or reduced. In Greece, these reductions were over 20 per cent. The wage-setting system was decentralised (fewer industry-wide deals, more company-specific deals). Coverage of employees by collective agreements has declined, as statutory extension mechanisms have been weakened and company-specific exemptions facilitated.

In Portugal, the number of industry-wide tariff agreements decreased from 200 in 2008 to 46 in 2012, while the number of employees with collective agreements fell in the same period from 1.9 million to 328,000. In Greece, the number of sectoral contracts declined from 202 (2008) to 14 (2013) and Spain in the same period from 1,448 to 543. The benefits from unemployment insurance and pension insurance were reduced and the retirement age increased. In Greece, pensions, which amounted to more than 1,000 Euros a month, were reduced by five to 15 per cent, the usual Christmas allowance was abolished, and the retirement age increased from 65 to 67.

The reductions in government expenditures did not just affect social expenditures. Between 2009 and 2014, health care expenditures in Greece also fell by 48.6 per cent, in Spain by 13.6 per cent, Portugal by 21.5 per cent; spending on education dropped by 20 per cent in Greece, 14.9 per cent in Spain, and 16.1 per cent in Portugal. Cuts in the health system led to serious problems in many hospitals, particularly in Greece.

These measures are embedded in broader sets of measures, such as the Euro Plus Pact and the Six Pack, which point in a similar direction. The Euro Plus Pact applies to EMU countries and seeks – in the context of budget consolidation and improvement of competitiveness – to abolish wage-indexing systems and adapt pension systems to demographic trends. The six-pack, which applies EU-wide, monitors nominal unit labor costs and the unemployment rate besides many other indicators of debt, competitiveness and inflation.

EMU AND SOCIAL DEVELOPMENT IN THE EUROZONE

What contribution has Economic and Monetary Union made to social development registered at the outset by its structural conditions (single currency, centralised monetary policy) and specific measures (policy coordination and monitoring, bailout programmes with conditions attached)? Before this question can be answered, different influential factors must be examined (see previous section). The answer depends upon where one starts in order to improve the social situation in the Eurozone.

Two simple answers can be ruled out at once: Neither the EMU nor national structures can be held responsible alone. If EMU were the sole cause, social developments between countries and in different time periods would not be so divergent. If national structures were solely responsible, different social developments in the individual periods would be difficult to explain. If countries such as GIPS and Italy were fundamentally unsuitable for membership in EMU because of their economic and social structure, their development by 2008 should not have been so dynamic. Some of the countries considered here also adopted the Euro very late, in particular the Baltic States (2011, 2014, 2015) and the other new Member States (2007-2009). Their currencies were already previously tied to the Euro, however.

The two extremes: Germany and the programme countries

The two extreme cases of the Eurozone, Germany and the programme countries, provide complementary examples of interrelations between internal and external factors.

Germany responded to its problems (unemployment and budget deficits) at the beginning of the Euro era in 2003 with Agenda 2010. Pressure was only applied by Brussels because the budget deficit exceeded the Maastricht limit of 3 per cent. Accompanying wage stagnation and wage dispersion (facilitated by cooperative trade unions and works councils) and real internal devaluation enormously improved an already good current account balance ("export world champion"). Local demand was curtailed and price competitiveness grew, functioning like a turbocharger for otherwise good structural competitiveness (optimal specialisation capitalising on global demand trends). Were there not the common currency, a nominal appreciation of the Deutsche Mark would soon have reduced these price advantages – although probably with the advantage of relatively higher purchasing power at home.

The programme countries, on the other hand, saw no reason to change their policies when their economies were growing dynamically in the pre-crisis phase. The above-average increases in prices and wages hardly undermined competitiveness: Exports continued to grow, with world market shares remaining relatively stable except for Ireland. High current account deficits were due not to declining exports, but to strongly expanding domestic demand. Outside of the EMU, however, they might have led to a devaluation. The budgetary situation was relatively stable (Ireland and Spain even had surpluses), which is why the EU expressed little criticism of the growth model.

With the triple crisis of banks in 2008, the great recession in 2009, and the sovereign debt panic, the picture changed suddenly. In the context of the bailout programmes, creditors also expected budget consolidation and real internal devaluation. The two goals were difficult to reconcile, since falling wages at least lowered tax revenues in the short term. Negative multiplier effects of reduced government expenditures reduced growth further. As a result, wages and social protection declined. Since these national policies were clearly pursued because creditors (the Troika) insisted on them, the link between social problems and EMU membership is clear. However, the question is whether national alternative scenarios (exit from the Euro and/or state bankruptcy) would have been less painful.

Impact on wage development, social security and income distribution

The impact of EMU on three key social challenges, namely wage development/labor market, social security and income distribution/poverty, can be summarised as follows:

First, EMU is obviously compatible with very different wage developments. However, it prevents diverging wage developments from affecting the external value of the currency, i.e. appreciations correcting wage restraint and devaluations compensating for rising wages (wage changes always relative to trading partners). As a result, imbalances can build up over longer periods of time. This will only be problematic for deficit countries, however, if financing of the current account deficit is no longer feasible. Surplus countries will in the worst case lose their savings (claims against foreign countries).

Secondly, Economic and Monetary Union can also be reconciled with different types of welfare states and social protection levels. In almost all countries, social security expenditure has risen, in the short term especially during the recession of 2009. Deficits and debt limits do not necessarily lead to cuts in social spending. What has been problematic is the deep cuts that were imposed on the programme countries, reducing their spending during periods of social crisis.

Thirdly, the EMU has had little impact on income distribution in the Euro countries. However, inequality and poverty rose in phases of internal devaluation, for example in Germany from 2003, and in the programme countries from 2010 onwards. In the programme countries, the Troika can be held responsible; in Germany this development was chosen by Berlin itself – albeit as a reaction to perceived adjustment pressures in EMU.

The basic compatibility of membership in EMU with various social developments (wages, social policy, income distribution) does not mean that common policies or standards would be superfluous. Mutual dependencies are too great for this. Because of the integration of markets and the coordination imperative underlying European policy, national policies are often no longer in a position to react optimally. National initiatives are not only less effective than common ones, but they also risk being successful at the expense of other countries. European monitoring of national developments and support in critical times can prevent or at least mitigate problematic social developments in EMU.

Notes

1 | The Gini coefficient is an indicator of inequality that varies between zero (full equality) and one (all income belongs to an individual or household).
2 | The figures are based on Eurostat data, from the last available year (as indicated); for the wage share: Ameco Database.

PART II: POLITICS, POWER, IDEAS

5. Germany's own special path?
Fundamental economic principles underlying German policy

Mark Schieritz

There is a story about former Italian Prime Minister Mario Monti that goes like this: At the peak of the Euro crisis he was visiting Barack Obama in the White House in Washington. The President asked him why international negotiations with Germany on economic issues are often so tedious and why the Germans so stubbornly refuse to do more to strengthen domestic demand. Whereupon he, Monti, answered that for Germans economics is not a social science. Economics, rather, has "always been more of a branch of moral philosophy".

This brief episode underscores the special status assumed by Germany in the international economic debate. In macro-economic discussion groups of global institutions such as the G20 or the G7, German negotiators rarely find any allies, while in the Anglo-Saxon world German economists are usually considered to be outsiders who are no longer in tune with the times. Martin Wolf, chief columnist of the *Financial Times*, summed up the prevailing mood in many of Europe's capital cities with the words Germany is "the biggest problem" in the Eurozone.

The aim of this Chapter is to sketch out the idiosyncrasies of the German economic debate and explore the causes of these peculiarities in detail. After this, we examine what consequences it all has for progressive political strategies in Europe.

'TWAS THE STATE

Angela Merkel issued a government statement in the Bundestag on 29 June 2012. The topic: The Euro crisis. Delegates had to vote on the introduction of the Fiscal Treaty, which among other things would obligate the Member States of Economic and Monetary Union to have balanced budgets and to enact a debt cap in national law based on the German model. The German Chancellor called it a "milestone in the history of the EU", paving the way to a "sustainable Union of stability".

This wording reflects the first quirk in the German debate. It reveals where Berlin views the roots of the crisis to be found: In excessive sovereign debt. This diagnosis also accounts for the therapy prescribed: The most important aim in Germany policy towards the crisis – at least in its initial phase – was at any rate stricter European budget rules. The Council of Experts for the Assessment of Overall Economic Development, for instance, proposed a "long-term regulatory framework" to deal with the "sovereign debt crisis" in Europe in its annual review for 2011, while the Federal Government advocated stricter rules for the Stability and Growth Pact on top of its efforts to gain acceptance for the Fiscal Treaty.[1]

Of course, by that point in time a more differentiated interpretation of the crisis had long since gained currency at the international level. After all, the crisis had by then also hit countries like Spain and Ireland, which in contrast to Greece, for instance, had relatively low debt ratios. The focus shifted, for example, to the role of the financial markets in speculative excesses in real estate markets. Thus, in the years following the introduction of the Euro, large amounts of foreign capital – not least from Germany – flowed to countries like Spain or Ireland because investors expected greater yields there. This capital was not invested in productive undertakings, however. In Spain, for instance, there was a tremendous expansion in the award of mortgaged loans and building activity. It was only after the bubble burst and ailing banks had to be bailed out that sovereign debt skyrocketed.

Another cause of the crisis addressed in the international debate was also the decision-making mechanism of investors in financial markets, who suddenly pulled out their money when the crisis hit, thereby exacerbating the situation because as a result countries that had maintained relatively solid fiscal purses like France all of a sudden faced financing difficulties. According to this perspective from game theory, there is not only one, but several stable conditions or balances in economic variables. The situation before the crisis constituted such a balance: Investors provided the Southern countries cheap money, which is why these states were able to always service their debt on time. As a result of the panic in the financial markets, interest shot up because nobody wanted to invest money in the periphery any longer due to fear of impending insolvency. Precisely this crash became probable as a result of the increasing costs of debt-servicing. The European Central Bank assessed the risk of such a scenario materialising at such a high level that the Board of the Central Bank felt forced to take counter-measures in the early summer of 2012. Within the framework of the Outright Monetary Transactions (OMT) programme, the Central Bank announced that it would intervene if the interest level in individual Member States moved significantly upwards as a result of irrational market movements. In doing so, it made a significant contribution to the stabilisation of the financial markets.

5. Germany's own special path? 71

These different manners of interpretation became evident in a debate among experts triggered by a paper published by the Center for Economic Policy Research. In November 2015 a group of international economists under the leadership of Richard Baldwin and Francesco Giavazzi attempted to spell out a consensus in the analysis of the Euro crisis. In their article, they stated that the crisis should "not be viewed as a sovereign debt crisis". Instead, they argued, it had been triggered by a reversal of significant flows of capital to states in the periphery.[2] In Germany this interpretation has remained controversial down to the present day. In their response to the paper, the members of the Council of Experts argued that the consensus did not adequately address the role of the state and one-sidedly viewed actors in the financial markets as to blame for the skewed behaviour. In Greece and Portugal, for instance, the state also accepted cheap credit from abroad, expanding its debt. In Spain and Ireland government institutions had approvingly gone along with the booming real-estate market instead of taking decisive action to contain it. In its essence, the crisis was thus once again a case of state failure.[3]

Statements like these reflect a fundamental distrust of state action in the European context. This distrust marked the German line in the negotiations over the Treaty of Maastricht and also impacted the specific design of Economic and Monetary Union, which concedes the financial markets a key role in the exercise of controls over national fiscal policy. Based on these notions and ideas, the interest level is to assume the function that the exchange rate is no longer able to perform as a result of the launch of the common currency. A sustainable budget management is accordingly rewarded with low interest, while an expansive policy in government expenditures is penalised with higher interest. Because this mechanism is threatened by being put out of commission by interventions of the Central Bank, the Bundesbank has rejected the OMT programme down to the present. In June 2013, the President of the Central Bank, Jens Weidmann, argued before the German Federal Constitutional Court that the answer to the question as to whether the interest level is distorted by market forces would always have to be framed in a "highly subjective" manner. Given this, purchases of bonds by the ECB would pose "considerable problems for stability policy" which would "undermine the disciplinary role of market interest and governments' own responsibility for financial policy.

HEY THERE: INCENTIVES!

An American military twinjet touched down at Westerland airport on 12 July 2012. On board: Timothy Geither, at the time U.S. Secretary of the Treasury. He had come to Sylt to meet Wolfgang Schäuble, who was spending his summer holiday on the island just like every year. Schauble told Geithner that he was willing to exclude Greece from the EMU because the country simply did not stick to the rules. Geithner was shocked, as he was sure of one thing: That this would exacerbate the crisis. That is how Geithner described it in his memoires, revealing another peculiarity in the German debate over economic policy: The significance of incentive effects. While in particular the Americans and French repeatedly urged intervention to calm the situation in the financial markets, the German government argued that this would reward skewed behaviour and lay the foundations for a new crisis.

Fears of false incentives in the form of generous assistance measures run through German crisis policy like a scarlet thread. In the negotiations over the first rescue programme for Greece in the early summer of 2010, Berlin urged that especially drastic savings requirements be applied to deter potential copycats. The restrictive design of the programme was intended to prevent other crisis countries from also demanding financial support. The rejection of debt relief for Greece was justified by the German government among other things by arguing that if generous debt relief were offered, Portugal or Spain would demand the same. And when the European Central Bank fell in line behind other major central banks in January 2015, announcing that it would seek to decrease long-term interest levels by purchasing government bonds, this was also criticised in Germany by arguing that cheaper financing costs would reduce pressure on the Member States to carry out reforms.

The incentive problem also dominated the German position in previous crises. In reaction to the worsening economic crisis in Latin America and Asia in the 1990s, the International Monetary Fund (IMF) put together major rescue packages. These were supposed to compensate for the outflow of private capital, which was threatening the stability of banks in the respective countries. In the case of Mexico and Indonesia, the assistance amounted to almost 20 per cent of Gross Domestic Product. The measures taken, not least at the behest of the American government, were sharply criticised by the Bundesbank – which together with the Federal Ministry of Finance is responsible for German relations with the IMF. The strategy opted for was "subject to extreme misgivings from a stability-policy perspective," according to an article in a monthly report published in September 2000. The incentive structures were "distorted in the direction of high-risk behaviour", making "future financial crises" more likely.[4] This behaviour, dubbed "moral-hazard fundamentalism" by former Treasury Secretary Timothy Geither, is not to be witnessed in this form in virtually any other industrialised country.

No experiments

In February 2008, Dominique Strauss-Kahn travelled to India. The Managing Director of the IMF was to hold a speech there – and Strauss-Kahn used the opportunity to announce a radical change in course. He called upon the community of states to support overall economic demand within the framework of "target-oriented fiscal stimulus". This statement marked a departure from financial policy orthodoxy, which had characterised IMF policy for decades – and which was advocated by most economists. The use of monetary and financial policy instruments to steer the economy experienced a global renaissance as a result. In several country reports, the IMF called upon Germany to leverage discretionary latitude in public budgets to encourage more investment, even if this led to the government taking on more debt.

In Germany this approach continues to meet with reservations. Although at the climax of the international financial crisis the German Government also instituted two economic-stimulus packages, when the crisis reached EMU, the stabilisation of demand was subordinated to the aim of fiscal consolidation in line with the interpretation of the crisis as a sovereign debt crisis as described in the foregoing. As the crisis unfolded, scepticism grew over expansive policy measures. In particular, Minister of Finance Wolfgang Schäuble repeatedly lashed out against the mechanical notion – in his view – that the state could compensate for sagging demand by means of expansive policy measures. Decreases in interest rates were problematic, in his opinion, because they offered fertile soil for new speculative excesses in the financial markets. Government expenditure programmes could even throttle economic growth if companies and consumers were made insecure by an increase in indebtedness. And low interest rates, it was argued, would also lead to speculative excesses in the financial markets.

German policy-makers therefore emphasised the need to create the preconditions for long-term sustainable growth through structural reforms. Even though such reforms might be associated with decreases in transfer payments, they could also have an impact in the short term if trust and confidence in the state's ability to act effectively grows. This perspective is shared by most economic policy advisory institutions. The German Council of Experts, for instance, writes in its 2015 Annual Report that relaxation of the austerity course in the crisis countries would "jeopardise the credibility of consolidation and its effect of strengthening the supply side." A "new economic-stimulus package in Germany financed with debt" must be rejected for this reason.[5] How wide the divide was between Germany and the rest of the world in fiscal policy is illustrated by a statement made by Olivier Blanchard, former head economist of the International Monetary Fund, to the effect that during his term he had to fight time and time again against the "Hoover-German line" (American President Herbert Hoover insisted on rigid financial policy during the Great Depression in the USA), according to which a decrease in budget deficits in and of itself has a stimulating effect on the economy.[6]

The Myth of the Global Market

In January 2013, Angela Merkel was a guest at the World Economic Forum in Davos. As is so often the case these days, the future of Europe was at stake. European states could only grow "if they also offer products that can be sold globally," asserted the Chancellor. That is why competitiveness was "important". The view that only exports create true prosperity is widespread in Germany. The legislative programme of the CDU and the CSU in the Bundestag elections in 2013, for instance, posited that Europe had to "secure opportunities in international markets" and for this reason resolve a "pact for competitiveness". This view is based on the assumption that a country, like an enterprise, can conquer new markets if it reduces its costs – in this case usually wage costs. For this reason as well, the call for pay cuts for workers has been a mainstay in German crisis policy.

It has repeatedly been noted in the international debate, however, that this strategy can very quickly run up against its limits in a large economic area like the Euro area. In small or very open economies, it may be possible to stimulate the economy through low wages and an increase in unemployment. The precondition for this is that advantages in the export branch are not negated by negative developments in the domestic market as a result of low wage increases. This is the case in Germany, which has an export quota of 46 per cent.

With exports of goods accounting for 19.5 per cent of economic performance, Economic and Monetary Union is more like the USA or Japan than Germany. In comparison to the individual Member States, as the European Central Bank writes, it is "a much more closed economy" and sells by far the predominant share of its goods internally and not abroad. This also means, however, that an improvement in external competitiveness does not have a positive effect on the overall economy as it does in the case of Germany. Viewed economically, the continent is simply too large to be able to restructure and recover by wage-dumping at the expense of its trading partners – all the more so because Europe's trading partners would defend themselves against this at the mere attempt. The Americans are increasingly annoyed by Europeans' burgeoning foreign-trade surpluses, for instance, and it is only a question of time until they take counter-measures. They could impede access to their market for European products, for example, or devalue the dollar.

In his analysis of German crisis policy, the Dutch political scientist Matthias Matthijs comes to the conclusion that the German government has assumed the role of a *coercive hegemon*. Germany has only been able to preserve its claim to leadership in Europe by coercive means – such as penalising countries by withholding financial assistance or by threatening them with termination of their membership in EMU – because the German view of the crisis is not shared by most of the other European states. He compares the role of

Germany with the USA, which in the wake of World War II was able to rise to a position of global leadership as a *benevolent hegemon* because American political ideas were viewed as useful and in the own interest of many Western countries. Based on this analysis, Matthijs then goes on to forecast that Germany's hegemonic position in Europe will not be of a lasting nature. An order based on coercion is unstable over the long term.[7] But why are Germans different than everybody else?

Ideas

The German economic policy debate cannot be understood without analysing the historically conditioned dogma upon which it is founded: Ordoliberalism. Its inception goes back to a group of economists led by Walter Eucken, Alexander Rüstow and Franz Böhm, who sought an answer to the undeniable phenomenon of crises in the capitalist mode of production in the 1930s. They found one in a sort of "third alternative" between a planned economy of the Soviet type and radical liberalism. In the view of ordoliberals, on the one hand an economic policy based on state intervention is doomed to failure because the state does not have all the information and the power to impose its will that would be necessary in order to centrally steer economic processes. On the other hand, a market economy left to itself would lead to a concentration of economic and hence also political power through the formation of cartels and mergers. In the words of Eucken: "There is only a small difference between American trusts and Russian central planning."

The task of economic policy, argued the ordoliberals, was therefore to develop a regulatory framework that ensures that market economy forces in the end work to the benefit of everyone. One key role in this is played by the principle of liability, i.e. the notion that market actors bear complete responsibility for their actions and cannot escape this responsibility in the face of negative developments. Even though ordoliberalism can be subsumed under liberalism, the state plays a central role in ordoliberal conceptions, as is underscored by Alexander Rüstow's call for a "strong state [...] above the economy, there, where it belongs". At the heart of an ordoliberal regulatory conceptualisation are – for historical reasons in part – usually fair competition and the combatting of monopolies. Above and beyond this, Eucken also sees a need for socio-political measures, or for "precautions to fill in the gaps and cushion hardship" – a concept that was explored in more detail by economists like Alfred Müller-Armack, head of the Department for Basic Issues at the Ministry of Economics under Ludwig Erhard and co-founder of the programme for the Social Market Economy.[8]

Nowadays there is practically no professorship for ordoliberal policy at German universities to be found, and German economists are now also assessed in terms of whether they publish in international journals that only address ordoliberalism at most from a historical perspective. Nevertheless, ordoliberal principles have a major impact on the economic policy debate even today – and this across all political party lines. These principles have penetrated deeply into the institutional minds of key economic-policy institutions like the Bundesbank and Council of Experts and continue to have a major influence on policy in actual practice through economic advisory committees in ministries and active policy-makers. When German economists reject monetary policy or fiscal policy intervention to stabilise the economy, this is always associated with a general unease based on the ordoliberal tradition toward every form of process policy. The German emphasis on incentives and the belief in the binding nature of rules also have their roots in ordoliberalism: The Stability and Growth Pact and the Fiscal Compact are from the German perspective an attempt to specify a framework for economic action by the state at European level.

As a result of the European economic constitution's emphasis on economic freedoms, many ordoliberals were initially open to European integration.[9] Almost all ordoliberal currents are based on a sceptical view of human beings, strongly emphasising the fallibility of political decision-makers – for example their proclivity towards lobbying interests and political party tactics. For this reason, ordoliberals have little confidence in the rationality of political processes in general, which is expressed at the political level in certain reservations about the process of democratic opinion-formation. The expansion of joint competencies in the areas of environmental protection and social legislation has been accompanied by a change in attitudes towards the governing institutions of the EU, which have been increasingly viewed as a threat to economic freedom. This rejectionist stance has been reinforced by the crisis. A communitisation of risks, for example in the form of Eurobonds, is viewed as problematic, for example, because it could undermine the principle of responsibility: While financial political control remains in national hands, liability is being centralised. Thus, in the worst-case scenario, all countries taking part in the EMU would have to share responsibility for individual member countries that do not stick to the rules. In the opinion of the Bundesbank, the biggest risk to the stability of the currency union is that "first of all joint liability is being expanded, thus widening the existing institutional framework considerably, while on the other hand control and intervention possibilities are lagging behind".[10]

Ordoliberalism nevertheless dodges the most common international economic policy scheme. Its internationally conservative image stems from its rejection of discretionary intervention. Active steering of the economy is one of the central features of the progressive stream of Anglo-Saxon tradition, while in many cases ordoliberal strategies are completely void of any macroeconomic dimension.[11] In the left's criticism of neoliberal philosophy, however, the progressive potential of this movement is usually scarcely perceived. Thus, ordoliberalism definitely allows a redistributive social policy, as discussed above – as long as this redistribution is not implemented in a discretionary manner, but rather as part of the regulatory framework (for instance in the form of tax allowances or transfer payments that are pegged to income levels). Part of the problem German and international economists have in understanding each other can probably also be explained by different models of the social state that are implicitly assumed in the debate. In the Anglo-Saxon states, with their tendency towards a low level of social security, stabilisation of the economy by means of monetary and fiscal policy is assigned a much greater importance than in the Federal Republic, where the social state guarantees minimum social security in crises. That is why American policy-makers are under considerably greater pressure to quickly resort to macro-economic instruments to counter crisis situations. It should at least be discussed whether this automatically produces better results from a progressive perspective.

Interests

As important as economic policy tradition is in Germany – this alone cannot explain German crisis policy. After all, political struggles do not take place in a vacuum. They are driven by interests (whereby here interests are taken to mean what actors perceive their interests to be and not what can be defined as interests from an observer's perspective). What is special about the German debate can therefore also be attributed to special aspects of the German economic structure. Germany differs from the crisis states through its enormous savings surplus, reflected in a positive current account balance amounting to almost ten per cent of economic output. The peripheral states, in contrast, have run deficits in their current accounts until recently, i.e. they have saved less than they have invested and have been net importers of capital from abroad.

A decrease in the prime rate has a different impact in a country with a surplus than a country with a deficit – all the more so when in Germany savers have placed a large part of their assets in fixed-interest bonds and a relatively low percentage of the population has real estate, thereby profiting from low interest rates through the mechanism of rising real estate prices. Against this background, it is not unusual that the crisis policy of the ECB is viewed more critically in Germany than in the other countries in Economic and Monetary Union. This is all the more the case because a country like Germany, in which there is almost full employment and the sovereign debt ratio has been steadily declining for years, views the need for a macroeconomic stimulation of the economy differently than a country like Greece, with an unemployment rate of more than 20 per cent.

The economic debate is moreover influenced by the specific mix of economic sectors in Germany. The high level of dependence on exports and considerable international networking of the Germany economy have led to some enterprises that are specialised in exports, such as in the automotive industry, having much better access to the political arena than, for example, service companies. This also explains why international criticism of high German export surpluses – the reverse side of the savings surplus – largely falls on deaf ears in Germany.

Experience

In its essence, the EU is an example of a multi-level system with a complex structure of horizontal and vertical decision-making lines. Germany's rather cautious approach can be explained by the fact that entire generations of German politicians and economists have gained experience with the problems involved in governing such systems: By virtue of everyday political life in Germany's federalist system.

Relations between the federal government and the *Länder* exhibit a high degree of similarity to relations between the Member States of the EMU and the European level. These relations are marked on the one hand by a high level of risk-sharing in the area of financing because the financing costs of the *Länder* only differ minimally from those of the federal government and there is a transfer mechanism in the guise of financial compensation paid to the *Länder*. At the same time, the *Länder* also have considerable autonomy in several areas of policy. The German debate over a mutualisation of risks in Europe has been shaped by the experience that this dichotomy has proven to be a problem and *Länder* like Bremen or Saarland have become permanent recipients of transfer payments. In centralised states like France, such considerations scarcely play any role; nor are such ideas as salient in federal countries with more elements of competition, such as the USA, as in Germany. The flat rejection of Eurobonds and other instruments for spreading risk is accordingly also a result of unsolved problems in the German federal system.

What is to be done?

The Council of Experts made a remarkable proposal in its 2011 annual assessment: It argued that part of the old debt of Member States should be placed in a debt-repayment fund with joint liability and gradually reduced, which would have been associated with considerable interest-related advantages for the southern States. In return, the participating States would put up collateral and adopt binding consolidation plans.[12] This proposal was remarkable because it contained a clearly progressive element by virtue of the distribution of risk, but was devised by the Council of Experts, which is heavily influenced by ordoliberal ideas, and as a result was also criticised by conservative economists. Even though no debt-repayment fund was ever established, an important lesson can be learnt from its genesis: The German economic mainstream can also be persuaded to accept progressive strategies if in addition to short-term stabilisation goals such an approach also takes into account the long-term incentive problem.

In the last few years, economists, who – with all their scepticism towards Anglo-Saxon ways of thinking – are interested in solving problems and therefore have a certain openness to innovative ideas, have been appointed not only to the Council, but also to the Bundesbank, ministries and major economic-research institutes. In addition to reaffirming the Treaty of Maastricht and the principle of individual responsibility, the Bundesbank, for instance, has also broached the notion of an alternative to "pure fiscal union" with a far-ranging sacrifice of national sovereignty, which would in its view also be compatible with the incentive approach – and at the same time characterised German wage policy as not ambitious enough in view of the price stability objective of the European Central Bank.

Against this background, the demand for a European fiscal capacity, for example, would need to be supplemented with advocacy of a European steering capability so that liability and control are not situated on two different levels and to maintain consistency in the framework within which action is taken. Perhaps a combination of ordoliberal regulatory policy aspects and progressive elements even holds out an opportunity to move the debate over the future of Economic and Monetary Union out of the ideological trench warfare it is bogged down in at present and in a more progressive direction.

Notes

1 | Sachverständigenrat zur Begutachtung der gesamtwirtschaftlichen Entwicklung (2011): Verantwortung übernehmen. Jahresgutachten 2011/2012.
2 | Baldwin, Richard et al. (2015): Rebooting the Eurozone. Step I – Agreeing a Crisis Narrative. Policy Insight 85, Center for Economic Policy Research.
3 | Feld, Lars et al. (2016): Causes of the Eurozone Crisis: A Nuanced View. VoxEU (22 March 2016)
4 | Bundesbank (2000): Die Rolle des Internationalen Währungsfonds in einem veränderten Weltwirtschaftlichen Umfeld. Monatsbericht September 2000.
5 | Sachverständigenrat zur Begutachtung der gesamtwirtschaftlichen Entwicklung (2015): Zukunftsfähigkeit in den Mittelpunkt. Jahresgutachten 2015/2016.

6 | Blanchard, Olivier (2016): How to Teach Intermediate Macroeconomics After the Crisis. Real Time Economics Watch (2 June 2016), Peterson Institute for International Economics.

7 | Matthijs, Matthias (2015): Reading Kindleberger in Washington and Berlin. Ideas and Leadership in a Time of Crisis. Annual Meeting Paper, APSA, 2014.

8 | Eucken, Walter (2004): *Grundsätze der Wirtschaftspolitik*. Stuttgart: UTB.

9 | Joerges, Christian (2010): Europa nach dem Ordoliberalismus: Eine Philippika. Postneoliberale Rechtsordnung. Suchprozesse in der Krise, in: *Juridikum* 4/2010.

10 | Bundesbank (2015): Ansätze zur Stärkung des Ordnungsrahmens der Europäischen Währungsunion. Monthly Report for March 2015.

11 | Bofinger, Peter (2016): German Macroeconomics. The Long Shadow of Walter Eucken. VoxEU (7 June 2016).

12 | Sachverständigenrat (2011).

6. Which reform path for the Eurozone?
A mapping of political actors and their influence in the German debate

Björn Hacker and Cédric M. Koch

INTRODUCTION

The heated nature of debates surrounding the crisis of the Eurozone repeatedly gives the impression of unprecedented controversy. In tracing out positions of key actors in the German debate, however, it will become evident that a cornerstone in the sharp divide between champions of a stability union and advocates of a fiscal union was laid very early on. Specifically, an age-old conflict in international economic policy is being rekindled, with trust in a rule-based, self-disciplining market in one corner squaring off against the conviction that the state must intervene to correct and shape an imperfect market in the other.

Already in the founding phase of the Economic and Monetary Union (EMU), it became apparent how sharp the dichotomy was between these two economic paradigms for a currency union. One can characterise the first initiative for a monetary union – the 1970 Werner Plan – as having been dominated by Keynesian notions of economic dirigisme. Ideas included synchronising national budgetary procedures, harmonising tax systems and coordinating economic stimulus policy in an economic decision-making committee to be set up at the Community level. Although the report submitted by Commission President Jacques Delors in 1989 calling for a renewed attempt at establishing the EMU, which was eventually undertaken in 1999, still pointed to the need for a macro-economic framework and common policy, the monetarist-ordoliberal argument for budgetary disciplining of national fiscal policies had at the same time come to occupy centre stage in the eventual design.[1]

In the domestic German debate, it is not difficult to identify a long-standing majority position endorsing a rules- and market-based version of a transnational monetary area. Although scattered observers repeatedly drew attention to the dangers of integrating monetary policy if fiscal policy remains a national preserve, the internal German debate over the architecture of the EMU went quiet aside from a brief controversy over budgetary policy rules when Germany violated the pact in the years 2002 to 2005. This changed when the Eurozone was hit by the crisis in 2010, where calls for more ambitious reform projects from European partner countries were thwarted by Germany. When during the global financial crisis in 2008 the French President and presiding chairman of the EU Council, Nicolas Sarkozy, made the case for a common bank bailout package and a European economic government, he received little applause in Germany. An initiative in favour of common European bonds for major infrastructural projects, launched by Italian members of the European Parliament at the time, once proposed by Jacques Delors, and also advocated by the head of the Euro group, Jean-Claude Juncker, was rejected in Germany by representatives of the Bundesbank and the German government under Angela Merkel. Before a public debate could get underway, the idea was discarded by the European Commission in early 2009. Even an initiative by the French government to strengthen the Euro group through regular joint meetings was brushed aside by Germany before the end of 2009.

The historical schism between backers of a stability union and proponents of a fiscal union emerged again during the crisis[2] and has been augmented by a new position calling for a roll-back of the EMU. All three camps of actors and their arguments are presented in the following Chapter. Afterwards, the factors shaping the German debate over a viable reform of the Eurozone and the stability offered by sticking with the status quo are discussed on this basis.

Positioning for a Reform of the Eurozone in Germany

While the grouping advocating a stability union would like to carry on with the same model of the Economic and Monetary Union as in the past while strengthening its reach and closing the gaps in it, those favouring fiscal union are calling for the development of complementary institutions and instruments lacking in the present model to date. Above and beyond this, a heterogeneous field of actors critical in principle of EMU and formed during the period of the crisis in the Eurozone would essentially like to see a (partial) roll-back of monetary integration.

Carry on! Main advocates of a stability union

Proponents of a stability union undisputedly hold the high ground in the field of German actors – with the two governments under Angela Merkel's CDU leading the way since the outbreak of the crisis in 2009/10. Conceived under the CDU-CSU-FDP coalition government, the resolute line of preserving, deepening and strengthening the stability union has also been carried on by the Grand Coalition that came to power in 2013. Under the banner of "budget consolidation and structural reforms to promote growth", a twin-track strategy was since pursued, and was summed up in the negotiations over loan conditions with the so-called "crisis states" as the dictum of "solidarity only with solidity". On the one hand, this strategy of preserving and maintaining the Eurozone is an essential element, pointedly couched by Merkel herself in terms of an existential imperative using the words "if the Euro fails, Europe fails". On the other hand, the government camp stubbornly refuses to budge from its rejection of any and all forms of financial communitarisation – as exemplified by the statement of the Chancellor that there shall not be any Eurobonds while she is still alive – as well as the insistence on strict conditionality being tied to the rescue packages that have become unavoidable to preserve the Euro. The fundamental reasons for the crisis in the Eurozone are from this angle to be blamed on the failure to stick to existing rules and economic policies of the crisis states, thereby undermining their competitiveness. Accordingly, the paramount aim and objective in combating the crisis and further developing the Eurozone has been to correct these purportedly "wrong" national policies and close possible loopholes in the rules.

There are a whole host of measures along these lines, from the launch of national debt brakes as part of the Fiscal Compact to pushing for automatic sanctions for breaking the Eurozone public debt rules and laying down structural reforms promoting competition and fiscal consolidation in the Euro Plus Pact and in the European Semester and enforcing these if necessary within the framework of credit assistance programmes. On top of all this, additional reforms continue to be up for debate such as, for instance, an orderly insolvency procedure for states as well as tools for stronger intervention in national economic policy, including outside the programmes provided for in the European Stability Mechanism such as, for example, the so-called "contractual arrangements" for supply-side structural reforms between Member States and the European Commission.

The key actors on the side of both Merkel governments past and present in both Merkel governments are the Federal Chancellery, acting as the command-and-control centre for European policy, and the Ministry of Finance, headed by Wolfgang Schäuble. In the case of the Ministry of Finance, this has above all been a result of this ministry's responsibility for this domain – after all, the Eurozone involves the currency and the issue of how German tax revenue is used. The key role of the Federal Chancellery can largely be explained by the fact that all the most important forums and decisions in the Eurozone crisis then and now have been made at the level of the heads of state and government. Only agreements between states at the highest level could deliver far-reaching decisions with the required speed while keeping a half-way manageable number of parties in the negotiations.

Although by no means inconceivable in principle, the line laid down by the Chancellery and Ministry of Finance has not been aggressively countered or actively moderated by other important actors in the government. Under the CDU-CSU-FDP coalition, for instance, the Foreign Office under Guido Westerwelle left European policy almost completely in the hands of the two CDU-led institutions, whilst the FDP-led Ministry of Economics under Rainer Brüderle actively supported the market-based course that had been adopted and under Philipp Rösler generally exercised restraint regarding topics involving EMU. This basic line, after the other ministries in charge of the economy had vacated the field, leaving European policy solely up to the CDU, was for the most part continued in the Grand Coalition as well.

The Bavarian sister party of the CDU, the CSU, has played the role of an admonisher in both coalition governments, at times clambering loudly that no elements of a transfer or liability union must be allowed in the reform of the Eurozone. However, although it adopted a tone that was considerably shriller and more strongly permeated with grudges against the "Club Med states", the CSU ultimately supported the course staked out by the Chancellor, viewing itself more as a corrective against excessive concessions to European partners.

This resolute government line has been and still is buttressed by a whole host of actors from the fields of scholarly research, the media, the business community and societal actors, most prominent among them employers' associations. The German Council of Economic Experts is considered to have major influence on the economic debate in Germany and is among the main architects and supporters of European policy à la Merkel. Embedded in wide stretches of the ordo-liberal tradition, it provides the theoretical and economic underpinnings both for the specific analysis of the causes of the Eurozone crisis as well as the reform course devised in response and aiming at a consolidation and strengthening of the stability union. Other important economic institutes and their representatives can be added to this list such as, for instance, the head of the Munich ifo-Institut for many years, Hans-Werner Sinn, or the employer-funded Cologne Institute for Economic Research and the lobby initiative Neue Soziale Marktwirtschaft. Above and beyond this, also deserving mention is the role of the Deutsche Bundesbank, which as a result of its similar economic ideology and its position as a traditional bastion of stability-oriented economic policy offered its support in the debate over reforms of the Eurozone. In its capacity as the most important monetary-policy institution in the country and the biggest shareholder in the European Central Bank (ECB), it also has considerable weight in actual political reform processes.

While these actors have espoused this course over the last few years especially out of ideological and economic conviction, employers' organisations such as the Bundesverband der Deutschen Industrie (BDI) or its umbrella association, the Bundesvereinigung der Deutschen Arbeitgeberverbände (BDA), have also lent their support to this policy, motivated of course more by interests, as it were. The German export economy profits as a whole from an open internal market and the micro-economic advantages offered by a single currency as well as the undervaluation of the Euro in comparison to the alternative "Deutsche Mark 2.0", which would make products and services "made in Germany" significantly more expensive in the world market and thus pose problems for sales abroad – so business and industry share an interest in preserving the Eurozone. Understandably enough, the focus on structural reforms to promote competition in Europe is also supported by employers. After all, these include reforms of the labour market which are usually interpreted as business-friendly. This aligns with the same perspective from which Germany's labour market reforms ("Hartz IV") have been and still are touted as the key to Germany's economic success. If the Eurozone is now moving closer to the German export model due to outside pressure and internal devaluation in the form of wage cuts, this is from an employers' perspective to be welcomed as an additional legitimation of employer-friendly domestic policy just like attitudes towards the asymmetrical treatment of current account surpluses: These are held to be less problematic than respective deficits, as they are considered to be an indicator of "competitiveness" achieved by virtue of structural reforms.

Wielding particular clout in constellations of actors from academia and employers' groups are furthermore prominent parts of the German media world, which largely back the course taken by the government in the direction of a stability union and do not assume a fundamentally critical position questioning it. This is demonstrated not only by drastic examples such as the widely-read *BILD-Zeitung*, which ran memorable polemic headlines in early 2010, but also editorials and reports in *F.A.Z., Welt, FOCUS, Wirtschaftswoche* or *Handelsblatt*. Nor have *DER SPIEGEL* and *Süddeutsche Zeitung* made much of a contribution to expanding the debate and offering a more prominent voice to criticism of the government's approach in the debate. Only later, in the course of the crisis and in connection with individual topics such as the austerity dogma, has a certain rethinking become discernible in parts of the media.

Furthermore, a heterogeneous set of actors has been speaking out with regard to isolated issues that they consider to be game-changers. Thus, for instance, the Association of Savings Banks in Germany is an important player in discussions over the banking union, enjoying considerable clout with the population and media in its self-styled role as guardian of German savers. The same applies to the association of taxpayers, which loudly vents its opinion in the discussion over reforms on a regular basis, warning especially against fiscal communitarisation and lending German tax revenue to crisis states.

Finally, deserving mention is also the fact that German trade unions have at least an ambivalent position in the landscape of actors. On the one hand, they step forward as clear advocates of an alternative vision of the Eurozone along the lines of a fiscal union (see the next section), while on the other hand many trade unions, especially IG Metall and IG BCE, are profiting from the buoyant economic situation at present, which Economic and Monetary Union brings for German employees in industry and manufacturing. An end to the Eurozone and revaluation of the German currency that would accompany it would hit many exporting companies and their employees hard. Especially in the area of wage-policy coordination within the Eurozone, employers and trade unions have spoken out strongly against greater integration of economic policy: Any and all attempts in this direction have been stamped as an attack on the autonomy of collective bargaining and for this reason rejected out of hand – ironically enough even though influences at the European level in the current situation have been pressing especially for significantly higher pay to be agreed upon in collective agreements and an end to chronically lagging wages in Germany.

Forward! Main advocates of a fiscal union

In view of the phalanx of champions of a stability union described in the foregoing, actors in favour of a fiscal and political expansion of the EMU have had their work cut out for them. Conceiving of the crisis in the Eurozone as a manifestation of a design flaw at the heart of the Treaty of Maastricht, which integrated monetary policy without sufficiently doing the same to other areas of economic policy, may well be a truism in other countries. In Germany, however, those urging this route would appear at best to be non-conformist idealists – if not misinformed wastrels. Completing the EMU to rectify deficits that have become woefully apparent during the crisis in essence involves cross-border liability and a coordinated economic policy for the Eurozone. It is not difficult to make out that this would be associated with a curtailment of national sovereignty and a major financial commitment on the part of Germany. Entrenched in a position of relative economic strength, the public debate closes its ears to many of the economic and political arguments for an expansion and reform of the EMU towards a fiscal union. For those actors that want to rectify the systemic failure that occurred in the crisis, on the other hand, leaving it all at a hardening of individual components in the existing EMU architecture is not a sustainable alternative.

Many specific proposals calling for a broader reform of the EMU, especially from German scholars, have been published dating back to when the crisis broke out. In its essence, the prevailing negative or market-creating integration mode is supposed to be supplemented with elements of positive or market-shaping integration. By the same token, it has been emphasised how insufficient monetary policy of the ECB is in countering asymmetrical shocks. Not trusting in the adjustment of macro-economic imbalances that goes hand in hand with austerity, deeper fiscal integration is considered to be necessary. This includes specific instruments such as an external trade Stability Pact, different forms of Europeanised debt management and automatic stabilisers for the Eurozone in the form of insurance mechanisms or a common budget. To curb and contain asymmetrical shocks and compensate for eroding demand, investment initiatives encompassing Europe in its entirety and close coordination of wage and social policies are furthermore proposed. Because a coordination of policies solely based on rules is considered to not be adequately specific or legitimised, the Eurozone will need to be politicised and democratised in this view.

In the public debate in the political arena and media, these notions of fiscal and political integration have only been seized upon in isolated cases, however – usually when neighbouring states or European institutions have directed demands along these lines at Germany. This has been due to only a small group of Keynesian or heterodox economists opposing the hegemony of neo-classical or ordoliberal theory. Only scattered representatives of these views work at major research institutes and universities, with those that do being concentrated at universities of applied science, think-tanks and foundations such as the trade-union-financed Hans Böckler Foundation's Macroeconomic Policy Institute. Even if, as the crisis proceeded, more and more critical voices were to be heard forwarding proposals for reform in the direction of a fiscal union – worth mentioning here, for example, is the German Institute for Economic Research, but also institutions closely aligned with the political arena, such as the German Institute for International and Security Affairs – these only account for a minority compared to those researchers that hold a stability union to be the optimum solution for the EMU.

Alternative interpretations of the crisis in the Eurozone or formulas for progressive changes in the Economic and Monetary Union have accordingly received scant attention in the news and on talk shows. Well-known intellectuals have tended to be more successful in garnering media attention, for instance Jürgen Habermas, Ulrich Beck or Gesine Schwan. Their formulas are often macro strategies, however, which more strongly emphasise the aspect of political integration and remain general with regard to the economic changes regarded as necessary. Academic concepts – a European unemployment insurance[3], a cyclical shock insurance[4], a debt redemption fund[5] and the Blue Bond/Red Bond concept[6] – are often very complex models that defy depiction in simple terms in the media.

Nevertheless, a change in reporting can be witnessed in the German media environment since 2010. The longer the crisis in the Eurozone has dragged on and the more unsolvable it has appeared, the more the dominant academic and political position has been discarded and the more frequently critical voices have been heard, increasingly from commentators and interview guests from other countries, such as were featured already at an early point in Financial Times Deutschland until it went out of print at the end of 2012. In many print media, like *Handelsblatt*, *DIE ZEIT* or *Süddeutsche Zeitung*, pro and con arguments are now juxtaposed on specific reform steps.

Without being politically embedded, media exposure to alternative viewpoints on the crisis in the Eurozone inevitably remains weak, although at the onset of crisis management in 2010 three opposition parties – the SPD, the Greens and the Left Party – were prepared to cast off Merkel's course in the direction of a stability union because they did not believe it to be sustainable. While this was only to be expected given the platforms of the three parties calling for an expansion of European cooperation while at the same time roping in the excesses of transnational markets exposed by the financial crisis, in de facto terms the opposition parties have appeared to be overwhelmed by it all. Only late in the game did they realise the opportunity offered by a European strategy aiming at fiscal union directed against the CDU/CSU/FDP government. Citing the austerity policy going hand in hand with this, the Left Party's parliamentary party group refused to provide its consent to the rescue package adopted by the Bundestag from loan assistance to the crisis states – except for an extension of assistance to Greece in February 2015 out of solidarity with their fellow party comrades in Syriza, which had just been elected to power. At the same time, the Left Party was not successful, however, in offering a convincing concept for the future of the Eurozone in the political debate, as the party itself appears to be split into advocates and opponents of the common currency. The parliamentary party groups of the Greens and SPD vacillated between voting for or abstaining in the first resolutions adopted by the Bundestag in the crisis, but then with the exception of a few renegades swung into line behind the government course beginning in 2011.

Especially remarkable is the behaviour of the Social Democratic Party. With the support of the majority opinion in the German trade unions and backing from most of the welfare associations, it stuck to its programme of fiscal union in a targeted manner at the outbreak of the crisis. The influential former chancellor Helmut Schmidt explicitly called for fiscal and political integration, acting as a link between the party and a host of intellectuals that also backed this course. At a party congress held in Berlin in 2011, Schmidt was speaking to the delegates. He read the riot act to the "crisis Chancellor" to thundering applause from the Social Democrats, urging them to live up to their historical, economic and European political task of offering something of substance as an alternative to the flawed narrative of a sovereign debt crisis.

The Party has only responded to this call in sporadic instances, however. At times, it has supported plans sponsored by Keynesian and heterodox scholars as well as the trade unions, for instance suggesting Eurobonds or a new Marshall Plan in the form of a European investment programme. It has also showed an understanding for civil society protest movements – which have remained relatively modest in Germany – like Occupy, which set the crosshairs on unregulated financial capitalism as the main culprit in the crisis of the Eurozone. But in the wake of negative headlines and survey results, the SPD leadership usually beat a retreat with its ideas for fiscal and political integration, assuming nebulous positions firmly ensconced in the realm of majority opinion. Overall, then, it can be considered to be within the fold of the CDU-CSU-FDP government's policy.

Upon its entry into the Grand Coalition in 2013, the SPD then abandoned with verve all positions in favour of a fiscal union that it was still clinging to, falling into line behind a stability policy course for the remainder of the legislative period. With the exception of scattered initiatives by the Minister of Economics[7] and the Foreign Minister[8] as well as the State Minister for Europe[9], usually in tandem with their respective counterparts in neighbouring countries, particularly France, SPD-led ministries with a say in the reform of the Eurozone have touted the line laid down by the CDU-run Chancellery and Ministry of Finance.

Summing up, the camp of supporters for a fiscal union in Germany would appear to be rather lacking in contours. Conceptual strategies for fiscal integration of the EMU, although certainly available, merely account for a minority position in the realm of academia and, because this would mean a shift in paradigm from the current crisis-management approach, are only advocated with passion by a handful of political actors.

Retreat! Main advocates of rolling back Eurozone integration

Not all actors in the German debate over a reform of the Eurozone want either a strengthened stability union or a swing towards fiscal union. The constellation in Germany is rounded off by a very heterogeneous grouping that is demanding that EMU be dismantled partially or completely rolled back. This view, which did not enjoy much backing before the crisis, has experienced a surge in support over the last few years. The motives underlying this demand can be split up into two diametrically opposing camps: On the one side a conservative-liberal critique of the Eurozone, according to which Germany has much too strong economic ties to purportedly crisis-prone and heavily indebted states, which constitutes a threat to German taxpayers either already or in the future. This camp categorically rejects the transfer of sovereignty away from the German Bundestag that goes hand in hand with EMU. There is a fear that Germany's economic success will be undermined and that fundamental principles of stability are endangered by, for instance, the rescue packages during the crisis or the monetary policy of the ECB.

This faction has without a doubt had the biggest impact on the debate so far. Originally the brainchild of Professor Bernd Lucke and Joachim Starbatty as well as ex-BDI President Hans-Olaf Henkel, this strategy led to the founding of the "Alternative für Deutschland" (AfD) Party and, following its split, has been laid down both in the AfD's and "ALFA" party platforms. These actors have called at various times for individual members to exit the Eurozone (Greece, the crisis states, but also Germany) or for the split-up of the monetary zone into economically homogenous parts such as, for instance, a northern and southern Euro or a "core Euro" with Germany at its nucleus. Over the course of the crisis of the Eurozone, members of other parties also sided with positions like these, however, supporting for example legal action challenging the rescue packages before the German Federal Constitutional Court; in the case of CSU delegate Peter Gauweiler, this even led to him breaking with his own party. Other defectors such as e.g. Wolfgang Bosbach in the CDU or Frank Schäffler in the FDP pop up periodically in the debate, but in spite of major media exposure have not obtained a large enough following at any point in time to pose a threat to the respective course of the government.

Looking more closely at this grouping, it is striking that in terms of analysis and demands there is considerable overlap with the camp advocating a stability union. Thus, in various instances key proponents of this line call for (in some cases) the exclusion of certain countries from the Euro, most prominently among them no doubt Finance Minister Schäuble with regard to Greece in the summer of 2015. CSU members such as the Bavarian Finance Minister, Markus Söder, or the Secretary General and later Federal Minister of Transport, Alexander Dobrindt, have called for Greece in particular to be excluded from the Eurozone; a demand in which they are also supported in part by scholars such as Hans-Werner Sinn or his successor as head of the ifo-Institut, Clemens Fuest. Attacks against the policy of the ECB to preserve the currency union in some cases also take on dimensions bearing similarity to the camp of opponents to the Euro in the vicinity of the AfD. This view is shared inter alia by political actors such as the ex-President of the Bundesbank, Axel Weber, or the ex-ECB Chief Economist, Jürgen Stark, both of whom resigned in protest against the policy of the central bank.

This faction of advocates of winding down the Euro contrasts fundamentally with criticism of the Eurozone coming from the left of the political spectrum. From the latter's perspective, the Economic and Monetary Union in its current variant of a stability union, which has been reinforced by the crisis policy, is an arrangement which due to its liberal market nature contributes to an erosion of national welfare states and undermines existing mechanisms to contain socially negative and undemocratic market outcomes, thereby threatening to shake European cohesion at its roots. Among other things, criticism is levied against the substantial privileges afforded to market actors such as banks and companies operating at the international level in the European project as well as a tendency within the Economic and Monetary Union to impel members to adopt a competition-based course in conformity with the market. The lack of supranational elements to combat tax competition and the perceived downgrading of social aspects and employee interests while a competitiveness mantra is chanted enshrining deregulation and liberalisation are according to this view equally problematic results of a half-baked Eurozone as is the muscling through of an austere fiscal policy and the de facto acceptance of long years of mass unemployment and stagnation across large stretches of Europe. The manifestation of these aspects in crisis and reform policy and the imposition of an economic policy that is viewed to be unsocial, uniform and supply-sided in a Union in which there are justifiably different models of capitalism casts fundamental doubt on the legitimacy of the monetary project. Because the ability of the EMU to carry out internal reform and the presence of political majorities required for such is questionable, it is recommended that it be dismantled.

This view has been forwarded in a particularly cogent manner by the former Director of Cologne's Max Planck Institute, Wolfgang Streeck[10], who has been making a case for at least a partial return to national currencies since 2012 to be able to put an end to the skewed deflationary policy, which from his perspective is a logical consequence of a monetary zone conceived along liberal market lines and that has been drastically radicalised in the crisis. The Euro in its current manifestation leads to Europe being split up between debtors and creditors, condemning a whole host of countries to economic stagnation, while Germany profits from it all – a situation that cannot be sustainable over the medium term. Additional advocates of this approach from academia and the media such as the political scientist Martin Höpner, the economist Heiner Flassbeck or the journalist Wolfgang Münchau have subscribed to this analysis and position in various ways over time and view at least a partial dismantling of the Eurozone to be the sole sustainable and realistic solution. In the political arena, this case has been made above all by a wing of the Left Party and injected in the debate by the party's former Chairman, Oskar Lafontaine, in 2013. Since then an internal dispute has been raging between different wings of the party, with one grouping around Gregor Gysi championing the Euro squaring off against a host of persons behind the current Chairwoman of the parliamentary party group, Sahra Wagenknecht, who is now also calling for the Euro to be abandoned. While this bleak view on the Euro is being discussed in the trade unions and among other critical actors in the field of scholarly research and the media, the conclusion that the Euro itself is the problem and should therefore be sent to its grave has not been taken up broadly beyond these circles.

With all the differences mentioned, the opposing political poles among advocates of dismantling the Euro have one thing in common: Criticism of the crisis and reform policy, which in their view has gone in the wrong direction and is from a democratic perspective profoundly problematic. While one side laments the stealthy introduction of a transfer and liability union at the expense of Germany, their opposites are rebelling against the demolition of Europe's welfare states, the cementing of disparities between successful creditor states and stagnating crisis countries through the common currency and against the democratic disempowerment of the crisis states. Both poles dismiss the further development of the Eurozone along the lines of deeper integration as a possibility – either because this would be undesirable and would mean additional losses of sovereignty over German tax revenue, or because a correction of the unsocial Euro construct does not have any realistic chance of fruition in view of experience and majorities to date.

Beyond these commonalities, however, this block of actors is extremely divided both in terms of their analysis of the causes as well as their conclusions and demands based on this analysis. There is thus no consensus whatsoever over whether the right answer would be complete liquidation of the Eurozone, its split-up into different currency regions or only the expulsion of individual countries. The modalities of the transition also remain controversial: While some actors consider the introduction of parallel currencies to be absolutely essential, others plea for the immediate institution of national means of payment. The politically crucial question as to what economic upheavals this would bring about and hence what spill-over effect there would be on other aspects of European integration such as freedom of capital or the internal market is also assessed very differently. Conservative-liberal critics moreover regularly run the danger of degenerating into an openly nationalist narrative towards the crisis countries or fanning the flames of resentment against the European project, a drastic example of which is the AfD. Both camps have in common that they are criticised for groping for populist, simplistic solutions, which has constituted a significant obstacle to this current of actors becoming a mainstream force capable of assembling a majority in the political debate thus far.

DETERMINANTS FOR A REFORM OF THE EUROZONE WITH GERMANY'S BACKING

On the basis of the three groups of actors discussed in the foregoing and their main demands, we identify four determinants for a reform of the EMU that is seen as viable in the German debate and could also be forwarded as a promising direction in Brussels. These determinants are:

1. Path dependencies of reforms since the crisis;
2. Economic developments;
3. The behaviour of EU partners and EU institutions;
4. Coalition-building in the German discourse.

Path dependencies of reforms since the crisis

For Angela Merkel and the dominant government position in the discourse, a *volte face* in the crisis of the Eurozone and a swing towards notions of fiscal union or break-up of the Eurozone scarcely constitute an option any longer. The appearance of the AfD on the political scene means that the roll-back position on the right of the political spectrum is already occupied, only allowing the CDU to concentrate on its calling card of coordination of European policy in the EMU – understood primarily in terms of budget policy and supply-side structural reforms. The CSU, on the other hand, wants to continue its watchdog role guarding against greater communitisation, also in view of the votes being captured by the AfD, which means that the fiscal union position of the CDU is a dead letter as well. What is more, an abrupt U-turn would discredit the course steered by the Chancellor thus far.

The conservative parties will therefore most likely not venture away from the path opted for in the management of the crisis since 2010. On the one hand, they have themselves to thank for it all, as down to the present they have justified their measures to cope with the crisis to the public as "without alternative". Secondly, no compelling alternative vision to a stability union has been able to gain currency in the political arena, civil society or the media. The enduring nature of the crisis and fundamental new conflicts regularly flaring up between European partners have tarnished the stability camp's "prerogative of interpretation", but zig-zagging actors advocating fiscal union have profited less than the advocates of a hard break with European policy in the form of a roll-back of integration to date. Even though as discussed this group is more heterogeneous than the proponents of fiscal integration, its proposals are much more attractive due to their radical nature in the eyes of sections of the population disenchanted with the Merkel crisis mode.

On the left of the political spectrum, above all the SPD has had to wrestle with the problem posed by dependence on the path once taken. It has not been possible to argue for a course inspired by the objective of fiscal union any longer in the public debate as a consequence of implicitly backing the policy of crisis management laid down by the CDU-CSU-FDP coalition government. The cleft in the SPD between its party programme and actual political actions when it comes to the future of the Eurozone has not been bridged yet, reflecting the fragmentation characterising fiscal unionists and gridlocked public opinion in the German debate over the crisis. While conceivable given his past at the helm of the European Parliament, new party leader and candidate for the general elections Martin Schulz has not made clear to date to what extent the SPD might indeed turn towards the fiscal union approach in the run-up to the elections in September 2017. Instead, he remains cautious in trying to balance the opportunity for clear differentiation from Merkel's CDU in European policy with the hostile discourse over financial communitisation in Germany.

Future economic developments

A second determinant for an EMU reform capable of obtaining a majority in Germany is economic developments. In contrast to what worrying reports on the situation of the Eurozone and many of its Member States would suggest, the German population does not perceive any deep crisis. In the collective minds of Germans, the global financial and economic crisis has been relatively mild as a result of the specific model of the Social Market Economy and resolute intervention and steering of the Grand Coalition at the time. Years of self-doubt as to the future viability of the "German model", played up by the media as it were, has given way to self-satisfaction as the predominant mood at the industrial core, from employee co-determination all the way to export surpluses being taken for granted. The economic woes being experienced in the periphery of the Eurozone, but also plaguing Germany's neighbour, France, have been successfully branded as "their own fault" in the political arena. This explains the lack of understanding for the never-ending crisis, which although impacting Germany in the form of relative low growth rates, is scarcely perceived in a conscious manner by the population.

The German economy has concentrated more on selling export products in the world market since the collapse in demand in other European countries with the onset of the crisis of the Eurozone. If a politically induced, enduring stagnation in the EMU coincides with a slump in the global economy, however, it could lead to an economic downturn in Germany as well. This may boost willingness to consider alternative crisis modes. It remains unclear, however, whether European cooperation would receive a new chance as a result of recession in Germany or whether the apologists championing a return to the national state would be reinforced by a throng of additional supporters. The latter is not improbable, as one can foresee that an answer to the "debt question" in an economic crisis – prepared by long years of debate – would be found in the lagging willingness of European neighbours to carry out reforms. This can already be discerned at present in the form of the discontent being expressed by the population over ECB policy. Low interest on savings are not being discussed as a consequence of the restrained fiscal policy crisis course conceived in Berlin, but rather ascribed to a monetary policy that damages "us" and benefits the crisis states in spite of their transgressions.

Positioning of EU partners and institutions

Not only internal German factors bear relevance to the formation of a reform position towards the EMU by Germany. The behaviour of European partner countries and EU institutions may be decisive. Although the German government has had its way in negotiations in Brussels pretty much across the board with its vision of a stability union, this vision is far from being shared by all the actors in the European round. On the contrary, a majority of countries can be identified that are seeking a fiscal union, at least over the medium and long term. Here as well, the longer the crisis lasts, the more loudly the call for alternatives to austerity and internal devaluation will become. And in contrast to Germany, ongoing stagnation with high levels of unemployment in the crisis states ensures a keen awareness of the crisis and pressure for change. Thus, the electoral gains registered by radical leftist parties in Greece, Portugal and Spain and their membership in coalition governments pose an antithesis to the dominance of the stability approach and at the same time the genie that Merkel herself let out of the bottle and cannot get back in. The banking union was initiated in the face of opposition by German interests through a skilful alliance between the governments of France, Italy and Spain. A similar approach could find copycats in the direction of fiscal union in future reform plans, possibly boosted by the election of Macron as French President if he follows up on his fiscal union-leaning election programme for Europe. The aggressive stance of the Italian government in coping with refugees and the spill-over onto topics relating to Monetary Union (i.e.: "refugee bonds") in the EU emanates from the mounting internal political pressure resulting from a crisis policy perceived as being both wrong and foisted upon Italy. Whether and how long this all remains limited to demands for stronger fiscal integration cannot be said. Leftist parties in EU partner countries have for some time now been facing the question as to whether they should resort – not void of frustration – to a roll-back of the Eurozone in order to preserve their welfare states.

The reform agenda of the EMU is also being castigated by the European Commission. After an initial run-up to wide-ranging institutional changes in 2012 had to be seen as a failure, the President of the Commission, Jean-Claude Juncker – with the support of the European Parliament and the ECB – would like to move forward with his reform paper presented in 2015 while introducing elements of a fiscal union[11]. The German government found itself forced – if under protest – to tolerate the more relaxed implementation of the Stability Pact successfully brought about by the Commission. The IMF and OECD are also applying pressure to the German stance of a "lack of alternatives" by drawing up a critical balance sheet on their own recommendations in the crisis, which had for some time been aligned with those of Germany.

Above and beyond this, Germany could see itself in a tight spot if right-wing populists and opponents to the Euro continue to register successes in elections in many Euro states. Fear of an impulsive, one-sided roll-back of the Eurozone could unleash a discussion over whether the solution is a leap forward in integration or, on the other hand, a controlled multi-lateral roll-back. A first taste of the possible economic and political disarray triggered by unilateral centrifugal movements can be seen in developments in the wake of the outcome of the Brexit referendum held on 23 June 2016 as well as in the heated Eurozone debates surrounding the French electoral campaign in 2017, where presidential finalist Marine Le Pen threatened to put a Frexit on the political horizon. While averted in this election, such calls are likely to continue to resonate with the French electorate without a brighter economic outlook in upcoming elections.

Coalition-building in the German discourse

The fourth determinant in the positioning of Germany regarding more far-reaching reforms of the Eurozone are coalitions between groups of actors which may be successful in having a sustained impact on the discourse. Academia will probably remain the most static voice in Germany. Although the group of Keynesian or heterodox economists may increase in number and internationalisation of scholarly work may blow a fresh wind into faculties, the long shadow cast by ordo-liberal economics will not dissipate that quickly. The presence of this school of thought in many relevant groups of actors continues to lend credibility to the vision of a stability union. Even though the Chancellor has gone down for the count as a result of Europe's inability to solve the plaguing problems of the refugee crisis, she will be able to rely on the closed ranks of the stability camp in the foreseeable future.

There could be movement in the debate if mounting economic uncertainties lead German business to ratchet up pressure on policy-makers through employer's associations to steer things in the direction of fiscal union, as recent position papers such as that of the BDI[12] would suggest. This could in particular lead to a correction in the course within the CDU. On the other hand, the solidification of intergovernmental European interventionism in national economic and social policies in the trade unions distilling out of the ad hoc crisis mode could shift tendencies in the direction of a roll-back of the EMU – out of fear that national employee rights and the achievements of the welfare state might have to be sacrificed. This would influence the future course of the SPD.

Fundamentally speaking, the positioning of the Social Democratic Party is the crucial key to whether a reform debate gets under way and in what direction it goes. All other political forces are too weak to be able to forcefully posit a departure from the perspective of a stability union in the debate. The Greens,

Liberals and the CSU would probably not attach priority to any fundamental reorientation of European policy in conceivable coalition negotiations with the CDU in 2017 due to internal political considerations. It is very likely that support will continue to swell for the camp of advocates of a roll-back of the EMU as long as there are no viable solutions for the Eurozone in sight, particularly in the Left Party. Additional actors could be tempted to divert this groundswell of support in their direction by adopting a comparable position – a phenomenon that can be witnessed between the AfD and the established parties over asylum policy. But the heterogeneity of actors and demands being forwarded by the roll-back camp will prevent a majority crystallising in spite of commonalities in the current constellation. What is important for the SPD, then, is: Just like the minority position of fiscal unionists has been due in large part to the alternating positioning of the party in the debate since the onset of the crisis, it could now – either in the form of a repeat of the Grand Coalition, or even a coalition government made up of the SPD, Left Party and Greens – fuel a departure from the status quo.

Conclusion: The Deceptive Stability of the Status Quo

The German debate over the reform of the currency union resembles a frozen landscape. The realisation of a stability union is based on a stable grouping of actors and profits from the lack of crisis awareness in the German population. As long as growth and employment in Germany remains higher than in many neighbouring states, a change of policy in spite of a stagnating economy, deflation and high levels of unemployment in many crisis countries is highly unlikely. If another major crash does not take place in financial markets or in the global economy which causes the economic situation of the Eurozone and Germany as well to unravel, the stability vision could continue to stumble along mired as it were in persisting stagnation: The crisis would not be bad enough for sufficient pressure to build in neighbouring states and within Germany to lead to a swing in the direction of fiscal union. But at the same time the economic situation could be perceived as insufficient to contain the continued rise of radical proponents of roll-back.

This is precisely where the danger of sticking to the status quo lurks: The stability union cannot help to quickly surmount the crisis in the Eurozone, nor does it have sufficient instruments to prevent or mitigate the next crisis. The sustainability of the approach produced by the German debate is an illusion. It is foreseeable that the question of expansion or roll-back of the currency union will become ever more pressing. The growing attractiveness of the camp of those supporting a roll-back reflects the political explosiveness of the situation.

It would therefore be advisable to make a decision in the near future on whether to steer towards a fiscal union or to terminate the project of a common currency. Both scenarios are replete with imponderables and uncertainties that are difficult to assess. Both approaches face tough going in establishing a secure footing in the German debate not only due to the dominance of the stability version, but also because a departure from the currency union could cast doubt on Germany's openness to integration or because a fiscal union would very probably be associated with an end to Germany's privileged position in the EMU and a loss of sovereignty and financial transfer. This is, understandably, a difficult sell to voters!

It is not helpful in this context that many actors in both camps are oversimplifying things with an idealistic world view by either promising that the end of the Euro or the establishment of a "United States of Europe" would solve all the problems being faced at the moment. A sensible point of departure for a progressive reform of the Eurozone, instead, would be to spell out what a prospective reform would offer in terms of proper functioning of the Economic and Monetary Union. These prospects would have to be measured in terms of their realistic chances of overcoming the deceptive status quo – because it cannot and thus will not hold for ever.

NOTES

1 | Pisani-Ferry, Jean (2006): Only One Bed for Two Dreams: A Critical Retrospective on the Debate over the Economic Governance of the Euro Area, in: Journal of Common Market Studies, Vol. 44, no. 4, pp. 823–844.
2 | Hacker, Björn (2013): On the Way to a Fiscal or a Stability Union? The Plans for a "Genuine" Economic and Monetary Union. International Policy Analysis. Berlin: Friedrich-Ebert-Stiftung, December 2013.
3 | Dullien, Sebastian (2008): Eine Arbeitslosenversicherung für die Eurozone. Ein Vorschlag zur Stabilisierung divergierender Wirtschaftsentwicklungen in der Europäischen Währungsunion. SWP-Studien 2008/S 01, February 2008.
4 | Enderlein, Henrik/Guttenberg, Lucas/Spiess, Jann (2013): A Blueprint for a Cyclical Shock Insurance in the Euro Area. Paris: Jacques Delors Institute Note Europe, September 2013.
5 | Council of Experts (2012): After the Euro Area Summit: Time to Implement Long-term Solution (12 July 2012).
6 | Delpla, Jacques/von Weizsäcker, Jakob (2011): Eurobonds. Das Blue Bond-Konzept und seine Implikationen. Berlin: Friedrich-Ebert-Stiftung, June 2011.
7 | Gabriel, Sigmar/Macron, Emmanuel (2015): Warum Europa zu einer Sozialunion werden muss, in: Die Welt (4.6.2015); http://www.welt.de/ wirtschaft/article

141919414/Warum-Europa-zu-einer-Sozialunion-werden-muss.html (called up on 29 June 2016).

8 | Auswärtiges Amt (2016): Gemeinsamer Beitrag des französischen Außenministers Jean-Marc Ayrault und Außenminister Frank-Walter Steinmeiers: Ein starkes Europa in einer unsicheren Welt (24.06.2016); http://www.auswaertiges-amt.de/DE/Infoservice/Presse/Meldungen/ 2016/160624-BM-AM-FRA.html (last accessed 13/07/2016).

9 | Auswärtiges Amt (2014): Joint statement of the Ministers for European Affairs of France, Italy and Germany: For a European Union of values and solidarity, of prosperity and competitiveness (30.07.2014); http://www. auswaertiges-amt.de/cae/servlet/contentblob/682830/publicationFile/ 195152/140730-StMR-Desir-Gozi_Erklaerung.pdf (last accessed 29/06/2016).

10 | Streeck, Wolfgang (2013): Gekaufte Zeit. Die vertagte Krise des demokratischen Kapitalismus. Berlin: Suhrkamp Verlag.

11 | Juncker, Jean-Claude (2015): Completing Europe's Economic and Monetary Union (22.6.2015); https://ec.europa.eu/priorities/sites/beta- political/files/5-presidents-report_en.pdf (last accessed 29/06/2016).

12 | BDI (2015): Die Vollendung der Wirtschafts- und Währungsunion. Reformoptionen in der Diskussion. Integrationsbericht Europa; http://bdi.eu/media/presse/publikationen/Vollendung_der_EWWU_ September_2015.pdf (last accessed 29/06/2016).

7. The legal framework for reform projects and the role of the German Federal Constitutional Court

Franz C. Mayer

Since the outbreak of the sovereign debt crisis in the Eurozone in May 2010, legal issues have been a permanent fixture of the Euro debate. Accordingly, legal questions also play a key role in all reform considerations applying to Economic and Monetary Union (EMU).

A distinction can be made between more general framework conditions already existing in applicable European law at the level of the founding Treaties (on these, see the section "Requirements laid down in the founding Treaties"), as well as legal framework elements that have been added on in the course of the Euro crisis (on this, see the section "Rebuilding the ship on the high seas?"). In addition, numerous constitutional law requirements have also been derived from case law developed by the German Federal Constitutional Court (BVerfG) (on this, see the section "Underlying constitutional law conditions").

REQUIREMENTS LAID DOWN IN THE EUROPEAN TREATIES (TEU, TFEU)

Economic and Monetary Union is spelled out in more detail in the Treaties founding the European Union: The Treaty on European Union (TEU) and the Treaty on the Functioning of the European Union (TFEU). All the legal requirements that have also played a key role in the Euro crisis are contained in these. This is because they set the framework for reforms or even simply new elements below the threshold of amendment of the Treaties (on the underlying legal conditions for implementation of the proposals presented in this work, see also Chapter 12). Worth mentioning are the prohibition of bailouts, the prohibition of monetary financing of governments, general stability requirements and the fundamental principle of the independence of the European Central Bank (ECB).

No bailout – each state is responsible for itself

The so-called bail out prohibition is of pivotal importance in law governing Economic and Monetary Union. Accordingly, neither the EU nor individual Member States are "liable" for the commitments of other Member States and "shall not assume such commitments ". This is meant to ensure that no state lives beyond its means. To quote Art. 125, section 1 TFEU verbatim:

"The Union shall not be liable for or assume the commitments of central governments, regional, local or other public authorities, other bodies governed by public law, or public undertakings of any Member State, without prejudice to mutual financial guarantees for the joint execution of a specific project. A Member State shall not be liable for or assume the commitments of central governments, regional, local or other public authorities, other bodies governed by public law, or public undertakings of another Member State, without prejudice to mutual financial guarantees for the joint execution of a specific project."

Of course, there may be emergency situations in which assistance might be possible after all by way of exception. Pursuant hereto, Art. 122, section 2 TFEU provides as follows:

"Where a Member State is in difficulties or is seriously threatened with severe difficulties caused by natural disasters or exceptional occurrences beyond its control, the Council, on a proposal from the Commission, may grant, under certain conditions, Union financial assistance to the Member State concerned. The President of the Council shall inform the European Parliament of the decision taken."

In the responses to the Euro crisis, this exception has of course not played any role to date. Thus, it was assumed in the case of Greece, for instance, that the reasons for the situation that came about there were by no means beyond the control of Greece. The prohibition of bailouts means that creditors of Member States, or these Member States themselves or even the EU or other Member States cannot automatically be held liable for the debts of these Member States in the same way as an ordinary citizen. There is in principle no joint liability scheme and no Member State has any claim to the EU or other Member States assuming or redeeming its commitments. The intention here is that assessment of the creditworthiness of individual Member States is left up to the financial markets, which means that sloppy budget policy is penalised with risk premiums.

The bailout prohibition does not proscribe financial assistance to Member States in general and without any exception, however: The assistance provided to Greece and the aid offered within the framework of the rescue packages (see below) therefore do not violate Art. 125 TFEU because, based on the language of Art. 125, section 1 TFEU, a Member State is only barred from entering into a debt relationship between another Member State and its creditors. Voluntary assistance, on the other hand, is tantamount to an independent new commitment and is hence per definition not deemed to constitute entry into an old existing debt relationship. In other words: One does not have to offer assistance – but it possible to voluntarily do so.

The example of Eurobonds aptly illustrates the consequences of this Treaty situation:[1]

Eurobonds are most probably incompatible with the "no bailout" clause as it stands at present. The launch of Eurobonds would bring about joint liability on the part of all Member States of the Monetary Union because every Member State would enter into the debt relationship of the other Member States. In contrast to voluntary assistance within the framework of the rescue packages, for instance, there would be no basis for new commitments by Member States. From this perspective, the crucial difference between the rescue packages and Eurobonds would be that Eurobonds would specifically also involve a communitarisation of debt relationships with third-party creditors. Moreover, Eurobonds with joint and several liability on the part of all members of EMU would automatically translate into an unlimited liability Union (and hence closer to a "transfer Union"). This can be viewed as incompatible with the meaning and intent of Art. 125 TFEU.

Because they would be a permanent mechanism, so to speak, Eurobonds cannot be justified *mutatis mutandis* by application of Art. 122, section 2 TFEU, either, as this provision at any rate only makes reference to a stabilisation mechanism that is to be activated in emergencies. There is much to suggest that the launch of Eurobonds – regardless of whether under current primary law or in separate new Treaties – would require amendment of Art. 125, section 1 TFEU and hence amendment of the Treaties. If it involves an "expansion of the competences and powers of the Union", this amendment of the TFEU would have to be carried out through the regular procedure to amend the Treaties under Art. 48, sections 2 to 5 TEU – an undertaking that would take several years.

The prohibition of monetary financing by Member States

To prevent states in the EMU from living beyond their financial means, the founding Treaties also proscribe so-called monetary public-sector financing through the ECB. The Euro States cannot directly finance themselves through the ECB. To quote Art. 123, section 1 TFEU verbatim:

"Overdraft facilities or any other type of credit facility with the European Central Bank or with the central banks of the Member States (hereinafter referred to as 'national central banks') in favour of Union institutions, bodies, offices or agencies, central governments, regional, local or other public authorities, other bodies governed by public law, or public undertakings of Member States shall be prohibited, as shall the purchase directly from them by the European Central Bank or national central banks of debt instruments."

Prohibition of the "direct purchase" of debt instruments, however, does not affect the possibility for the ECB to carry out bond-purchase programmes in the so-called secondary market, the resale market for government bonds (on this, see the following). The ECB is thus not automatically barred from purchasing bonds. Of course, purchases in the secondary market are harder for a state to calculate, a situation that is hence offering fewer incentives to rely on purchases of bonds by the ECB and its effects.

The fundamental principle of stability as orientation

One central objective in the European Monetary Union is the stability of the currency. Art. 126 TFEU lays down a series of requirements in this regard, assigning the main supervisory role to the European Commission. To quote Art. 126, section 1 TFEU verbatim: "Member States shall avoid excessive government deficits." The European Commission is in charge of monitoring this under Art. 126, section 2 TFEU. Section 3 stipulates:

"If a Member State does not fulfil the requirements under one or both of these criteria, the Commission shall prepare a report. The report of the Commission shall also take into account whether the government deficit exceeds government investment expenditure and take into account all other relevant factors, including the medium-term economic and budgetary position of the Member State. The Commission may also prepare a report if, notwithstanding the fulfilment of the requirements under the criteria, it is of the opinion that there is a risk of an excessive deficit in a Member State."

This fundamental requirement set out in the Treaty is supplemented by various levels and layers of rules and provisions pertaining to stability laid down in Protocol no. 12 on the procedure in the case of an excessive deficit, in the Euro Plus Pact and in the Six-Pack and the Two-Pack. While Treaty law and the Protocol can only be changed in accordance with the rules governing amendment of the Treaty (unanimously), the other levels and layers fall within the domain of law governing sub-aspects of Treaties and, depending on the legal form, can be amended by majority decision. The Treaty on Stability, Coordination and Governance in Economic and Monetary Union (also referred to as the Fiscal Stability Treaty or Fiscal Compact),[2] which was concluded in 2012 in the midst of the Euro crisis, essentially underscores the stability obligation once again. This agreement lies outside of the founding Treaties, however, because amendment of the founding Agreements was opposed by Great Britain. The Fiscal Compact illustrates how reforms can be instituted outside the founding Agreements by means of subsidiary agreements. At the same time, problems crop up when adopting such a strategy in this example, namely when institutions and mechanisms refer back to the founding Treaties. Thus, the assignment of the European Commission as monitoring institution in the Fiscal Compact was not without controversy. Great Britain originally intended to take the issue to the courts, but did not pursue the matter. If reforms are also to be agreed upon in the future outside of the Treaties in subsidiary Treaties while at the same time assigning roles to institutions of the EU, the question as to whether and in what scope this is allowed, which has yet to be conclusively resolved, will resurface.

The fundamental principle of the independence of the ECB

The independence of the ECB is explicitly laid down in Art. 130 TFEU. To quote the Article in its entirety here:

"When exercising the powers and carrying out the tasks and duties conferred upon them by the Treaties and the Statute of the ESCB and of the ECB, neither the European Central Bank, nor a national central bank, nor any member of their decision-making bodies shall seek or take instructions from Union institutions, bodies, offices or agencies, from any government of a Member State or from any other body. The Union institutions, bodies, offices or agencies and the governments of the Member States undertake to respect this principle and not to seek to influence the members of the decision-making bodies of the European Central Bank or of the national central banks in the performance of their tasks."

The ECB is designed as a "countermajoritarian" institution, similar to constitutional jurisdiction. The ECB is not supposed to be controlled by the majority political will. It is not subject to democratically determined will and desire (of the Parliament).

Independence of course does not mean doing whatever one pleases. The European Court of Justice established as far back as 2003 that the ECB is in principle subject to checks and controls by the European Court of Justice. In its ruling, it stated:[3]

"By contrast, recognition that the Bank has such independence does not have the consequence of separating it entirely from the European Community and exempting it from every rule of Community law. There are no grounds which prima facie preclude the Community legislature from adopting, by virtue of the powers conferred on it by the Treaty and under the conditions laid down therein, legislative measures capable of applying to the European Central Bank."

The ECB is not beyond the pale of law. National central banks work together at the European level in the ESCB, the European System of Central Banks. The Bundesbank is an independent national central bank within the Euro system and is hence not subject to orders and instructions, for instance from the Bundestag or the German federal government. Art. 130 TFEU stipulates that national central banks are not allowed to take instructions or orders from any government of a Member State or any other institution in the execution of the powers, tasks and obligations assigned to them in the Treaties and the statutes of the ESCB and ECB. It is recognised that EU law takes precedence over national law (primacy of application)[4] and even constitutional law. Art. 131 TFEU stipulates that Member States must act to ensure that their domestic legal provisions are in harmony with the Treaties.[5] Art. 131 TFEU provides that Member States must act to ensure that their domestic legal provisions are in harmony with the Treaties. To the extent that national central banks fail to act in conformity with European law, the ECB can take action against national central banks before the European Court of Justice under Art. 35, section 6 of the ESCB/ECB Statute.

The Banking Union that was initiated in the course of the Euro crisis is one example of how the independence of the ECB can pose a problem for reform strategies. Bank supervision is the task of the respective central bank in many countries. For the EU, the issue arises, however, as to whether the independent ECB can be entrusted with a role as bank supervisor in the first place. This question is only insufficiently answered in the founding Treaties in Art. 127, section 6 TFEU and is ultimately left unresolved. In bringing about Banking Union, an attempt was made to ensure a separation of supervision and monetary policy by instituting internal organisational measures in the ECB. This is not a completely satisfactory solution, however.

Preliminary conclusion

Treaty requirements pertaining to EMU are characterised by the fact that, just like all Treaty provisions, they can in principle be changed and amended, but only if all Member States – not only the Euro States – agree to such. With 28 Member States now (27 after Brexit), this means in de facto terms that a considerable political hurdle as well as unavoidable temporal barrier would have to be surmounted.

The example of the Fiscal Compact illustrates how progress can be made subsidiary to the Treaties. The example of Banking Union shows that there are also legal premises and foundations within the domain of the Treaties that have not yet been fully leveraged or clearly established (Art. 127, section 6 TFEU). Another example of Treaty powers that have not been fully explored within their range is Art. 136, section 1 TFEU.

REBUILDING THE SHIP ON THE HIGH SEAS?

The Euro crisis has been accompanied by a host of legal developments since May 2010. The legal framework laid down in the founding Treaties obviously did not suffice to deal with the crisis. By the same token, neither the temporal nor the political preconditions needed were in place to undertake a comprehensive process to amend the Treaties, which would have taken several years. This would have been tantamount to rebuilding the ship on the high seas.

Initially, assistance for Greece had been organised on the basis of coordinated bilateral arrangements, then the temporary rescue package in the guise of the European Financial Stabilisation Facility (EFSF) and after this the permanent rescue package in the form of the European Stability Mechanism (ESM) were instituted. Both rescue packages were designed outside the founding Treaties. The rescue packages were buttressed by the Fiscal Treaty (see above), which targeted the spending side, and a bond-purchase programme on the part of the ECB, whose legal foundations were not undisputed.

EFSF and ESM rescue packages

The EFSF was a joint stock company formed under Luxembourg law that set up an initial rescue package for a limited amount of time.[6] In the next rescue package, the ESM, which was set up on a long-term basis and based on the ESM Treaty,[7] more conventional institutional concepts were used in a Treaty governed by international law. The ESM still lies in a domain outside the founding Treaties, however. The ESM can provide money loans and other financial assistance to states experiencing difficulties – but only tied to strict conditions that these states have to satisfy. ESM instruments can be further developed and refined within the ESM Treaty by means of unanimous resolutions. In addition, amendments to the ESM Treaty are possible. It has been established for the sake of clarity in the founding Treaties that the ESM does not violate Union law by means of an amending clause in Art. 136, section 3 TFEU – this is expressly not a stipulation involving competences. In its Pringle Ruling, the European Court of Justice has confirmed that the ESM is compatible with Union law.[8]

Bond-purchase programme of the ECB

Although the EFSF and ESM rescue packages have usually been in the limelight of media attention, the ECB was a crucial actor in the Euro crisis from the very outset. It put a supporting bond-purchase programme in motion early on. The Securities Market Programme (SMP) was active from May 2010 to September 2012. In September 2012, ECB President Mario Draghi announced it would be followed by an Outright Monetary Transactions (OMT) programme[9], shortly after he had publically announced in the summer of 2012 that the ECB would do "whatever it takes" to defend the Euro. To relieve the pressure on Euro states that were facing difficulties, he said that the ECB would if necessary purchase government bonds in the secondary market under the OMT programme. The precondition for this was at the same time supposed to be that these states assume an obligation to participate in an ESM programme and to adhere to strict conditions, generally reform and austerity measures. This was laid down in a resolution adopted by the ECB Governing Council on 6 September 2012 regarding "Technical Features of Outright Monetary Transactions" and outlined in a press release. In effect, the OMT programme has the same impact as the ESM, namely ensuring the liquidity of States facing difficulties – except that in this case the ECB decides – without any involvement of governments or parliaments. The press release itself announcing the OMT programme in 2012 was in and of itself enough to calm down markets at the time. The programme has not been activated down to the present day.

The OMT programme has nevertheless preoccupied the courts. In a ruling handed down in June 2015,[10] the European Court of Justice upheld the compatibility of the OMT programme with European law. The highest European court held that the OMT programme is part and parcel of monetary policy and hence within the domain of competence of the EU and, with it, the ECB. As there is no definition of "monetary policy" in the Treaties, the ECJ tried to clarify the realm of monetary policy by pointing to aims and instruments. With regard to aims and objectives, the argument hinges on the OMT programme being intended to ensure the proper transmission of monetary policy and its uniformity. If the impetus provided by monetary policy decisions is no longer transmitted and fails to impact parts of the Economic and Monetary Union, this also has a negative effect on the ability to ensure price stability. In the opinion of the European Court of Justice, the fact that such a programme also has indirect economic-policy effects is not detrimental to the issue of competences.[11] The ECJ also deems it possible to establish legal grounds for "selectivity", i.e. the fact that only some Member States are covered by the OMT programme – in essence the crisis States seeking protection through the rescue package of the ESM – if there are only some States in which there are disturbances in the monetary policy transmission mechanism.¹² Purchases of bonds may be viewed as a means of pursuing economic policy within the ESM system, but the ECB is not the ESM, thus the ECB can nevertheless use this instrument for monetary policy (see Art. 18 of the ECB Statute). The ECJ very clearly established that the OMT programme may only be conducted as long as problems with the transmission of monetary policy continue.¹³ The ECJ furthermore subjected the OMT programme to a proportionality test in order to review its suitability and its necessity.¹⁴ Here the ECJ assigned the ECB a "broad discretionary latitude" limited by obvious errors in assessments – "taking into account that monetary policy issues typically are a subject of dispute".¹⁵

One recurring criticism is that through the purchase of government bonds the ECB would ultimately be financing the budgets of States, which would then no longer have any incentive to maintain budget discipline (monetary state financing). The ECB is definitely empowered to purchase government bonds in the secondary market under the Treaties, however, although not in the primary market (Art. 123, section 1 TFEU). Pursuant hereto, the ECJ established that no circumvention of these requirements may be tolerated. For this reason, the ECB, if it purchases government bonds in the secondary market, must take sufficient precautions to ensure that such is in conformity with the prohibition of monetary state financing.¹⁶ In particular, market actors and the Member States may not assume with any certainty over the long term that certain government bonds will be quickly swept up by the ECB in the secondary market, and a standstill period between primary emission and purchase in the secondary market must be respected.¹⁷

Amendments of the Treaties as a result of the Euro crisis?

As a result of the Euro crisis, primary law was even amended by inserting Art. 136, section 3 in the TFEU.¹⁸ This is of interest in the reform debate because it provides some idea of the time frame involved in the event of any and all reforms in an EU of 28 (or 27 after a Brexit) Member States. The new Art. 136, section 3 TFEU, inserted by amending primary law, is the least ambitious amendment to the Treaties that is thinkable. Under this provision, the Member States which have the Euro as their currency can set up a stability mechanism which will be activated when absolutely necessary to preserve the stability of the Euro currency area as a whole. It is thus laid down in purely declaratory terms without any transfer of competences that Member States are not prevented from creating a rescue package such as, for example, the ESM outside the realm of EU primary law (law laid down in the Treaties). Even this minimal amendment to the Treaties took two and a half years from the draft bill to its entry into effect. And there was no review by a national constitutional court, which would have meant an additional delay. So when institutional reforms and changes in primary law are contemplated today, it must be taken into account that there is a time factor of at least two years.

Preliminary conclusion

The legal mechanisms that have come into play in the efforts to rescue the Euro constitute reactions to aspects of the crisis. They do not stand in the way of reform plans and considerations.

UNDERLYING CONSTITUTIONAL LAW FRAMEWORK CONDITIONS AND CASE LAW HANDED DOWN BY THE GERMAN FEDERAL CONSTITUTIONAL COURT

Further progress in European integration can be considered from at least two constitutional perspectives in Germany. The enabling perspective stresses the objective of a united European state (Preamble, Art. 23, section 1 of the Basic Law) as well as the openness of the Basic Law to European and international cooperation (friendly relations with Europe).[19] The defensive perspective, which predominates in case law developed by the German Federal Constitutional Court, emphasises the borderlines laid down by the Constitution.[20] This also applies to the entire area of Economic and Monetary Union.

The German constitution

Art. 23, section 1, subsection 2 of the German Basic Law allows the transfer of sovereign rights by law (Law Approving the Treaty of Lisbon) "to bring about a united Europe", thereby making the Constitution permeable.[21] The state objective of a "united Europe" and the openness of the Basic Law to international cooperation permeating the entire Constitution are by the same token the key dictates.

The German Federal Constitutional Court

Constitutional texts only explain the constitutional situation in part, however. Case law handed down by the courts having jurisdiction also play a crucial role. In European comparison, rulings handed down by the Federal Constitutional Court in connection with the Euro crisis assume a paramount station in both quantitative and qualitative terms. At the beginning, the admissibility of, and preconditions for, Euro rescue measures through the EFSF and ESM rescue packages from a legitimacy and procedural perspective were at the forefront of attention.[22] In recent decisions issued by the Federal Constitutional Court on the Euro crisis, attention has increasingly turned to the ECB and its crisis-related measures (purchase programme).

Ultra vires controls

In the Maastricht Ruling from 1993[23], the Federal Constitutional Court spelled out an *Ultra vires* doctrine with reservation of a right to perform checks and controls on the exercise of EU competences. According to this ruling, the Federal Constitutional Court can review whether measures taken by European institutions are within the limits implied in the German ratification statute to the Treaties that transfers sovereign rights to the EU. In its Maastricht Ruling handed down in 1993, the Federal Constitutional Court formulated the consequences of an *Ultra vires* case as follows:

"If European institutions use or further develop the Union Treaty in a manner that is no longer covered by the Treaty upon which the Law Approving the Treaty of Lisbon is based, such legal acts going above and beyond the Treaty would not be binding on sovereign German territory. German institutions would be prevented by reasons of constitutional law from applying these legal acts in Germany. The Federal Constitutional Court accordingly reviews whether legal acts of European institutions remain within the frontiers of sovereign rights granted to them or whether they overstep such."[24]

The court takes its checks-and-controls powers on *Ultra vires* acts (the Federal Constitutional Court initially referred to "break-out legal acts" in its 1993 ruling[25]) from its jurisdiction over the integration limits laid down in the Basic Law. According to the Federal Constitutional Court, there is an "integration programme",[26] circumscribed in the German Statute Law Approving the Treaty of Lisbon and the founding Treaties (the "act of assent"), which cannot be substantially altered subsequently by means of European *Ultra vires* acts without losing the coverage of the act of assent.

The legal effect of a European measure being held to be *Ultra vires* – i.e. in violation of competences – is the loss of its binding nature as a legal act in Germany. *Ultra vires* acts are purely and simply non-binding in the scope of the Basic Law. Whether in such case it is possible for German authorities to obey the authority of Union law voluntarily depends on whether the act in question would violate the Basic Law beyond the competence issue. The overall result of this line of jurisprudence is a German constitutional law-based reservation on European acts, which ultimately limits the scope of EU law primacy. The Federal Constitutional Court thus asserts that it has the last word in matters regarding the legality of Union law and hence its role as last instance in issues relating to Union law in Germany.

Probably not least as a reaction to the largely negative criticism of the Lisbon ruling confirming its *Ultra vires* approach,[27] the German Constitutional Court reformulated its *Ultra vires* doctrine in its 2010 Honeywell ruling.[28] There, the preconditions for a German *Ultra vires* ruling, which would declare Union law to be irrelevant in Germany, are formulated in such a strict manner that in the wake of Honeywell the possibility of the Federal Constitutional Court ever declaring Union law to be *Ultra vires* appears quite hypothetical: In addition to the fundamental requirement that *Ultra vires* controls be exercised in a manner that is "friendly to Europe",[29] the measures under discussion must be obvious violations of EU competences, this includes that there has to be a structural shift in the structure of competencies between the EU and the Member States as a result, and the European Court of Justice must have the possibility of reviewing the EU measures under attack. This implies that the Federal Constitutional Court will at any rate consult with the ECJ by means of a prior preliminary referral if it intends to declare a measure of the EU to be *Ultra vires*.

As far back as the 1993 Maastricht ruling, borderlines were also laid down in the area of Monetary Union spelling out the *Ultra vires* reservation for this area in more detail:

"This conception of Monetary Union as a community of stability is the foundation and subject of the German Act Approving the Treaty of Lisbon. If Monetary Union is unable to continue developing in the meaning of the agreed-upon stability task, it would depart from the conception of the Treaty."[30]

The fields of topics that are to remain under national control are described in more detail in the 2009 Lisbon Ruling:

"Particularly sensitive for the ability of a constitutional state to democratically shape itself are [...] fundamental fiscal decisions on public revenue and public expenditure, the latter being particularly motivated, *inter alia*, by social policy considerations (3), decisions on the shaping of living conditions in a social state [...]."[31]

In a decision rendered on 14 January 2014,[32] the Federal Constitutional Court called upon the European Court of Justice in a preliminary ruling procedure under Art. 267 TFEU for the first time in its history.[33] The subject of the submittal was the ECB's OMT programme (see above) and its compatibility with European and constitutional law. In essence, this involved an *Ultra vires* accusation directed at the ECB, which was held to be acting above and beyond its competences with the OMT programme.

After the ECJ held the action of the ECB to be lawful in June 2015 (see above), the Federal Constitutional Court accepted this ruling.[34] At the same time, it made clear, however, that it continued to doubt the competence of the ECB as well as the legal opinion of the ECJ, but ultimately did not deem the case to be sufficiently serious to establish it as an *Ultra vires* act.

In terms of reform plans and considerations, this means that the compatibility of all additions to, and remodelling of, Economic and Monetary Union with existing Treaty law can be reviewed by the German Federal Constitutional Court. This can at any rate mean a time delay as a result of court proceedings. Nor can opposition to the actual content of acts in the form of an *Ultra vires* decision be ruled out in spite of the strict requirements laid down for such. This of course does not relate to any changes in, or amendments to, the Treaty foundations of Economic and Monetary Union because the accusation of Treaty borderlines being overstepped does not apply if the Treaties are modified.

Identity control

In its 2009 Lisbon ruling, the Federal Constitutional Court developed an additional lever to control Union law above and beyond *Ultra vires* checks and controls:

"Furthermore, the Federal Constitutional Court reviews whether the inviolable core content of the constitutional identity of the Basic Law pursuant to Article 23.1 third sentence in conjunction with Article 79.3 of the Basic Law is respected. The exercise of this review power, which is rooted in constitutional law, follows the principle of the Basic Law's openness towards European Law (*Europarechtsfreundlichkeit*), and it therefore also does not contradict the principle of sincere cooperation (Article 4.3 Lisbon TEU); otherwise, with progressing integration, the fundamental political and constitutional structures of sovereign Member States, which are recognised by Article 4.2 first sentence Lisbon TEU, cannot be safeguarded in any other way. In this respect, the guarantee of national constitutional identity under constitutional and under Union law go hand in hand in the European legal area."[35]

And:

"The identity review makes it possible to examine whether due to the action of European institutions, the principles under Article 1 and Article 20 of the Basic Law, declared inviolable in Article 79.3 of the Basic Law, have been violated. This ensures that the primacy of application of Union law only applies by virtue and in the context of the constitutional empowerment that continues in effect."[36]

Responsibility for integration and the budget

In the Lisbon Ruling, the Federal Constitutional Court developed the notion of responsibility for integration through continued formulation of law by court rulings. "Responsibility for integration" (*Integrationsverantwortung*) is not expressly laid down in the Basic Law, other Member State constitutional systems or European primary law. It is based on an interpretation of constitutional law.[37]

The notion of responsibility for integration is further developed into a concept of responsibility for the budget by German parliament, the Bundestag, in case law on the rescue of the Euro. The Federal Constitutional Court held as far back as in the Lisbon Ruling that "[b]udget sovereignty is where political decisions are planned to combine economic burdens with benefits granted by the state"[38] and no "blanket empowerment" may be issued in this area.[39]

Accordingly, it does not suffice, for example, for the parliament to address rescue of the Euro once and for all. To be specific, according to the judges in Karlsruhe in their ruling on assistance to Greece and the Euro rescue package, it follows from the democratic foundations of budget autonomy "that the Bundestag may not conclude any inter-governmental or supranational agreements that are not bound to strict requirements and in terms of their effects involve automatic guarantees or payments which – once set in motion – cause it to lose its control and ability to intervene".[40] Obligations bearing importance to the budget and determination of the type and amount of taxes and levies to be borne by citizens must, rather, be subject to the discretionary latitude of the Bundestag – on an ongoing and continuous basis and not only at the outset.[41]

Involvement of parliament

The Federal Constitutional Court has consistently mandated close parliamentary monitoring by the Bundestag of Euro rescue measures. In exercising its budgetary rights and its overall responsibility for budgetary policy, the Bundestag must make the most important decisions itself.

Nothing important takes place in the ESM without prior consent being issued by a plenary assembly of the Bundestag. The Federal Constitutional Court allowed Germany to participate in the ESM in an injunctive legal protection proceeding in September 2012,[42] but only subject to the precondition that the Bundestag retain control over ESM measures at all times. This means, for instance, that the German government representative in the governing institutions of the ESM in charge of adopting resolutions requires the prior approval of the Bundestag before he can provide his consent to an ESM measure.[43]

The possibility that democratic legitimation can be achieved through the European Parliament (EP) as well does not play any significant role in the opinion of the Federal Constitutional Court regarding European democracy. More recent decisions of the Federal Constitutional Court on German EP election law have been interpreted by many observers as signifying that Karlsruhe has demoted the European Parliament in terms of its importance.[44] In the world of the Second Senate of the Federal Constitutional Court, democracy can apparently solely emanate from the peoples of the nation-states. Academic criticism

7. The legal framework for reform projects

of this very German perspective on "federal republican people's democracy"[45] has been mounting continuously since the 1993 Maastricht Decision. The Court has not been fazed by this so far. Nor does the Federal Constitutional Court explain why it on the one hand continues to view the EP as a representative of "peoples" – contrary to the wording of the Treaty[46] – while remaining deaf to the argument that the elimination of the blocking clauses in Germany would weaken the influence of Germany in the EP.

Quantitative borderlines
The concept of limiting authorisations to assume guarantees

The quantitative limits on the scope of authorisations to assume guarantees fundamentally were derived by the Federal Constitutional Court from the principle of democracy[47] in 2011 upon the occasion of the rescue of Greece. This involved the issue of whether and on what scope it is allowed for a sort of guarantee function to be assumed to rescue the Euro.

The Court did not spell out the limits in any certain scope. Instead, it held that determination of an alienation of budgetary autonomy with regard to the scope of the guarantee assumed must be limited to obvious violations and respect lawmakers' discretionary latitude in the assessment of such.[48] According to the Court, these borderlines had not (yet) been exceeded in the assistance to Greece in the amount of € 22.4 billion and the European Rescue Package of € 147.6 billion.[49]

Requirements applying to the ECB bond-purchase programme

The ECB's OMT programme (see above) has intensively preoccupied the Federal Constitutional Court. It considers there to be a functional parallel between rescue packages and bond-purchase programmes: Both are intended to safeguard the liquidity of states experiencing difficulties. ECB measures do not require either the consent of a national constitutional court or a Member State's parliament.[50] With regard to stock purchase programmes, the Federal Constitutional Court cannot order the Bundestag to participate in such if only because the ECB is independent. It is not difficult to understand why the Federal Constitutional Court was not exactly delighted by the fact that the ECB was able to override the sophisticated construct developed by the Federal Constitutional Court to secure far-reaching rights of intervention for the Bundestag in the ESM in order to protect German taxpayers by means of a court press release.

The Federal Constitutional Court laid down clear requirements in its first historical submittal to the European Court of Justice in Luxembourg for the

ECB's OMT bond-purchase programme. These have essentially been upheld by the European Court of Justice.

Included in these requirements is that the conditionality of the assistance programme in the rescue packages must not be undermined; the programme must be of a nature merely supporting economic policy in the Union. With a view to Art. 123 TFEU, in the opinion of the Federal Constitutional Court this requires that debt relief must be ruled out, that government bonds of individual Member States must not be bought on an unlimited scale and that interference with price formation in the market must be avoided to the greatest extent possible.

The bond-purchase programme following OMT under the rubric *Quantitative Easing* (QE) is not limited to Euro crisis States. It adopts a different strategy. OMT and QE differ at several levels. OMT not least has an impact on a psychological level. Its mere announcement suffices to reassure and calm the market. QE, in contrast, only has an impact when it is implemented as well. Wide-ranging bond-purchase programmes are part of the toolkits of central banks everywhere in the world. QE helps support banks, not least in the Crisis States, offering relief to public-sector and private debtors. Above all, however, a bond-purchase programme is generally associated with hope for an impetus towards general economic growth. None of the legal misgivings applying to OMT can be directed at QE. The objections of selectivity and liability risks for unlimited purchases do not apply because QE is not limited to government bonds from crisis states and its scope is clearly limited. Furthermore, national central banks are solely liable for government bonds of their Member States. Purchases are only effected in the secondary market, while it remains uncertain exactly which bonds will be acquired. Improvement in monetary-policy transmission is once again an argument[51], and, with the reasoning that the ECB must preclude deflation, QE is based on a verifiable monetary-policy criterion: The low inflation rate. Ultimately, categorising QE as monetary policy serving the aim of price stability is difficult to dispute.

CONCLUDING OBSERVATIONS

The underlying legal conditions for Economic and Monetary Union are laid down in a wide array of provisions and rules. Almost all requirements at the European level can be flexibly shaped, even if in part only through a consensus among the Member States. The framework conditions that are most difficult to change for Germany are to be found in the area of national constitutional law under the supervision of the Federal Constitutional Court. This applies, in particular, wherever the Federal Constitutional Court locates its review standards at the heart of the Constitution under Art. 79 section 3 of the Basic Law (the

7. The legal framework for reform projects 117

"eternity clause"), for instance via the core area of the principle of democracy. Then even an amendment to the Constitution could not achieve anything. A new constitution would then be needed in Germany.

What does this mean specifically for reform proposals like a European minister of finance, fiscal capacity or a debt-restructuring mechanism? This ultimately boils down to the design of proposals in specific detail and in each individual case. Blanket statements are not expedient here (for a legal assessment of individual reform projects see Chapter 12).

If for instance a European minister of finance and fiscal capacity were associated with new European competences, a constitutional amendment would be necessary at the European level. This is required under the principle of conferral (Art. 5 TEU), according to which the EU may only take action if it is also assigned competences. The path selected for the ESM and Fiscal Treaty was to organise new institutions and mechanisms outside of the EU Treaty and TFEU. The advantage with this route is that one does not have to need all 28 Member States on board, and that the conditions governing its entry into force can be freely selected. A certain conception of Economic and Monetary Union is unmistakable – a conception that is focused on stability and in which the bailout prohibition sets the tone. If the founding Treaties are amended, this conception can also be altered. If all the Member States are involved, a separate new Treaty with several argumentative acrobatics and arabesques can be viewed as a conceptual change – there might then possibly be an amendment procedure for the Treaties in which not all States participate. As soon as all the States are no longer involved, however, Treaties outside the founding Treaties probably no longer violate the founding Treaties and must uphold and abide by the principles stipulated therein. In the case of fiscal capacity, it would have to be weighed out whether Art. 125 TFEU (bailout prohibition) could be circumvented, at any rate whenever resources are supposed to be used for the "communitisation" of existing debts of the Member States. It is probably also questionable from the perspective of European law how compatible fiscal capacity is with Art. 311 TFEU (the Union's own resources). The basic conception (to be specific, in this case the range of the bailout prohibition) can only be changed by unanimous agreement of all the States. But ultimately everything can be structured and shaped at the level of European law if there is a will to change the Treaties.

Looked out from an overall perspective, German constitutional law probably sets the greatest barriers. The decision-making powers of the Bundestag with regard to important budgetary issues and with regard to the financial burden on citizens as a whole must remain a permanent fixture under case law handed down by the Federal Constitutional Court to date. It would thus not be possible to assign sovereign rights to the EU, which would mean important budgetary decisions being taken without the involvement of the Bundestag within the framework of the Basic Law. Nor would it be possible to achieve such by amending the Constitution if core elements of the principle of democracy that cannot be altered were affected by this (Art. 79, section 3 of the Basic Law in connection with Art. 20 of the Basic Law – constitutional identity). This would, in particular, also include empowering constructs outside the domain of German sovereignty and thus institutions that cannot be subject to direct checks and controls by the German Bundestag – for example, a European minister of finance – to exert influence on the German budget by means of recourse. At the same time, it should be noted that the Federal Constitutional Court has to date never established that any European law is in violation of the German Constitution. The question is thus what would happen if the Basic Law was amended to allow far-reaching alterations to EMU. For the court, opposing lawmakers moving to amend the Constitution with qualified majorities in the Bundestag, which is directly legitimated by the population, and in the Bundesrat would then probably require a very clear violation of the "eternity clause". And it may be difficult to justify this with a view to the requirement set out in the Basic Law that constitutional amendments take European integration into account. It will not be possible to carry out significant changes with regard to the common currency without a broad political consensus. If such a broad consensus is found, this will also be reflected or be able to be reflected in the further development of constitutional law.

Notes

1 | Mayer, Franz C./Heidfeld, Christian (2012): Verfassungs- und europarechtliche Aspekte der Einführung von Eurobonds, in: *Neue Juristische Wochenschrift* (NJW) 2012, p. 422.
2 | Vertrag über Stabilität, Koordinierung und Steuerung in der Wirtschafts- und Währungsunion, BGBl. (Federal Gazette) 2012 II, p. 1006.
3 | European Court of Justice, case C-11/00 (Commission vs. ECB), ECR 2003, I-7147 par. 6.
4 | European Court of Justice, case 6/64 (Costa vs. ENEL), ECR 1964, 585 (English special edition).
5 | European Court of Justice, case 11/70 (Internationale Handelsgesellschaft), ECR 1970, 1125 (1134); see also German Federal Constitutional Court, 2 BvR 2728/13, ruling handed down on 21 June 2016 – OMT, par. 118: "In principle, the precedence of application of Union law before national law also applies to conflicting national constitutional law and as a rule, in case of conflict, leads to the national law being inapplicable in the specific case".
6 | www.efsf.europa.eu.
7 | www.esm.europa.eu.
8 | European Court of Justice, case C-370/12 (Pringle), ECR 2012, I-13.
9 | Outright Monetary Transactions.

7. The legal framework for reform projects 119

10 | European Court of Justice, case C-62/14 (Gauweiler et al.), ruling from 16 June 2015.
11 | European Court of Justice, case C-62/14 (Gauweiler et al.), ruling from 16 June 2015, par. 51f.
12 | European Court of Justice, case C-62/14 (Gauweiler et al.), ruling from 16 June 2015, par. 55.
13 | European Court of Justice, case C-62/14 (Gauweiler et al.), ruling from 16 June 2015, par. 62, 112.
14 | European Court of Justice, case C-62/14 (Gauweiler et al.), ruling from 16 June 2015, par. 66.
15 | European Court of Justice, case C-62/14 (Gauweiler et al.), ruling from 16 June 2015, par. 68 and 74.
16 | European Court of Justice, case C-62/14 (Gauweiler et al.), ruling from 16 June 2015, par. 93.
17 | European Court of Justice, case C-62/14 (Gauweiler et al.), ruling from 16 June 2015, par. 104ff, 113.
18 | European Council Decision of 25 March 2011 amending Article 136 of the Treaty on the Functioning of the European Union with regard to a stability mechanism for Member States whose currency is the Euro, 2011/199/EU, adopted in the simplified treaty amendment procedure in accordance with Art. 48, section 6, sections 2 and 3 of the EU Treaty, Official Journal no. L 91 from 6 April 2011.
19 | See in this regard the dissenting opinion Lübbe-Wolff, Federal Constitutional Court 113, 273 (336ff.) – European Arrest Warrant.
20 | For instance, in Federal Constitutional Court 123, 267 – Lisbon.
21 | Wendel, Mattias (2011): *Permeabilität im europäischen Verfassungsrecht*. Tübingen: Mohr Siebeck.
22 | In Germany: Federal Constitutional Court 129, 124 – Greece/EFSF; Federal Constitutional Court 130, 318 – Committee of Nine; Federal Constitutional Court 131, 152 – ESM and parliamentary controls; Federal Constitutional Court – ESM and Fiscal Treaty (injunctive legal protection); Federal Constitutional Court 135, 317 – ESM and Fiscal Treaty (main case); Federal Constitutional Court 134, 366 – OMT (preliminary reference); Federal Constitutional Court, 2 BvR 2728/13, ruling from 21 June 2016 – OMT (final ruling). Older proceedings that play a role with regard to the Euro are Federal Constitutional Court 89, 155 – Maastricht, Federal Constitutional Court 97, 350 – Euro; Federal Constitutional Court 123, 267 – Lisbon.
23 | Federal Constitutional Court 89, 155 – Maastricht.
24 | Federal Constitutional Court 89, 155, 188 – Maastricht, see for an English translation 33 I.L.M. 388 (1994). See also the pertinent passage of the Honeywell Decision, Federal Constitutional Court 126, 286 (302) – Honeywell.
25 | For the definition, see Federal Constitutional Court 75, 223 (242) – Kloppenburg.
26 | "Integration program" including in the context of NATO, Federal Constitutional Court 104, 151 – New Strategic Concept of NATO.

27 | Federal Constitutional Court 123, 267 – Lisbon.
28 | Federal Constitutional Court 126, 286 (303-307) – Honeywell.
29 | Federal Constitutional Court 126, 286 (303) – Honeywell.
30 | Federal Constitutional Court 89, 155 (205) – Maastricht.
31 | Federal Constitutional Court 123, 267 (359) – Lisbon.
32 | Federal Constitutional Court 134, 366 – OMT (preliminary reference).
33 | See pursuant hereto Mayer, Franz C. (2014): Rebels without a cause?, in: *German Law Journal* (Special Issue), p. 111 (= EuR 2014, 473 and RTDE 2014, 683); Steinbach, Armin (2013): Die Rechtsmäßigkeit der Anleihekäufe der Europäischen Zentralbank, in: *Neue Zeitschrift für Verwaltungsrecht* (NVwZ), p. 918; Wendel, Mattias (2014): Kompetenzrechtliche Grenzgänge: Karlsruhes *Ultra vires*-Vorlage an die EuGH, in: *Zeitschrift für ausländisches öffentliches Recht und Völkerrecht* (ZaöRV), 74, p. 615.
34 | Federal Constitutional Court, 2 BvR 2728/13 ruling from 21 June 2016 – OMT
35 | Federal Constitutional Court 123, 267 – Lisbon.
36 | Federal Constitutional Court 123, 267 (253ff.) – Lisbon, par. 240.
37 | Federal Constitutional Court 123, 267 (355f.) – Lisbon.
38 | Federal Constitutional Court 123, 267 (361) – Lisbon.
39 | Federal Constitutional Court 123, 267 (351) – Lisbon.
40 | Federal Constitutional Court 129, 124 – Greece/EFSF, par. 127.
41 | Federal Constitutional Court 129, 124 – Greece/EFSF, par. 126.
42 | Confirmed in Federal Constitutional Court 135, 317 – ESM and the Fiscal Agreement (main proceedings)
43 | For details on the Act on Financial Participation in the European Stability Mechanism, (ESM Financing Act [ESM-Finanzierungsgesetz]).
44 | See, for instance, Federal Constitutional Court 135, 259 – three per cent blocking clause.
45 | Bryde, Brun-Otto (1994): Die bundesrepublikanische Volksdemokratie als Irrweg der Demokratietheorie, in: *Staatswissenschaften und Staatspraxis*, Heft 3.
46 | Under Art. 14, section 2 of the EU Treaty, the EP is composed of representatives of the citizens of the Union.
47 | Federal Constitutional Court 129, 124 – Greece/EFSF, par. 131.
48 | Federal Constitutional Court 129, 124 – Greece/EFSF, par. 130.
49 | Federal Constitutional Court 129, 124 – Greece/EFSF, par. 135.
50 | The Senate majority made it very clear that it views the ESM and OMT to be functionally parallel to one another, Federal Constitutional Court 134, 366 – OMT (preliminary reference), par. 40 and 78.
51 | Second recital of Decision (EU) 2015/774 of the European Central Bank of 4 March 2015 on a secondary markets public sector asset purchase programme (ECB/2015/10).

PART III: REFORM OPTIONS

8. Rethinking economic policy – a better fiscal framework for the Eurozone

Jeromin Zettelmeyer[1]

Budgetary policy decisions in the EU have been governed by certain fiscal rules as well as monitoring and coordination mechanisms ever since the launch of the Euro. In spite of repeated attempts at reforms, this framework has not achieved its economic policy objectives and has led to mounting tensions among the Member States of the Economic and Monetary Union (EMU) as well as between the EU Member States and the European Commission.

This Chapter proposes an alternative fiscal framework. Its aim is not to define new objectives (for instance, centralised allocation and distribution tasks that would be typical in a fiscal union), nor does it presuppose additional political or structural convergence between the Member States. The goal is merely to more effectively achieve the aims of the original framework: The stabilization of economic shocks[2] and fluctuations while avoiding crises and conflicts between Member States, within the existing political framework. Even these relatively modest aims and objectives cannot be attained without major reforms, however, and they require a resolute political will.

THE LOGIC OF MAASTRICHT

The Economic and Monetary Union created by the Treaty of Maastricht is based on centralised monetary policy on the one hand and – within the Stability and Growth Pact (SGP) – a decentralised fiscal policy. This coexistence of centralisation and decentralisation is not necessarily a contradiction. The task of the European Central Bank (ECB) is to ensure price stability and hence guarantee the cyclical stabilisation of the Euro area as a whole. This does not necessarily ensure that the specific stability needs of individual Member States are met (see Chapter 3); but as long as every Member State has an individual stabilisation instrument in the form of effective fiscal policy, this does not pose a problem. The precondition for this is that Member States have fiscal space, i.e. that they can take on debt in the financial market without difficulties. The fiscal rules of the SGP, according to which the national debt is in principle to be limited to 60 per cent and government deficits to three per cent of GDP, constitute an attempt to maintain this space by preventing excessive debt, while also allowing Member States some flexibility to conduct counter-cyclical fiscal policy.

The macroeconomic framework of Maastricht is hence not without logic – but it has nonetheless not functioned properly. Its failure became evident by 2010 at the latest, when in the wake of the global financial crisis first Greece and then additional members of the Euro area lost access to debt markets (or were on the brink of losing it) and were forced into abrupt reductions in public spending and/or tax hikes – the opposite of a counter-cyclical stabilisation policy. There were two key reasons for this failure:

- The SGP focused exclusively on official public debt and deficits. The possibility that private debt could be changed into government debt in the course of the financial crisis because of a collapsing banking system (as happened in Ireland or Spain) was overlooked. As a result, the Pact was vulnerable in this area.
- The SGP did not prove to be very effective even in its core mission. Of the twelve Euro Member States before 2007, seven exceeded the Pact's maximum deficit levels at least once, with five of these Member States violating limits frequently (Germany, France and Italy) or every year (Greece and Portugal). Even in the economic boom years of 2006 and 2007, in which members should have built up fiscal space, only roughly half of the Member States were able to produce fiscal surpluses. The overall debt-to-GDP ratio in the Euro area therefore scarcely dropped between 1998 and 2007 (see Diagram 1).

In reaction to these problems, a host of reforms and modifications of the EMU have been instituted since 2011, without however questioning the basic elements of the Maastricht framework: A central monetary policy and a decentralised fiscal policy constrained by rules. The most important amendment has been the (partial) establishment of a European banking union (in the form of joint supervisory and resolution authorities) as well as bank bail-in rules according to which losses are to be borne first by the shareholders and creditors of these banks. These reforms are supposed to make future banking crises less likely in the Eurozone and protect public budgets from the impact of financial crises. At the same time, incentives to adhere to SGP rules have been strengthened, fiscal rules have been focused more on medium-term debt reduction, and the monitoring of national economic policy has been expanded to cover non-fiscal crisis risks (see Diagram 2). Finally,

Diagram 1: Debt ratios in EMU and its five biggest Member States

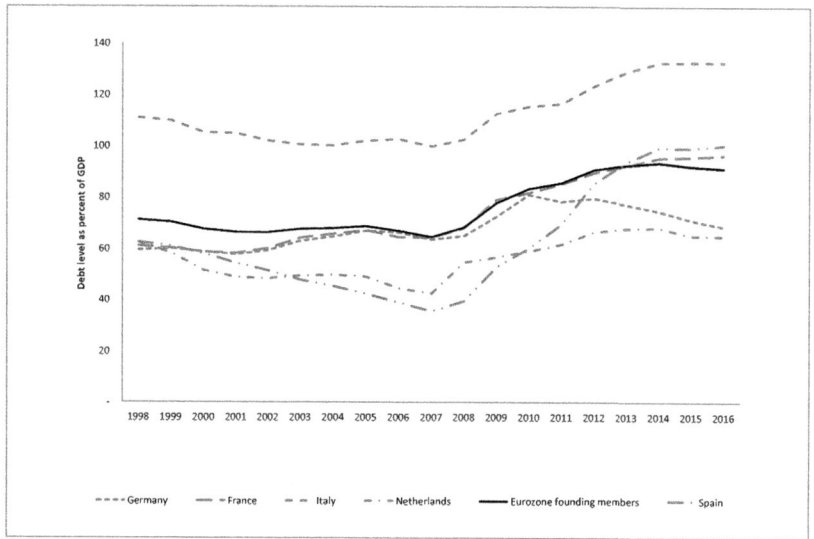

Source: AMECO, own calculations.

a public fund was set up in 2012, the *European Stability Mechanism* (ESM), which can make public bridging loans available in the event of an impending loss of market access, giving Member States time to consolidate their budgets and institute reforms.

In sum, a set of ambitious reforms have been implemented that appeared to offer an answer to almost every problem that cropped up during the first decade of the Euro. This raises the question as to why the debate over reform of the EMU has not subsided but instead – quite to the contrary – reignited,[3] why anti-Euro parties have sprung up or are gaining support in many EMU Member States and why public sentiment in favour of joining the Euro among non-EMU members waned by ten percentage points between 2010 and 2015 (see Diagram 3). Three factors appear to play a role:

1. In part, disenchantment with the EMU is no doubt a consequence of the fact that many problems faced by the Euro area since the beginning of the debt crisis in 2010 continue to persist. Reforms were primarily intended to prevent *future* crises. At the same time, however, some of these reforms have made it more difficult to surmount the *ongoing* crisis. Fiscal policy in the Eurozone was "pro-cyclical" in the years 2011-2013 (Member States increased consolidation in times of weak growth), thereby probably contributing to the intensity and duration of the Euro crisis.[4] This pro-cyclical behaviour was particularly salient in States that were obligated to undertake

Diagram 2: Reforms and amendments to EU fiscal rules, 2011-2013

December 2011: Six-Pack
(one EU Directive, five EU regulations)

1. **Reforms of the SGP**
   - **Reverse qualified majority** procedure: Recommendations by the European Commission are deemed to be approved by the Council if it does not reject the Commission initiative with a qualified majority.
   - **Debt-reduction rule**: EU Members whose debt ratio exceeds the reference value of 60 per cent of GDP have to reduce the difference to the reference level by one-twentieth per year.
   - In the event that the medium-term budgetary objective is not attained, an adjustment path is set that is designed to reduce the structural deficit by at least 0.5 per cent of GDP per year.
   - **Imposition of financial sanctions** (interest-bearing deposit of 0.2 per cent of GDP) is already possible in the preventive arm if, following a recommendation being issued by the Council, a Member State fails to take effective action.

2. **Launch of an "early warning system for macro-economic imbalances"**
   (Macroeconomic Imbalance Procedure)
   This is intended to expose and correct possible skewed economic developments early on by means of a scoreboard (which the European Commission produces for each Member State with "macro-economic and macro-financial indicators").

January 2013: Fiscal Compact
(Treaty governed by international law)
This obligates the (25) signatory States to introduce a so-called "debt cap" in their respective national legal systems (unless debt is below 60 per cent of GDP, while the annual structural deficit must not exceed 0.5 per cent of nominal GDP).

May 2013: Two-Pack
(two EU regulations)
This relates to stricter monitoring of EU Member States' economic and budgetary policies when they face serious difficulties in preserving their financial stability, when they have already received financial support, or when the support from a financial assistance programme (for example, ESM) is scheduled to expire in the near future. The Euro states are obligated to submit their budget plan to the European Commission for it to be checked and reviewed before adoption by the national parliament.

fiscal adjustments within the framework of the SGP.[5] Even though it is impossible to say whether the fiscal policy of the Euro area would have been different without the reforms of the SGP since 2011, it is at least clear that these reform measures have not addressed the pro-cyclicality of European fiscal rules.

2. An additional reason for dissatisfaction with the EMU is the practical experience gained with fiscal rules since 2011. Countries which are in (or near) the corrective arm of the SGP often perceive the application of consolidation rules as harmful at least in the short term and have therefore attempted to delay the adjustment imposed by the SGP.[6] This then triggers criticism from Germany and other fiscally orthodox members, which is directed not only at countries running excessive deficits, but also at the European Commission, which has been accused of leniency and "politicised" decisions.[7] Finally, the rules themselves have been criticised as complicated because they do not appear to function well in technical terms.[8] This is partly a consequence of the – in and of itself sensible – attempt to define the adjustment effort required by the SGP in structural terms, i.e. adjusted for the economic cycle. This is intended to avoid a pro-cyclical fiscal policy: The more the deficit is due to a recession, the less the need for adjustment imposed by the SGP. In practice, however, the separation of cyclical and structural components of the deficit has been highly imperfect, with the consequence that the adjustment required by the Member States could be partly or wholly based on measurement error.[9]

3. Finally, a new problem has been crystallising since 2013 against which the reformed EMU appears to be powerless – independently of whether members comply with the rules or not. At the heart of the Maastricht Treaty is the notion that fiscal policy in the individual EU Member States needs to worry only about discrepancies between the member-specific cyclical position and the Euro area average. Euro area-level stabilisation of the Euro area is meant to be the task of the ECB. In the last three years, however, the ECB has had a tough time performing this task in spite of an extremely expansionary and in part unorthodox monetary policy. For this reason, the European Commission, the International Monetary Fund (IMF) and the OECD have called upon Germany and other fiscally strong EMU members to support the ECB with a more expansionary fiscal policy. In these countries, this call usually falls upon deaf ears, however – among other things, because a neutral fiscal policy is perceived as appropriate given the *domestic* economic situation in these countries. At the same time, frustration over the monetary policy measures of the ECB, which for its part feels misunderstood and left alone, is mounting.

Diagram 3: Rejection of the Euro, 2010-2015

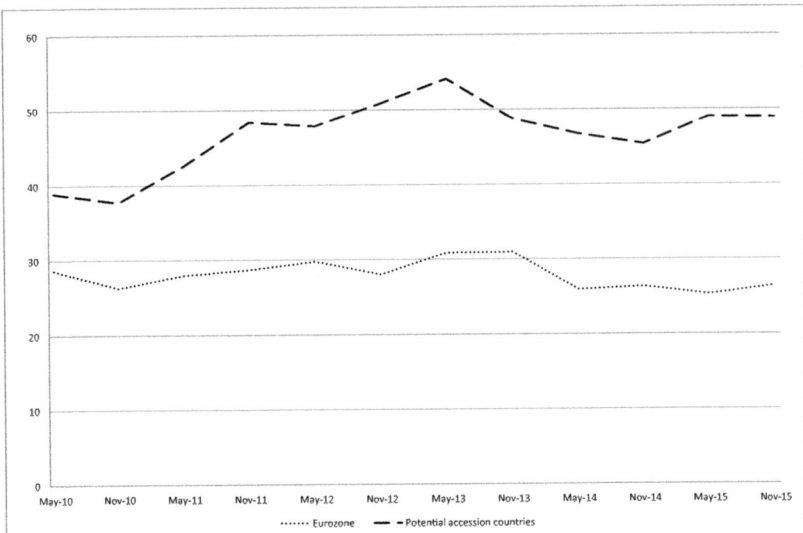

Note: The diagram shows the average share of negative answers to the question: "What is your opinion regarding the following proposals? Please state whether you support or oppose each proposal. European Monetary Union with a common currency, namely the Euro."

The group of countries "potential countries of accession" designates all EU members that are not members of the Euro, but which are generally speaking obligated to accede to the Euro (all non-Euro EU Members except for Great Britain, which voted to leave the EU altogether, and Denmark).

Source: Euro barometer of the European Commission

Conditions for Effective Reform

Despite repeated reform attempts, the macroeconomic framework of Maastricht – uniform monetary policy together with a decentralised fiscal policy that is constrained by rules – has not proven effective: Neither at the level of the Euro area, nor at the level of individual States, neither in the sense of crisis prevention nor in the sense of effective stabilisation. Instead, it has fuelled discontent and acrimony among the Member States of the Euro area as well as between Member States and institutions such as the European Commission and the ECB.

To solve these problems, we need a reform of the macroeconomic framework of the EMU which goes significantly beyond the reforms of the SGP to date, while also anticipating and taking into account conflicts of interest, political frictions, and difficulties in implementation. The aim of these reforms

8. Rethinking economic policy – a better fiscal framework for the Eurozone

should be to create a well-functioning stabilisation function for the Euro area and its members that can be implemented within the existing political system of the Euro area – i.e. without presupposing a "political Union" which may only be realised in the distant future (if ever). Three requirements follow from this.

1. One element in the new macroeconomic framework should be a central fiscal capacity for the Euro area – an institution that is able to contribute to the stabilisation of the Euro area using fiscal instruments. Fiscal policy decisions at the level of the Member States could be either too expansionary for the Euro area as a whole (as was the case in 2006-2007) or too restrictive (as in 2011-2014), even when fiscal rules are fully adhered to. The hope that this inconsistency can be resolved by means of better "coordination" between national fiscal policies has not materialised. Nor is anything else to be expected in an EMU in which sovereignty over national fiscal policies remains at the national level: One cannot call on the Member States to adjust their fiscal policies above and beyond what the fiscal rules require if this appears to contradict their national interests. In particular, Germany cannot be expected to assume the role of a central fiscal capacity for the EMU – if only because the additional debt that would be caused by this would have to be borne solely at the national level.

2. The macroeconomic framework must not lead to permanent transfers between members – except via separately legitimated, administrated and limited functions, such as those that already exist in the form of the EU structural funds. If automatic transfers take place – for example because a Member State especially hard hit by a domestic recession becomes a net fiscal recipient – these must be temporary and balanced out again in the course of a few economic cycles. Otherwise there is a danger that incentives will be created for poor economic policy, triggering new distribution conflicts between the Member States.

3. While fiscal rules have a role to play, they must not be the only pillars supporting the regulatory framework, and they must be much better constructed than has been the case to date. The micro-management of national fiscal policy laid down in the SGP cannot for the most part be justified in economic terms and causes considerable political costs: A growing aversion to "Brussels" and the EMU. The pro-cyclical nature of the current rules must be eliminated and with it situations in which governments find themselves either forced to act against the interests of their own population in the short term or face the risk of sanctions. Furthermore, the effectiveness of fiscal rules should not depend on whether cyclical and structural components of growth and other variables that depend on or are pegged to the economic cycle can be accurately estimated "in real time".

These three requirements have direct consequences for the ongoing debate over reform of the EMU. The three most frequently discussed models for a central fiscal capacity for the Euro area are:

- A budget for the Euro area,
- European unemployment insurance and
- An automatic stabilisation mechanism in which payments are effected between States depending on their respective "output gaps".[10]

To begin with the latter, the notion of an automatic stabilisation mechanism would not seem to meet the aforementioned requirements. In its pure form,[11] it violates requirement 1, as it does not stabilise the Euro area as a whole, but only Member States with above-average output gaps.[12] Requirement 3 would be violated as well because the procedure is only effective if cyclical ups and downs can be correctly measured in real time. As a result, a question mark must also be placed behind requirement 2: If output gaps are not measured correctly, there could be transfers to the benefit of one State over a lengthy period that are difficult to stop.

A European unemployment insurance[13] is also difficult to reconcile with requirements 2 and 3. Structural unemployment – i.e. joblessness that is not related to the economic cycle – differs considerably from one EMU Member to another. Uniform unemployment insurance that does not take these differences into account would lead to semi-permanent transfers to the benefit of Member States with high structural unemployment, potentially giving rise to moral hazard. In principle, this problem can be solved by linking transfer payments only to cyclical unemployment (the difference between actual and structural) or by requiring higher unemployment insurance premiums from States with higher structural unemployment. This would mean, for example that much greater premiums would have to be paid for a Spanish employee than a German employee, which may be politically difficult. And if these premiums are incorrectly calculated because the cyclical component of unemployment in Spain turns out to be greater (or lower) than assumed, this could lead to unintended transfers on a massive scale at the expense of (or to the benefit of) Spain. Such errors could be balanced out to a certain extent by means of retroactive correction mechanisms (comparable with a retroactive tax claim when fiscal authorities have made a mistake) – but only if the mistakes are not very great, as possibly irreversible decisions on expenditures may have been made in the intervening period.

For these reasons, a European unemployment insurance system that meets requirement 2 will be plausible only after the structures of national labour markets in Europe have converged to a great degree. European unemployment insurance should be the aim and objective of a European fiscal and social union, but only following reforms that lead to a reduction in structural unemployment and a convergence of other structural factors at the level of the best performers in the Euro area.

Given the existing economic and political structure of the Euro area, this leaves only one approach for creating a central fiscal capacity: A Euro area budget. In the public debate, it is often assumed that the scope and complexity of federal budgets put this option into the class of politically unrealistic federalist dreams. The remainder of this Chapter will challenge this assumption. In particular, the next section will argue that a Euro area budget might not only be desirable but also realistic over the medium term if

- its volume is smaller, its tasks are much simpler and involve less discretion than the central budget of a federal state and
- it is not the only reform of the fiscal regulatory framework of the Euro area, but rather one of several, mutually reinforcing reforms.

How a reform could succeed

In the following, a reform project is outlined that could commence immediately and be completed over the medium term – within five to ten years. It includes a minimalist Euro area budget, a legal framework that would allow the orderly restructuring of government debts of the EMU Member States if they were to become unsustainable, the emission of a significant portion of new government debts in the form of bonds pegged to growth and a fundamental reform of the SGP. This project is almost as ambitious as the institutional steps already taken to establish the EMU, i.e. the founding of the ECB, the creation of the ESM and the creation of joint bank supervision and resolution authorities. At least one of its building blocks, a budget for the Euro area, could require amendment of the EU Treaties. But with regard to political integration, it would only move slightly beyond the status quo, and it could be realised in roughly the same period of time as the original EMU project.

A Euro area budget for stabilization purposes

Government budgets have distributional and allocative functions (provision of public goods) and are accordingly large in scale. This applies even to the highest budgetary level (the federal level) in federal systems: Without taking into account social security, Switzerland has the smallest federal budget among the major industrialised nations, accounting for around 10.5 per cent of GDP. The corresponding figure in Germany is around 13 per cent of GDP. Including social security, federal budgets in Switzerland and Canada amount to 17 per cent (Germany is much higher, at 28.5 per cent, due to its pay-as-you go pension system).[14]

A budget of this type is inconceivable for the Euro area without a political union that goes considerably further than at present. This leads to the question of whether it is possible to define a budget for the Euro area which

- is much smaller than a federal budget, but at the same time can play a meaningful stabilisation role.
- has only a limited role in deciding the composition of public expenditures, and
- has no or only a minimal impact on long-term distribution between Member States.

Revenue side

To maximize the stabilisation effect of the budget, it is important that it draws its revenue from taxes that are as cyclical as possible. A corporate or profit tax is ideal because its reacts to economic fluctuations in an especially sensitive manner (see Diagram 4). This could possibly be supplemented by a small income

Diagram 4: Revenue from taxes on profits in selected countries, 2007–2010

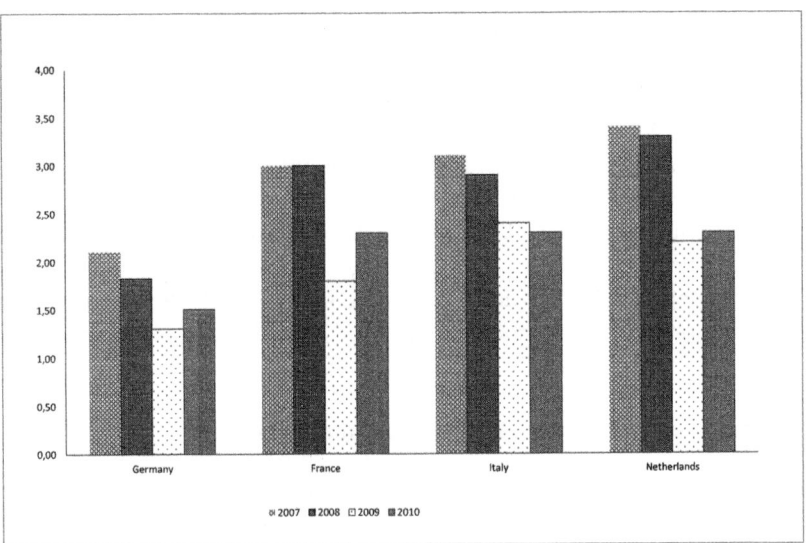

Note: This diagram shows the sum total from corporate and trade tax in Germany and for the other countries from the Eurostat series "Taxes on the income or profits of corporations"

Source: Federal German Government, Destatis, Eurostat, author's own estimates

or value-added tax. Two manners of execution are conceivable: A new tax at the European level which is compensated for by corresponding decreases in taxes at the national level, or the "diversion" of a small share of taxes imposed at the national level.

In either case, the tax level would need to be calibrated to result in a transfer of a certain percentage of national GDP (for example, two per cent, see below) when the economies of the contributing Member States are in a cyclically neutral position. The decision as to what exactly a "cyclically neutral position" means can hence not be avoided; however, it will only have to be taken once – in the course of the initial negotiations – rather than year after year, as required by current EU fiscal rules. Moreover, it could be reviewed and corrected after a few years if it is determined that a mistake has been made above a stipulated level.

Expenditure side

To fit in the existing policy and political framework of the Euro area, the Euro area budget should interfere with the allocation competences of Member States' budgets as little as possible. This could be achieved by limiting the expenditures of the budget to just two categories:

1. Infrastructure investments of a transnational nature (e.g. networks) or high-volume civil engineering projects meeting specified criteria. The European Investment Bank (EIB) could select and implement these projects – within the constraints of certain expenditure corridors for every member. Making this work might require an expansion of the EIB along federal lines. There are two arguments for carrying out infrastructure projects of this type at the European level. First, reaping gains related to integration (by strengthening the Single Market, for instance), and second, allowing countries with weaker institutions to benefit from best practices in the execution of major projects. Recent IMF research shows that the impact of greater public investments on short- and medium-term growth depends on the efficiency of public investments.[15] In this respect, there are significant differences between the Member States at present.[16]

2. A blanket transfer to the budget of the Member States, whose allocation would initially remain fully under national control (an understanding on broad areas in which the transfer is meant to be spent would be desirable, but is not essential).[17] These transfers could be interpreted as a precursor to shifting a portion of social or unemployment-related expenditures by Member States to the European level. They would not, however, depend on the level of unemployment or other social indicators that can be influenced by the economic or structural-policy measures of the Member States (changes conditional on demographic developments would be

conceivable, however). Instead, the transfers would be calibrated, for each Member State, such that the total amount of the transfer and investment budget is equal to the expected tax contribution of the Member State in a cyclically neutral position. The implication is that in recessions, transfers from the Euro area budget to the State would exceed taxes collected from that State, while the opposite would be true in booms. In addition, the Euro minister of finance or budget commissioner should be given the possibility of raising or reducing blanket transfers, without however changing the ratio of transfers across Member States. The level of transfers for a particular year would be notified to the Member States in the third quarter of the previous year so that it is can be taken into account on the revenue side of the Draft Budgetary Plan that the Member States submit by 15 October of each year.

Magnitude

The Euro area budget should be large enough to have an appreciable macroeconomic effect. This is deemed to be the case if it can exert a fiscal impulse (change in the structural fiscal balance) – of at least 1.5 per cent of GDP. The ability to produce a surplus of that magnitude depends on the scope with which expenditures can be reduced on short notice. In the expenditure structure proposed, this is true mainly for the transfer component, which could be set to zero in a year in which the Euro area budget wishes to impart a negative fiscal impulse. Hence, transfers would need to be calibrated at a level of at least 1.5 per cent of GDP in a cyclically neutral State. In addition, the Euro area budget would need to raise some revenues to finance the investment portion of the budget. In view of the investment volume of typical federal budgets (just one per cent of GDP in Germany, for example), it appears unlikely that investments financed by the Euro area budget would exceed 0.5 per cent of Euro area GDP. It follows that the "normal" volume of revenue and expenditures of the Euro area budget (in a cyclically neutral position) should be set at around two per cent of GDP.

Stabilisation effects

Changes in revenues and expenditures would arise from the following:

- Economic ups and downs that lead to greater or lower tax revenue
- Investment decisions within a stipulated floor and ceiling for each Member
- Decisions by the budget commissioner to scale transfers (and possibly expenditures on investment) to the Member States upwards or downwards within certain limits
- To the extent that transfers to the Member States are pegged to demographic developments: Changes in the size or structure of the population

Stabilisation would hence occur via three different channels:

1. Automatic stabilisers on the revenue side (Member States in a recession automatically pay less into the Euro area budget, while Member States automatically pay more in a boom)
2. Scaling of blanket transfers up- or downwards
3. Investment decisions within prescribed limits

Channel 3 would be modest in scope, as it requires suitable projects and would normally be associated with implementation delays of several years. In the event of persistent stagnation, it could play a role, however. Channels 1 and 2 would be suited to reacting to shocks or stabilising the economy at economic cycle frequencies. With a Euro area budget of just two per cent of GDP (which could probably be financed only in part with taxes that are highly sensitive to economic fluctuations, like a corporate tax)[18] the automatic stabilising effect of the budget would remain limited, however. The most powerful instrument would therefore be channel 2, the possibility of scaling transfers up or down or suspending them completely. While the contractionary impact of the budget would be limited by the difference between last year's transfer and zero, expansion could be larger, so long as the debt created by the budget remains sustainable.

Debt creation and governance

The stabilisation function implies that the Euro area budget would not normally be balanced, but would usually show a surplus or a deficit. Cumulative deficits could give rise to a Euro area debt stock, the sustainability of which will depend on the level of debt, expected Euro area growth, interest rates and the possibility of generating primary surpluses in the future. To retain flexibility for future stabilisation policy, the Euro area budget authority must use its discretionary power in a manner that the sustainability of Euro area debt is never questioned. This could be achieved by means of a debt cap that can only be exceeded in exceptional cases, for example, 25-30 per cent of Euro area GDP.[19] A democratically legitimated supervisory committee (a committee of the European Parliament, for example) would have to approve the investment budget proposed by the Euro area budget commissioner and determine if and when the debt ceiling can be violated.

Objections and unresolved questions

Would the construction just sketched deliver what it promises? Two possible objections appear to be particularly salient here.

1. Would a contractionary or expansionary stimulus by the Euro area budget be thwarted by offsetting behaviour of national budgets? In the event of a

contractionary impulse (transfers are reduced or suspended), it is conceivable that Member States would neutralise this by increasing their debt levels. However, this is unlikely to be fully offsetting, both because fiscal rules may be in place that restrict national fiscal expansion or because it matters whether fiscal expansion is financed by Member States taking on more debt themselves or by transfer. There could also be offsetting behaviour in the other direction: A conservative minister of finance who does not see any domestic macroeconomic reason to relax fiscal policy could refuse to spend the transfer from Brussels and instead use it to pay off debt. But again, full neutralisation is unlikely: To the extent that budget policy is not solely focused on stabilising the domestic economy, but also on avoiding new net debt (as has been the case in Germany over the last few years), the willingness to increase expenditures will depend in part on the source of financing. A call to spend € 15 billion will more likely lead to actual spending increases if it is backed up by a check for € 15 billion.[20]

2. Would the proposed procedure really be distributionally neutral across countries? As described above, the rules for the Euro area budget would not allow the budget commissioner to increase transfers to specific countries: She or he could merely decide on the amount of the transfer to the Euro area *as a whole*, which would subsequently be distributed according to a fixed key. Distribution effects could nevertheless come from two sources: The investment budget and the fact that some countries are growing faster than others and as a result pay greater amounts of revenue into the Euro area budget. The former is not problematic, as this budget is small, and discretionary latitude would also be restricted here (through specific spending corridors for individual countries) and be subject to democratic controls. The latter would only lead to permanent transfers if trend growth differs across countries (greater revenue as a result of a cyclically strong economy makes automatic stabilisation possible and would balance out over time). This effect is easy to neutralise, however: For example, by taking into account potential growth – as forecast by the European Commission or the IMF – when calibrating the allocation key. A new calibration could take place every five years, at which time differences between expected and achieved growth in the last period could be taken into account in the calibration for the next period.

Another important question relates to possible unintended consequences, in particular skewed incentives at the national level. This could include incentives to "free ride" on the Euro area budget by "shifting" certain investment responsibilities to the level of the Euro area, and of course slippages in spending in the hope that the Euro area budget would come to aid if something went awry. The first problem can be solved through a strong, multilateral governance structure that chooses the investment projects that are financed at the Euro area level. The second problem can be confronted by a clear, Treaty-based bailout prohibition especially focused on the new budget, a mechanism that ensures that debt crises are not resolved at the expense of European taxpayers, and more effective EU fiscal rules. The last two topics are explored in the following section.

COMPLEMENTARY REFORMS

A framework for restructuring excessive government debt

European fiscal rules aimed to prevent excessive government debts. This failed: In the case of Greece, even extreme fiscal adjustment and cheap credit from the European Financial Stability Facility did not suffice to restore the solvency of the public sector. An ad hoc restructuring of Greek government bonds took place in early 2012, in which (predominantly private) creditors lost about two-thirds of the net present value of their claims. Even this massive "haircut" was not sufficient, however, in part because it came too late.[21] Another restructuring of Greek government bonds therefore appears unavoidable – this time at the expense of public creditors.[22]

To avoid future debt crises being resolved either on the backs of the citizens of the crisis country or – if consolidation efforts fail – on the backs of Euro area taxpayers, the Euro area needs a procedure with which to restructure excessive government debt in an orderly manner. Such a procedure could have contributed to both the prevention and the resolution of the Euro crisis. It is also important as a complement to the Euro area budget. Experience from fiscal federations shows that the existence of a central budget can undermine the fiscal discipline of subordinate fiscal authorities.[23] Merely prohibiting a bailout will lack credibility, however, as long as the Euro area does not have any clear procedure with which excessive debt of a State can be reduced at the expense of private creditors. The possibility of an orderly restructuring of government debt would create a pressure valve to cope with extreme shocks affecting specific countries without having to make use of the Euro area budget.

There is by now a substantial literature addressing the question of what a European mechanism for restructuring excessive government debt could look like.[24] Proposals typically revolve around two components:

- A legal framework that legitimates a restructuring negotiated by creditors and the Member State (for instance, by consent of two-thirds of the creditors and/or the ESM) and protects the debtor against legal action by creditors not participating in the agreement ("holdouts"). This could be created, for example, by means of an amendment to the ESM Treaty.

- A criterion that requires a debt restructuring (or at least a maturity extension) of existing government bonds as a condition for new ESM loans or other fiscal assistance to very highly indebted Member States.

The introduction of such a framework would be associated with complications and risks. Even the best framework of this kind is not credible as long as a large portion of securities of a state are held by its own banks. To reduce these holdings, the regulatory treatment of sovereign debt on bank balance sheets will need to change, possibly in combination with the introduction of a "safe asset" that replaces national sovereign debt holdings.[25] Furthermore, an unavoidable and to some extent intended consequence of a debt-restructuring regime is that states with a very high level of indebtedness would have to pay higher interest and would lose access to the market earlier than is the case today. This implies that a debt restructuring framework could trigger a debt crisis if introduced during a period in which several states have very high levels of old debt, as is the case today.

For this reason, it is critical that the introduction of such a framework set reasonable transition periods and be combined with stabilising reforms, such as the launch of a Euro area budget described above and the reform of the SGP outlined below. This would improve the chances of highly indebted States to emerge from stagnation and reduce their debt mountain through a combination of growth and continued fiscal prudence.

Reform of the Stability and Growth Pact

The current fiscal rules for the Euro area are complex, prone to error and pro-cyclical. They need to be replaced by a governance structure that on the one hand prevents excessive debt and on the other retains sufficient space for a stabilisation policy geared to the specific needs of individual countries. A host of proposals along these lines have been made in recent years.[26] These proposals have in common that in order to avoid pro-cyclical influences they are not based on error-prone cyclical adjustment procedures, and instead assign the task of identifying recessions and crises to independent committees of experts. During these periods, Member States would be given more leeway to undertake countercyclical policies, or modified rules would apply that allow greater expenditures on the unemployed, higher investment or both. Furthermore, Andrle/Bluedorn et al. (2015) and Claeys/Darvas et al. (2016) call for fiscal rules which cap expenditure growth instead of the structural deficit in normal times, since the latter is much easier to measure and is under the direct control of the government.

An even more radical solution could be to dispense with rules-based consolidation requirements entirely and instead negotiate broad adjustment and reform programmes with countries that have exceeded specified debt or deficit levels. These programmes would not only lay down appropriate fiscal adjustment objectives and measures but also structural reforms and investment that foster growth. The more credible and better structured the reform package is, the less the need for consolidation in the short term. This strategy requires very strong and politically independent monitoring, however, by an institution that reviews the implementation of reform on a regular basis, ensures equal treatment of the Member States and in the case of sluggish progress reverts to a purely rules-based consolidation strategy.

Emission of GDP-indexed bonds

While a Euro area budget would create revenue-side automatic stabilisers, its power to deal with asymmetric shocks is likely to be modest due to the small level and limited cyclicality of the underlying revenue. For this reason, it would be worth considering adding an additional automatic stabilisation mechanism: The emission by Member States of GDP-indexed bonds, in which interest is pegged to growth.[27] There are historical examples for such bonds, although they remain rare. As Blanchard/Mauro et al. (2016) show, GDP-indexed bonds could be particularly helpful to members of the Euro area, whose stabilisation options are more limited than those of countries that retain control over their own currency.

GDP-indexed bonds impact the public finances of the issuer via two channels. Because economic growth risk is partly passed on to the creditor, they are usually more expensive for the issuer (higher expected yield) than normal government bonds. At the same time, however, in recessions they lead to significantly lower interest expenditures than would otherwise be the case. GDP-indexed government bonds thus contribute to economic stabilisation (they allow a more expansionary fiscal policy in a downswing) and/or slow down increases in government debt in deep recessions. As a result, they will generally support the sustainability of government debt and make it less likely that a debt problem would have to be solved by an ESM programme – or in an extreme case, by a restructuring of government debt. Blanchard/Mauro et al. (2016) show that GDP-indexed bonds would have made a significant contribution to the stabilisation of Spanish government debt in the face of the shocks that Spain had to withstand between 1999 and 2015.

Governments are often wary of emissions of GDP-indexed bonds because they would be somewhat more expensive than normal bonds and because the issuing government implicitly admits that future growth may be subject to a certain risk. But this is short-term thinking and fails to take into account the spill-over risk of an escalating debt crisis for other members of the Euro area. An agreement in which all members of the Euro area assume the obligation to issue a minimum proportion of their future bonds (for example, one-third) as GDP-indexed bonds would be both in the collective interest of the Euro area and in the long-term interest of the individual members.

Conclusion

The proposed reform of the fiscal regulatory framework for the Euro area consists of four elements:

1. A Euro area budget of around two per cent of GDP that finances investment in specific infrastructure categories and entails a transfer mechanism that can be used to stabilise Euro area-wide shocks;
2. A mechanism for the restructuring of government debts that makes the bailout prohibition credible and puts some of the burden associated with debt crises on the shoulders of private creditors rather than just taxpayers;
3. A reform of the SGP to avoid pro-cyclical fiscal policy and investment and improve incentives for structural reforms;
4. An agreement to issue a portion of Euro area debt via GDP-indexed bonds to create an additional channel for automatic stabilisation and improve the sustainability of government debt in phases of stagnation.

None of these reforms is politically easy. This is due in part to the fact that their opportunities and risks differ across Euro Member States. The risk that a mechanism for restructuring government debts that is launched in an inept manner will cause government debt to become more expensive and possibly trigger a new crisis is much greater in Italy than in Germany, for instance. It must be minimised by a carefully structured transition mechanism.

When it comes to the establishment of a Euro area budget with a capacity for issuing debt, the biggest potential loser is often seen to be Germany. In the form proposed here, however, the function of the budget would be so tightly circumscribed that it could scarcely become an instrument for redistribution in Europe. The only reason to nevertheless reject the proposal as a sort of invitation to additional redistribution is the fear that it could be abused: If something went wrong – and a European debt mountain remained – Germany in its capacity as the strongest fiscal Member State would be liable.

However, if the "South" rejects every reform idea that would lead to an increase in market discipline – even in the distant future – and Germany and others in the "North" reject any idea aimed at stabilisation, even if this is designed to avoid redistribution, EMU reform will continue in gridlock. But gridlock means further stagnation, the brunt of which continues to be borne by the general population, particularly the unemployed. The only beneficiaries will be parties that assail the European integration project and offer deceptive and illusory solutions.

There is another way: A reform path in which risks to both sides are both minimised and distributed symmetrically between the "North" and "South".

The reform elements outlined may contribute to a grand bargain along these lines. The alternative would be standstill – and continued standstill is the greatest risk of all.

Notes

1 | This article reflects the private opinion of the author. I would like to express my gratitude for the support and commentary to the editors of this book, Philipp Steinberg and Alexander Schellinger, as well as Agnès Bénassy-Quéré, Henrik Enderlein, Agata Grzeszewski, Katharina Marsch, Jean Pisani-Ferry, Felix Probst, Xavier Ragot and the participants in a workshop on the strategy for France that took place on 7 June 2016.
2 | In this article, the term "stabilisation" denotes demand-side policy in the broadest sense: To smooth out economic cycles, to promote stabilisation after shocks, but also to overcome lengthy phases of deflation or stagnation.
3 | Juncker, Jean Claude/Tusk, Donald et al. (2015): Die Wirtschafts- und Währungsunion Europas beenden; http://ec.europa.eu/priorities/sites/beta-political/files/5-presidents-report_de_o.pdf (called up on 20 June 2016); Sachverständigenrat zur Begutachtung der gesamtwirtschaftlichen Entwicklung (2015): Anhang zum Jahresgutachten "Zukunftsfähigkeit in den Mittelpunkt"; www.sachvertaendigenrat-wirtschaft.de/fileadmin/dateiablage/gutachten/jg20516/wirtschafts-gutachten/jg15_ges.pdf (last accessed 20/06/2016).
4 | Barbiero, Francesca/Darvas, Zsolt (2014): In sickness and in health: protecting and supporting, in: Bruegel Policy Contribution 2, February, http://bruegel.org/wp-content/uploads/imported/publications/pc_2014_02.pdf (called up on 20 June 2016); to what extent "austerity" has contributed to the European recession in 2012–2013 continues to be a source of controversy. It is no longer a subject of debate whether it had a contractionary effect. See Alesina, Alberto/Barbiero, Omar et al. (2015): Austerity in 2009–2013, in: Economic Policy, 30. Jg., July, pp. 383–437; http://scholar.harvard.edu/files/alesina/files/austerity_in_09-13_2014.pdf?m=1414170559 (called up on 20 June 2016) and the discussion by Taylor, Alan M. (2015): Comment on "Austerity in 2009–2013" by Alesina, Barbiero, Favero, Giavazzi, and Paradisi, in: Economic Policy, 30. Jg. July, pp. 383–437.
5 | Bénassy-Quéré, Agné/Ragot, Xavier et al. (2016) Which Fiscal Union for the Euro Area, in Bruegel Policy Contribution 5, February; http://bruegel.org/wp-content/uploads/2016/02/pc_2016_05.pdf (last accessed 20/06/2016).
6 | On France see European Commission (2015): Recommendations for a council recommendation with a view to bringing an end to the excessive government deficit in France; http://ec.europa.eu/economy_finance/economic_governance/sgp/pdf/30_edps/126-07_commission/2015-0w-w7_fr_126-7_commission_en.pdf (called up on 20 June 2016); on Italy, Portugal and Spain, see European Commission (2016): Spring

2016 European Semester package: Commission issues country-specific recommendations; http://europa.eu/rapid/press-release_IP_16-1724_en.htm (last accessed 20/06/2016).

7 | As was made very clear by the Chairman of the Euro Group, Jeroen Dijsselbloem, on 14 June 2016 in a statement of position before the Economic Committee of the European Parliament, in which he issued a reminder first of all regarding the role of the European Commission as "guardian of the Treaties" and the need to live up to this and at the same time warned against unequal treatment of large and small countries.

8 | Andrle, Michal/Bluedorn, John et al. (2015): Reforming Fiscal Governance in the European Union, in: Staff Discussion Notes 9, International Monetary Fund; https://www.imf.org/external/pubs/ft/sdn/2015/sdn1509.pdf (called up on 20 June 2016); Claeys, Grégory/Darvas, Zsolt et al. (2016): A Proposal to revive the European Fiscal Framework, in: Bruegel Policy Contribution 7, March; http://bruegel.org/wp-content/uploads/2016/03/pc_2016_07.pdf (last accessed 20/06/2016).

9 | Thus, for example, Claeys/Darvas et al. 2016 (op cit.) have determined that the typical annual measurement error (average correction of structural deficit measures between two years) is frequently higher than the consolidation of half a per cent of GDP typically required of the countries.

10 | Enderlein, Henrik/Bonger, Peter et al. (2012): Completing the Euro. A road map towards fiscal union in Europe (Report of the "Tommaso Padoa-Schioppa Group"), Notre Europe; www.notre-europe.eu/media/completingtheeuroreport-padoa-schioppagroupnejune2012.pdf?pdf=ok (last accessed 20/06/2016); Wolff, Guntram (2012): A budget for Europe's monetary union, in: Bruegel Policy Contribution 22; http://bruegel.org/wp-content/uploads/imported/publications/pc_2012_22_EA_budget_nal.pdf (last accessed 20/06/2016); Pisani-Ferry, Jean/Vihriälä, Erkki (2013): Options for Euro-Area Fiscal Capacity, in: Bruegel Policy Contribution 1, January; http://bruegel.org/wp-content/uploads/imported/publications/pc_2013_02.pdf (last accessed 20/06/2016); Allard, Celine/Koeva Brooks, Petya et al. (2013): Toward a Fiscal Union for the Euro Area, IMF Staff Discussion Note 13/09, September; Enderlein, Henrik/Guttenberg, Lucas et al. (2013): Blueprint for a Cyclical Shock Insurance in the Euro Area, Project "EU & differentiated Integration", September 2013, Notre Europe; www.notre-europe.eu/media/blueprintforacycli-calshockinsurancene-jdisept2013.pdf?pdf=ok (last accessed 20/06/2016).

11 | Enderlein, Henrik/Guttenberg, Lucas et al. (2013): op cit.

12 | One could also imagine a variant in which it is not deviations from the average output gap that trigger transfers, but rather the absolute size of the output gap. In this case, the mechanism would have to be linked to a fund or another type of debt-assumption capacities. Requirement 1 would be met, as the mechanism would then also have a stabilising effect if the Euro area as a whole slid into a recession. The error-proneness of the mechanism would be exacerbated by this, however, because the absolute amount of output gaps is more difficult to estimate in real time than the relative level of the output gap in one Member State in comparison to another.

13 | See for example Claeys, Grégory/Darvas, Zsolt et al. (2014): Benefits and drawbacks of European Unemployment Insurance, in: Bruegel Policy Brief 6, September; http://bruegel.org/wp-content/uploads/imported/publications/pb_2014_06_281114.pdf (last accessed 20/06/2016).

14 | Source: International Monetary Fund: Government Finance Statistics. The statistics for Switzerland are for 2013, for the other countries 2014. These are the last years for which information is available.

15 | International Monetary Fund (2014): Is it time for an infrastructure push? The macroeconomic effects of public investment, World Economic Outlook, Chapter 3, October, pp. 75-114; https://www.imf.org/external/pubs/ft/weo/2014/02/pdf/c3.pdf (last accessed 20/06/2016).

16 | The IMF study uses survey-based indicators from the World Economic Forum. Among the States of the Euro area, Finland attained the best rating in 2015 (almost five on a scale of one to seven, the best possible rating), while Italy merely attained a scale of barely two.

17 | This is similar to the "target grants for the attainment of common aims and objectives" from a Euro area fund to the Member States. See Enderlein, Henrik and Jean Pisani-Ferry (2014): Reformen, Investitionen und Wachstum: eine Agenda für Frankreich, Deutschland und Europa, ein Bericht für Sigmar Gabriel und Emmanuel Macron, November; www.bmwi.de/BMWi/Redaktion/PDF/Publikationen/empfehlung-enderlein-pisani-ferry-deutsch,property=pdf,bereich=bmwi2012,sprache=de,rwb=true.pdf (last accessed 20/06/2016). In contrast to Enderlein and Pisani-Ferry, the transfers proposed here would not be earmarked, however.

18 | In Germany, for example, the corporate tax only yields around 0.7 per cent of GDP.

19 | Assuming that no more than a quarter of the Euro area revenue flow (i.e. 0.5 per cent of GDP) is to be dedicated to debt service, a long-term real interest rate of 2 per cent and a long term real growth rate of 1 per cent, the standard stock-flow debt accumulation identity implies that the proposed revenue stream could sustain a maximum debt of just over 50 per cent of Euro area GDP. However, Euro area debt should be far less in normal times to give room for fiscal expansions in emergencies and maintain AAA status without requiring a joint guarantee.

20 | The manner in which the German Minister of Finance dealt with unexpectedly high revenue in the years 2014 and 2015 underscores this point: in spite of record employment and a surging economy, this additional revenue was for the most part ploughed into higher expenditures (for communities, public investments and, at the end of 2015, a reserve for refugees) instead of debt reduction. The additional investment and local community spending would not have taken place if it had been at the expense of a greater debt burden.

21 | Zettelmeyer, Jeromim/Trebesch, Christoph et al. (2013): The Greek Debt Restructuring: An Autopsy, in: Economic Policy, July, pp. 513-563; http://economicapolicy.oxfordjournals.org/content/economicpolicy/28/75/513.full.pdf (last accessed 20/06/2016).

22 | Eurogruppe (2016): Eurogroup statement on Greece, Press release, 25 May 2016; www.consilium.europa.eu/en/press/press-releases/2016/05/24-eurogroup-statement-greece/ (last accessed 20/06/2016).

23 | Rodden, Jonathan (2002): The Dilemma of Fiscal Federalism: Grants and Fiscal Performance around the World, in: American Journal of Political Science 3, pp. 670-687.

24 | See overview: Zettelmeyer, Jeromin (2016): A Sovereign Debt Restructuring Mechanism for the Euro Area?, in: Olli Rehn/Jermomin Zettelmeyer (ed.): Global Fiscal Systems: From Crisis to Sustainability, World Economic Forum, May, pp. 24-29; http://www3.weforum.org/docs/WEF_GAC16_Global_Fiscal_Systems_From_Crisis_to_Sustainability_report.pdf (last accessed 07/07/2016).

25 | Corsetti, Giancarlo/Feld, Lars/Koijen, Ralph/ Reichlin, Lucrezia/Reis, Ricardo/ Rey, Helene/Weder di Mauro, Beatrice. 2016. Reinforcing the Eurozone and Protecting an Open Society. Monitoring the Eurozone 2, May. London: CEPR; Brunnermeier, Markus K./ Langfield, Sam/Pagano, Marco/Reis, Ricardo/Van Nieuwerburgh, Stijn/Vayanos, Dimitri. 2016. "ESBies: Safety in the Tranches." ESRB Working Paper No. 21, September.

26 | Andrle, Michal/Bluedorn, John et al. (2015): op cit.; Bénassy-Quéré, Agnè/Ragot, Xavier et al. (2016): op cit.; Claeys, Grégory/Darvas, Zsolt et al. (2016): op cit.

27 | For example, interest equals the growth rate of GDP plus a fixed premium, see Borensztein, Eduardo/Mauro, Paola (2004): The Case for GDP-indexed Bonds, in: Economic Policy 38, April, pp. 165-216; Barr, David/Bush, Oliver et al. (2014): GDP-linked bonds and sovereign default, Bank of England, Working Paper 484, January; www.bankofengland.co.uk/research/Documents/workingpapers/2014/wp484.pdf (last accessed 20/06/2016); Blanchard, Olivier/Mauro, Paolo et al. (2016): The Case for Growth-Indexed Bonds in Advanced Economies Today, Peterson Institute for International Economics, Policy Brief 16-2, February.

9. An institutional framework for a reformed Eurozone

Daniela Schwarzer

When European Economic and Monetary Union (EMU) was launched in 1999, the European Central Bank (ECB) assumed responsibility for monetary policy in the Eurozone. But unlike other currency areas, the boundaries of which are generally those of nation-states, the ECB has no Eurozone government or Eurozone finance minister as counterpart. Instead, a multitude of national and European actors participate in economic governance alongside the ECB. This makes Eurozone governance a complex process that is often less than fully efficient, transparent and democratic.

When the Eurozone was founded, the ECB was its only dedicated institution. At the time the Maastricht Treaty was negotiated, it was assumed that a common currency excluding certain EU states would only be a transitional phase. Over the years it became clear that not only would the opt-out states – the United Kingdom and Denmark – remain permanently outside, but Poland and other Central and Eastern European states were also retreating from the goal of rapid accession. Therefore, differences in membership between the Eurozone and the EU are going to persist for the foreseeable future.

At the same time, the initial years of EMU underlined the need for considerably greater coordination and integration between Eurozone states than within the EU and the internal market. The series of Eurozone crises following the 2007/2008 financial meltdown in the United States left no doubt that the Eurozone lacked instruments and institutions. Now the question of its institutional arrangements has returned to the agenda. The structures have already experienced change in the course of the crisis management process, which created new formats and instruments in the European Stability Mechanism (ESM) and the Euro Summit. There are also far-reaching proposals for improving governance structures to enhance the democratic legitimacy and efficiency of Eurozone decision-making.

The issue became even more urgent in 2016. Firstly, the United Kingdom's "Brexit" referendum in June 2016 stimulated discussions about improving the transparency, efficiency and democratic legitimacy of decision-making. Calls for referendums on EU membership have been raised in other Member States as well. Secondly, there is growing acceptance of the idea that the EU's future will be a great deal more diverse than had once been thought. For some states, differentiation may mean "less EU". Others, like the Eurozone, see the possibility and functional necessity for deeper integration as the essence of the EU. This institutional dimension can only be addressed in conjunction with the questions of which economic, financial and budgetary instruments should in fact be located at federal level in a monetary union, and what the functional needs are in terms of coordinating and potentially monitoring national policies in order to underpin stable macroeconomic development. In connection with institutional reforms, it is also relevant whether the differences in membership of Eurozone and EU are expected to persist for the foreseeable future. This contribution assumes that they will. Thus, the Eurozone states should gradually create and strengthen institutions, forums and administrative structures of their own, and potentially seek their own Eurozone Treaty – while making sure that it all remains embedded in the EU.

The following section begins by describing the existing institutional structure of the Eurozone. Then the principles for reform and the places where action is required are outlined, along with concrete proposals for developing them.[1] Finally, the prospects for institutional reforms and the implications for the Eurozone's relationship with the EU are discussed.

THE STATUS QUO

EMU has only one federal institution: The politically independent European Central Bank. The ECB is responsible for monetary policy in the Eurozone, with a remit to preserve monetary stability. There has been no corresponding transfer of economic policy and budgetary powers to the European level. Therefore – alongside the European Commission – national governments still play a decisive role: They set their own national budgets – supposedly in line with the Commission's recommendations and within limits defined at the European level. They also legislate at the initiative of the European Commission, in many areas on an equal basis with the European Parliament.

Ecofin

The national governments of the EU Member States participate in law-making and economic and budgetary coordination through the Economic and Financial Affairs Council (Ecofin). Ecofin, comprising the national finance and economics ministers, is the decisive institution with regard to economic and financial legislation. It is responsible for coordinating and monitoring EU Member States, and rules on sanctions under the Stability and Growth Pact. Ecofin also decides whether to accept EU Member States into the Eurozone and approves the EU's annual budget jointly with the European Parliament.

In most cases Ecofin takes decisions by qualified majority voting; tax questions require unanimity. The European Parliament is consulted where it is not already involved as a co-legislator in the scope of the ordinary legislative procedure. Eurozone and non-Eurozone members have different voting rights to ensure that matters concerning the Economic and Monetary Union (EMU) (Art. 136 [1] TFEU) and securing the Euro's place in the international monetary system (Art. 138 [1] TFEU) are decided only by the ministers of the Eurozone states.

Eurozone-specific formats: Eurogroup and Euro Summit

Alongside Ecofin, the Eurogroup was established in 1998 as an exclusive forum for the Eurozone ministers in order to account for the specific interdependencies and needs for joint action within the Economic and Monetary Union. To date, however, it has no decision-making powers. Although it was originally created outside the Treaties, the Eurogroup is today a firm fixture in the Eurozone governance framework and plays a major role in economic and financial coordination. It is first mentioned in the Lisbon Treaty (Art. 137 TFEU) – with reference to the annexed Protocol No. 14 laying out the composition and objectives of the Eurogroup. The Eurogroup has had a chair since 1 January 2005, serving thirty-month terms, while the rotating Presidency of the Council of the EU chairs Ecofin and changes every six months.

As the debt crisis sharpened, the heads of state and government of the Eurozone states held increasingly frequent emergency meetings, generally immediately before or after the European Council. Initially, from 2008 onwards, the summits were ad hoc crisis management meetings. Not until the Euro Summit of 26 October 2011 did the Euro states agree on a Franco-German proposal to institutionalise the gathering as a regular forum to steer Eurozone development and economic cooperation at the highest political level. The plan was for the heads of state and government to meet at least once every six months. But in the crisis years 2011/2012 meetings were held considerably more frequently and the discussions often concentrated on operational questions.

The Euro Summit was given its own permanent chair, parallel to the office of the permanent President of the European Council. Currently both positions are held by Donald Tusk. The Eurogroup President's tasks are similar to those of the President of the European Council, for example in the field of organisation and seeking common ground before and during the meetings of the heads of state and government. Finally, in 2012, the Eurozone formats acquired their own administrative base, with a dedicated working group – comparable to the

Council working groups – to prepare the meetings of the Eurogroup and the Euro Summit and resolve technical questions in advance. After operating especially intensely during the worst phases of the crisis, the format has receded increasingly into the background since the acute crisis abated in 2013. The most recent Euro Summit was held on 12 July 2015.

European Commission

The European Commission has the right of initiative and presents draft legislation for approval by the Council of Ministers and the European Parliament in a codecision procedure where both of the latter have equal rights. The Commission also monitors the implementation of European legislation and may request the European Court of Justice to impose sanctions. It plays a decisive role in monitoring and coordinating the Member States' budget and economic policies. Under the Stability and Growth Pact the Commission works preventively to stabilise national budgets by formulating reform proposals for countries at risk of violating the deficit criteria. Wherever a violation occurs, the Commission may, with Ecofin's approval, initiate a deficit procedure. The role of the Commission was reinforced by the introduction of the European Semester in 2010, the reform of the Stability and Growth Pact, and macro-economic surveillance under the so-called Sixpack of 2011. The Commission assesses the overall economic development of each country, and – where emerging balances are identified – analyses the associated risks for the Eurozone and the EU. The Commission and Ecofin may recommend corrective measures to Member States. If an excessive imbalance is found, the Commission monitors the implementation of necessary reforms by the government in question. It also prepares an annual growth survey and evaluates the country reports and stability and convergence programmes that form the basis for discussion at the Spring European Council.

Hence, the Commission's role in economic and budgetary coordination has grown. On the other hand, it has come under pressure through the strengthening of the European Council and Euro Summit. For example, in the crisis years 2010 to 2013 the European Council, which under the Treaty of Lisbon "shall not exercise legislative functions" (Art. 15 [1] TEU), repeatedly asked its President, Herman Van Rompuy, to prepare proposals that undermined the Commission's monopoly right of initiative. Intergovernmental agreements, such as those to create the bailout mechanisms and the Fiscal Compact, also weakened the Union's supranational institutions and community procedures (for more on this see also Chapter 2). This weakening of its role sometimes made it hard for the Commission to fulfil its bridging function between the Eurozone and EU-28 and to operate as the "guardian of the Treaties".

European Stability Mechanism

In the course of the Eurozone debt crisis, the European Stability Mechanism (ESM) was created on the basis of an intergovernmental Treaty between the Euro states. The ESM is an instrument for providing financial assistance to governments and banks suffering liquidity crises wherever this is necessary to safeguard the financial stability of the Euro area (Art. 3 ESM Treaty). Assistance is conditional on reforms. The ESM replaced the temporary European Financial Stability Facility (EFSF) and European Financial Stabilisation Mechanism (EFSM) of May 2010.

The ESM can – preventively or in response to acute need – grant loans up to a maximum lending capacity of € 500 billion to fund state debt or recapitalise financial institutions. It may also purchase government bonds in primary and secondary markets. The ESM Treaty stipulates that as of 1 January 2013 all new government bonds in the Eurozone with terms longer than one year must contain collective action clauses because the Eurozone otherwise possesses no rules for state insolvencies.

Decisions on ESM assistance are taken by the board of governors, which comprises the finance ministers of the Member States and their deputies, who in turn appoint two representatives from each state to the board of directors and elect the executive director. As such, the board of governors is basically the same as the Eurogroup, except that here different voting rules apply: Votes are weighted according to financial contribution. Therefore, unlike in the Council of Ministers, there is no parity between France and Germany.

The board of governors makes decisions on financial assistance, altering the capital and credit facility, and mandating the Commission to negotiate terms and conditions for assistance by unanimous agreement. Abstentions are possible, but in urgent cases the European Commission and the ECB can bring about an emergency decision with a qualified majority of 85 per cent of votes cast. With 28 per cent of ESM capital and voting rights, the German government has a veto over such decisions.

When a Member State applies for assistance from the ESM, the chair of the board of governors asks the ECB and the European Commission to identify the funding requirements and the risks for the Eurozone and for the State in question. If financial support is approved on the basis of this assessment, the conditions are then negotiated with the European Commission, the ECB and the International Monetary Fund (IMF). In parallel the managing director prepares a proposal for a "financial assistance facility agreement" that lists the specific terms and must be approved by the board of directors. After the board of directors approves the release of the first funds, the Commission, the IMF and the ECB monitor observance of the conditions, which is decisive for release of further instalments. Fundamentally, the ESM is open to any EU state that complies with the Maastricht criteria; even without membership they may participate on an ad hoc basis.

European Parliament

The European Parliament participates in economic governance through the ordinary legislative procedures together with the Council of Ministers. On the basis of the Lisbon Treaty it is also involved in monitoring economic coordination, which occurs largely through Ecofin in discussion with the Commission (Art. 121 [6] TFEU). The Council and the Commission are required to inform the European Parliament regularly about the agreed objectives of common economic policy and the findings of multilateral surveillance.

The Parliament is also responsible for shaping the multilateral surveillance process in cooperation with the Council. In the European Semester it comments on the Commission's annual growth survey in February and the Council's autumn country-specific reform recommendations, in each case preceded by an exchange with the national parliaments.

In the scope of the economic dialogue, the European Parliament's Committee on Economic and Monetary Affairs (ECON) is entitled to summon the Presidents of the Eurogroup, the European Commission and the European Council. The European Parliament can also enter directly into dialogue with a Member State against which a procedure has been initiated for excessive deficit or macro-economic imbalances. The economic dialogue is, however, merely a non-binding communication platform that grants no veto to the European Parliament and involves neither a reporting duty on the decision-making organs and institutions nor any binding character of agreements reached with them.

With regard to the ESM, the Fiscal Compact and the Euro Plus Pact, the European Parliament has only very weak influence. It would generally be informed when these are applied, but has no influence. Its role in the management of the financial, debt and banking crisis was further restricted in the political aftermath by the shifting of central decisions to the intergovernmental level – the European Council and the Euro Summit. In the interests of rapid response to crisis, some of the newly created mechanisms, such as the ESM, were intentionally established outside the Union's institutional framework. Whereas the amendment to the Treaty of Lisbon required to establish the ESM (Art. 136 [3] TFEU) – using the simplified Treaty amendment procedure – provided only for non-binding consultation with the European Parliament, the ESM itself was founded through an intergovernmental treaty. The European Parliament's calls to be involved in the process of shaping and applying it have gone unheeded.

Thus, all in all the European Parliament holds a rather weak position in European economic governance. But cooperation between the European Parliament and national parliaments is attributed growing importance. Amongst other things, the Fiscal Compact provides for the European Parliament and national parliaments to discuss budgetary questions. But this does not resolve the problem that the European Parliament's lack of integration produces gaps in the legitimation process, both in the creation of new governance instruments and in their application, because these tasks cannot be accomplished by national parliaments, either.

Why improve governance structures?

As the analysis of the status quo shows, Eurozone-specific structures and mechanisms have developed incrementally since the introduction of the Euro, with the intention of enabling closer cooperation at all instances from working level through the Eurogroup to the heads of state and government. While not themselves making legally binding decisions, these institutions offer space to discuss relevant national and European questions. Closer exchange among the Eurozone states, with the participation of the European Central Bank and the European Commission, increases the likelihood of the Member States considering Eurozone matters from the most European perspective and at the same time being able to address problematic developments in individual states. Despite these advances, however, institutional weaknesses have become especially clear in the course of the crises. These can be summarised as follows:

- Complex surveillance with weak efficacy: Complex surveillance and coordination arrangements have emerged for the budget and economic policies of the Member States. Although there is an urgent need for coordination between national policies, no powers have been transferred. In many cases, rule-based coordination has not produced the desired results.
- Increasingly executive-driven decision-making: The need to respond rapidly to crises in the Eurozone has expanded the role of the Euro Summit and thus the executive bias of Eurozone governance. For example, the governments created the ESM as an instrument outside the Treaty framework, in whose governance the finance ministers play a decisive role – but the EU institutions are scarcely represented.
- Formats outside of the community framework: The ESM is an example of the way institutional reforms have been implemented outside of primary law and the Community institutions. The reform process has repeatedly been determined by ad hoc talks at the level of heads of state and government,

which are less transparent and more weakly legitimated than Treaty revisions, which must be ratified in the Member States.
- Weak parliamentary control and participation: Neither the European Parliament nor the national parliaments possess a unified or coordinated control mechanism (with sanctions) vis-à-vis the executive decision-makers of the European Council, its President and the Eurogroup. In many central questions the European Parliament remains an observer.

In the current Eurozone architecture, the European Central Bank is the only European institution with the ability to influence macroeconomic developments from a European perspective. But it is tied to a mandate that prioritises price stability over other economic goals such as growth and employment. This is an important fundamental principle: An independent central bank responsible for safeguarding the stability of the currency and the financial system, while governments are free to act democratically in other policy fields. But it becomes problematic when integration of monetary policy and pressure from the markets leaves the instruments at national level increasingly ineffective and the possibilities for democratic influence on macro-economic developments become very small indeed – while at the same time mechanisms at the Eurozone level are underdeveloped. In the course of the existing political processes, too little consideration has been given to Eurozone aggregates (for example when assessing budget policies), while fiscal instruments at Eurozone level, such as a Eurozone budget with allocative and stabilising functions, are lacking (see Chapters 3 and 8).

The expansion of rule-based coordination of national fiscal and economic policies also raises persistent questions as to the democratic legitimacy of measures and interventions. If excessively detailed and restrictive rules are laid down in secondary law – or largely designed to only be implemented at national level – this undermines the self-correcting function of democracy. This is especially problematic when the rule-based governance framework fails to supply solid macroeconomic results. The consequence of this situation is individual governments repeatedly refusing to follow the course imposed by "Brussels".

This course of action can also lead to legitimacy problems. Member States that actually abide by the rules and accept the financial risks associated with European bailout mechanisms (despite facing grave difficulties) feel cheated when other members decide to ignore the rules and objectives of budgetary and economic coordination.

The Eurozone thus has a dual legitimacy problem. On the one hand, the input legitimacy of the economic governance structures of the Eurozone, as a core area of European policy, is weak. On the other hand, the output legitimacy, which traditionally plays a major role in EU affairs, has suffered after almost a decade of Eurozone crises. The EU and most national governments have a poor track record in the areas of growth, employment and social security. Economic and Monetary Union is increasingly regarded as problem rather than a solution, both by its debtors and its creditors. In the light of generally weak economic prospects, global competition and demographic trends, this is not a transient, crisis-specific issue.

CONCRETE PROPOSALS FOR IMPROVING EUROZONE GOVERNANCE

If the legitimacy issues on the input and output sides of the system – as described above – are to be rectified, it will be necessary to develop new policy instruments at Eurozone level (see Chapters 8 and 10) and to expand the community's institutional structure. In the following, two central starting points are examined: A European finance minister and stronger parliamentary control.

A Eurozone finance minister

The proposal to introduce a Eurozone finance minister is mostly argued on the basis of improving governance capacity and executive functionality in the Eurozone's decision-making framework, which is presently exercised above all through Ecofin and the European Commission. This would make decision-making more effective, improve the enforcement of rules and principles and strengthen the European perspective on Eurozone affairs. The Eurozone finance minister would represent not just the interests of the Member States, but those of the Eurozone as a whole.[2]

The idea was first raised formally by ECB President Jean-Claude Trichet,[3] and subsequently discussed in various quarters with a range of differing emphases.[4] French Economy Minister Emmanuel Macron used the discussion over a possible Grexit to call for a Commissioner for the Euro, to coordinate the economic, financial and social policies of the Euro states and manage a Eurozone budget.[5] ECB Executive Board member Benoît Coeuré argued for a Eurozone finance ministry under the oversight of the European Parliament. Its responsibilities would include preventing economic and budgetary imbalances, managing crises in the Eurozone, controlling the budgetary capacity proposed in the Five Presidents' Report, and representing the Eurozone governments in international economic and financial institutions.[6]

The European Commission also proposes the introduction of a Eurozone treasury, to ensure strengthened, unified external representation of Eurozone interests and stronger collective decision-making in fiscal affairs, without seeking a complete centralisation of budgetary policy.[7] Finally, the idea of a

Eurozone finance minister and treasury is also likely to resurface in the European Parliament's own-initiative report on "improving the functioning of the European Union building on the potential of the Lisbon Treaty".[8]

In the discussion over a possible finance minister or a "Super-Commissioner" with special powers, the German government tends to concentrate on the aspect of monitoring rule-based coordination. The officeholder in Brussels should, Berlin argues, have the possibility to enforce binding measures in the Member States. In the discussion over fiscal instruments at European level, Berlin has to date concentrated above all on the question of how mechanisms could be coordinated to create incentives for reforms (see also Chapter 5).

Tasks

The possible tasks of a Eurozone finance minister relate to the various dimensions of the institutional development needs of the Eurozone as described above. Without establishing new instruments at Eurozone level, a Eurozone finance minister could – in the scope of more strongly rule-based cooperation and coordination – be responsible for conducting and enforcing budgetary and economic surveillance of Member States. Enderlein and Haas describe this function as "division of sovereignty".[9] A Eurozone finance minister could also strengthen the Eurozone dimension in all discussions so that for example an analysis of developments affecting the Eurozone as a whole flows into macro-economic analyses conducted by the Commission and the chair of the Eurogroup. This would prioritise European aggregates (over national considerations), for example concerning deficit trends and their macro-economic repercussions.

A Eurozone finance minister would be especially important if new European policy instruments were introduced, seeking to improve the effectiveness of economic governance in the Eurozone. If a Eurozone budget is instituted, somebody will need to be politically responsible for it. A finance minister could, for example, assume responsibility for a budget that provided investment spending and served to smooth out asymmetrical shocks through automatic stabilisers (see Chapter 8). Additionally, discretionary spending could give national governments – whose policies are otherwise still coordinated via rule-based mechanisms – incentives for reforms. Depending on which funding sources the budget tapped, the European Parliament or the national governments and parliaments would need to be included in the process. This would relativise the current asymmetry between uniform European monetary policy and much less closely integrated economic and budget policies.

A Eurozone finance minister could also chair the European Stability Mechanism – or a European monetary fund if the ESM were to develop in that direction. In both cases the Eurozone finance minister would largely share responsibility for Eurozone crisis management with the ECB. Depending on how the funding of the future crisis mechanism was structured, the European finance minister and the European Parliament would – in a potentially strengthened control function – take over tasks from national finance ministers and parliaments. The ESM is currently, as described above, an intergovernmental organisation, whose radius of action is circumscribed by national vetoes.

Finally, a Eurozone finance minister could assume the task of representing the Eurozone externally in economic and budgetary affairs. At present the ECB, in its responsibility for the currency, represents EMU in international forums and institutions. But there is no unified external representation on other economic policy matters; this has to date been fulfilled partly by a representative of the European Commission, but also by representatives of national governments.

Institutional anchoring

The European finance minister would ideally be a member of the European Commission, as vice-president for economic and financial affairs, and would strengthen its executive role. At the same time, he or she could be made chair of the Eurogroup and the European Stability Mechanism (ESM) for the duration of the Commission's mandate. The European finance minister would work closely with the European Fiscal Board, which was created to support the application of the Stability Pact (also in cooperation with national fiscal councils), and advise on questions of the direction of budget policy in the Eurozone. If a substantial deepening of the Eurozone were to occur, the tasks of the Eurogroup would change over time, and with them the weight of the Eurozone finance minister – for example if Ecofin's formal decision-making powers were transferred to the Eurogroup.

By combining the Commission post and the Eurogroup chair, the Eurozone finance minister would contribute to cohesion within the EU and the Eurozone because he or she would also be responsible for internal market affairs. The dual role of Commission vice-president and Eurogroup chair could be regulated through an inter-institutional agreement. The Member States would appoint the finance minister as chair of the ESM (which is located outside the EU Treaty framework). If the finance minister combined all three functions, he or she would have to be appointed simultaneously by the President of the European Commission and by the Member States of the EU (in the guise of the European Council). The European Parliament should ratify the appointment. Council, Commission and European Parliament should be able to force the finance minister to resign through a vote of no confidence.

Certain tasks of a Eurozone finance minister would require parliamentary control, especially the management of a possible Eurozone budget and an enhanced ESM. The specific arrangements for parliamentary control would depend on how the two instruments are structured on the revenue side. A Eurozone budget with European revenue sources would need to be scrutinised by a sub-group of the European Parliament. If, on the other hand, the ESM continues to be funded by national contributions, control should lie with national parliaments.

Strengthening parliamentary control

The discussion about a Eurozone finance minister, possibly equipped with more Eurozone-wide instruments and resources, thus nurtures the discussion about parliamentary participation because the democratic legitimacy of Eurozone decisions as a whole needs to be increased. But the minor role of the European Parliament in the development of an EU anti-crisis strategy and in the ongoing economic governance of the Eurozone – as described above – remains an issue (quite apart from the finance minister discussion) and is regarded as a reason for the weakness of its democratic legitimacy.

In order to enhance parliamentary control, especially in the event of the appointment of a European finance minister strengthening the executive and granting it new instruments, three different approaches are conceivable.

The most far-reaching form would be the creation of a Eurozone parliament as a new institution exercising parliamentary influence and control in matters of legislation and coordination affecting the Eurozone.[10] If a Eurozone parliament were actually to be created, the line dividing the Eurozone and the EU-28 would be very clear. There would be a danger of undermining the coherence of policies for the internal market and the EU-28. Much more promising and in the meantime more visible in the discussion is a second approach: The idea of founding a Eurozone committee within the European Parliament, for example as a subcommittee of the ECON Committee.[11] Here, only MEPs from Eurozone states would have full voting rights in areas like fiscal policy[12] and full rights of control over the Banking Union and the ESM.[13] MEPs from non-Eurozone states could attend, but would have no vote.

Thirdly there is a proposal to include national parliamentarians in the parliamentary representation of the Eurozone. Enderlein and Haas propose a joint committee of European and national deputies to exercise democratic control over the investment spending of a future European finance minister and European monetary fund.[14] This would account for the fact that these institutions are located at the interface between supranational and intergovernmental politics and have direct repercussions on national budgets. A parliamentary representation of national and European parliamentarians could also participate in economic and budgetary coordination. The prospective benefit of such a step would be not only to locate European objectives within a more democratic process in order to counteract the preponderance of technocratic decisions in the current governance framework. Over time, it could also strengthen insight into European interdependencies, especially among national parliamentarians, and deepen their understanding of developments in other Member States. They would also be integrated earlier and more closely into the coordination process, which could strengthen the application of rule-based coordination.

Outlook

In view of the aforementioned governance problems, the institutional structures of the Eurozone need to be developed and improved. In a first step, the influence of the European Parliament could be further expanded through informal channels, and national parliamentarians integrated in the process. The European Parliament has long been demanding stronger democratic legitimation of the process for coordinating national budget and economic policies. Further steps, such as the introduction of a Eurozone finance minister with a dual role as Eurogroup chair and Commission vice-president, could be implemented through inter-institutional agreements.

In order to equip a finance minister with far-reaching new powers, Treaty amendments may, however, be required (see Chapter 7 by Franz C. Mayer). This would apply for example if the finance minister was given the right to intervene in national political decisions or the power to manage a Eurozone budget. This transfer of powers could occur in the form of an amendment to the existing EU Treaty. A Eurozone Treaty would also be conceivable, affecting only the Eurozone states and requiring only their ratification.[15] In the course of such Treaty amendments, the ESM, which was set up on the basis of an intergovernmental Treaty, could be developed towards a European monetary fund. It could, like the IMF, take on additional tasks such as guaranteeing currency stability, promoting economic cooperation, and stimulating growth and employment in the various Member States.

The obvious window for further-reaching reforms begins after the German Bundestag elections in 2017, by which time France will also have elected a new president and parliament. But concrete proposals should be drafted without delay. The Brexit referendum led to a crisis of confidence in the markets, affecting not only the United Kingdom and the British pound, but also the Eurozone. It cannot be excluded that heightened pressure on the European periphery will persist and could increase – in particular in view of the political uncertainty in certain Member States. If the markets test the resilience of the Euro in this manner, the central Eurozone governments should issue a strong political statement of their commitment to preserving and developing the Eurozone.

In order to find broad support within the Eurozone, an institutional reform proposal would have to both take into account the concerns of those states that prioritise rule-based coordination (with less financial solidarity and risk-sharing) and respect the interests of those members which believe that the Eurozone can only operate successfully with greater risk-sharing. Transferring rights of intervention to the Eurozone level presupposes not only a Treaty amendment, but also ratification referendums in certain Member States. Moreover, the question of compatibility with the national constitution arises in a number of Member States.

The future relationship between Eurozone states and non-members will depend not only on the willingness of the Eurozone to integrate, but also on the extent disintegration will proceed. The decision of the UK to leave the EU may have political repercussions in other EU Member States. Not only the UK, but also the EU risks suffering the consequences of Brexit in political, economic and financial terms. From the Eurozone perspective, this situation increases the necessity and improves the political chances of pursuing the deepening of Economic and Monetary Union. Only as such can it become more resilient and create better preconditions for growth and employment.

The future EU will in all likelihood be increasingly differentiated. For reasons of democratic legitimacy as well as economic efficiency, the Eurozone needs to be developed as a strongly integrated and institutionalised core.

Notes

1 | Schwarzer, Daniela (2015): *Die Europäische Währungsunion: Geschichte, Krise und Reform.* Stuttgart: Kohlhammer Verlag.

2 | De Galhau, François Villeroy, and Weidmann, Jens (2016): Europa braucht mehr Investitionen, *Süddeutsche Zeitung* (online) (3 June 2016), www.sueddeutsche. de/wirtschaft/euro-raum-europa-braucht-ein-gemeinsames-finanzministerium1. 2852586; Schubert, Christian (2015): EZB fordert Finanzministerium für Europa, *Frankfurter Allgemeine Zeitung* (online) (last accessed 13/06/2016), www.faz.net/ aktuell/wirtschaft/wirtschaftspolitik/europaeische-zentralbank-will-ein-europaeisches-finanzministerium-13772228.html; (2015): EZB-Präsident: Draghi unterstützt angeblich Forderung nach Eurofinanzminister, *Spiegel Online* (last accessed 13/06/2016), www.spiegel.de/wirtschaft/soziales/eurozone-ezb-chef-mario-draghi-fordert-angeblich-euro-finanz minister-a-1050274.html

3 | Enderlein, Henrik, and Haas, Jörg (2015): *Was würde ein Europäischer Finanzminister tun? Ein Vorschlag*, Policy Paper 145, Jacques Delors Institute.

4 | EurActiv (2011): EU-Finanzministerium? Berlin ist skeptisch, www.euractiv.de/ section/prioritaten-der-eu-fur-2020/news/eu-finanzministerium-berlin-ist-skeptisch/ (last accessed 15/05/2016).

5 | Klimm, Leo, and Wernicke, Christian (2015): Refondons l'Europe, Interview mit Emmanuel Macron, *Süddeutsche Zeitung* (31 August 2015), http://international.sueddeutsche.de/post/128026249890/refondons-leurope (last accessed 13/06/2016).

6 | Coeuré, Benoît (2015): Lehren aus der Krise für die Zukunft des Euroraums: Rede bei der Semaine des Ambassadeurs, https://www.ecb.europa.eu/press/key/date/2015/html/sp150827.de.html (last accessed 13/06/2016).

7 | European Commission (2015): *Completing Europe's Economic and Monetary* Union (The Five Presidents' Report), https://ec.europa.eu/priorities/sites/beta-political/files/5-presidents-report_en.pdf (last accessed 16/12/2016).

8 | European Parliament (2016): *Draft Report on Improving the Functioning of the European Union Building on the Potential of the Lisbon Treaty*, 2014/2249(INI), http://www.europarl.europa.eu/sides/getDoc.do?pubRef=%2F%2FEP%2F%2FNONSGML%2BCOMPARL%2BPE-573.146%2B01%2BDOC%2BPDF%2BV0%2F%2FEN (last accessed 16/12/2016).

9 | Enderlein, Henrik, and Haas, Jörg (2015).

10 | Hollande, see Meier, Albrecht (2015): Unions-Fraktionsvize Friedrich erteilt Hollandes Vorschlag Abfuhr, *Tagesspiegel* (online), www.tagesspiegel.de/politik/regierung-fuer-die-euro-zone-unions-fraktionsvize-friedrich-erteilt-hollandesvorschlag-abfuhr/12080312.html (last accessed 14/06/2016); Schäuble, see Eur Activ (2014): Schäuble Advocates Separate Eurozone Parliament; www.euractiv.com/section/future-eu/news/schauble-advocates-separate-eurozone-parliament/ (last accessed 13/06/2016); Fossum, John Erik (2016): *Democracy and Legitimacy in the EU: Challenges and Options*, ARENA Working Paper 1/2016, https://www.sv.uio.no/arena/english/research/publications/arena-working-papers/2016/wp-1-16.pdf (last accessed 13/06/2016).

11 | European Commission (2012): *A Blueprint for a Deep and Genuine Economic and Monetary Union: Launching a European Debate*, http://ec.europa.eu/archives/commission_2010-2014/president/news/archives/2012/11/pdf/blueprint_en.pdf (accessed 15 June 2016); Simon, Frédéric (2014): UK Conservatives Balk at Plans for Eurozone Parliament, EurActiv, www.euractiv.com/section/uk-europe/news/uk-conservatives-balk-at-plans-for-eurozone-parliament/ (last accessed 15/06/2016).

12 | European Commission (2012); Duff, Andrew (2016): *The Protocol of Frankfurt: A New Treaty for the Eurozone*, www.epc.eu/documents/uploads/pub_6229_ protocol_of_frankfurt.pdf (last accessed 15/06/2016).

13 | Simon, Frédéric (2014).

14 | Enderlein, Henrik, and Haas, Jörg (2015).

15 | Bogdandy, Armin von, Calliess, Christian et al. (2013): *Aufbruch in die Euro-Union*, http://glienickergruppe.eu/de/aufbruch-in-die-euro-union/ (last accessed 18/07/2016).

10. Developing the social dimension

Peter Becker

The Euro crisis has demonstrated that the Economic and Monetary Union (EMU) needs to develop if it is to survive. In summer 2015 the five presidents of the EU institutions presented a report on strengthening the EMU. It proposed a three-stage model of incremental deepening to create an economic, financial and fiscal union, and by 2025 finally a political union. The beginning of this deepening process will involve further efforts to bring Eurozone economies closer together: Convergence within EMU is a precondition for lasting economic stability. The more convergent economies are, the smaller the inherent tensions and costs incurred in rectifying imbalances. The flip side of convergence is instability and imbalance. Nonetheless, it would be inadequate and short-sighted to regard these efforts for greater convergence as the solution for a permanently stable Monetary Union. Especially given that adequate and sustainable convergence is unlikely to be achieved in view of historical differences between national economic and welfare models.

After the French and the German general elections, i.e. at the end of 2017, at the latest, European heads of state and government therefore intend to return to the task of completing the EMU. Various EU reform and revision processes already coincide in 2017 and 2018.

Upcoming negotiations on the EU's next multiannual financial framework (MFF) in connection with the consequences of Brexit for the European budget will initiate a debate about adapting and restructuring spending priorities. This will implicitly also be associated with a debate about reweighting EU spending priorities; social and employment challenges could come to the fore. That discussion could in turn become intertwined with the question of changing the funding system for the EU budget and the issue of introducing an EU tax. The high-level group on own resources under the direction of Mario Monti already published its final report[1] at the end of 2016, which also adressed the tax question, including recommendations to establish new European own resources. Changing spending priorities and funding policies of the EU budget would require a consensus of all Member States and EU institutions. This also applies to the introduction of an EU tax, which would require an amendment to the Lisbon Treaty.

Article 16 of the Fiscal Compact provides for the Treaty to be reviewed by 2017, with consideration of the question of transferring its content into European primary law. Although today one hears little about this agreement and its obligations on states to introduce national debt brakes and continuously reduce public borrowing, and the Compact plays little role in Brussels debates and documents, the question will still arise whether the EU (and especially the German government) want to abandon the Compact.

And after Brexit the pressure on the EU to reform and adapt will increase in any case. A Treaty amendment is already inevitable in order to lastingly stabilise the EMU and deepen it into a social union. The various reform processes could then be pooled together into a comprehensive European reform package. Such a package will be necessary to serve and balance all interests involved, and make possible the required consensus for a reform of the European Treaties. 2017 will thus set the course for the future development of the EMU and European integration.

The EU and Member States will have to decide whether they wish to attempt a comprehensive reform of the EMU and the underlying Treaties, or whether they shy away from the associated risk of failure in national ratification referendums.

THE LONG AND OLD SEARCH FOR CONVERGENCE

Ever since the first discussions about founding a monetary union, German policy on Europe has sought to achieve the convergence required for lasting stability through rule-based discipline. The Maastricht convergence criteria, formulated during the creation of EMU, and the long-term agreement to observe the criteria associated with the Stability and Growth Pact are the results of this approach. The new instruments that Germany achieved in the course of European crisis responses – the Euro Plus Pact and the Fiscal Compact – also correspond to this ordoliberal regulatory concept of convergence.

It is, however, still unclear what form of convergence the EMU requires, and how far it needs to go. A distinction is usually made between nominal and real convergence, with real convergence meaning more backward economies catching up with the productivity of the more advanced ones, whereas nominal convergence describes movement towards specified targets (such as interest rates, inflation and income).

Formally, the EU has written both forms of convergence – nominal and real – into its Treaty objectives. Ever since the founding of the Economic Community, the European Treaties have proclaimed the goal of real convergence.

In the Preamble to the Treaty on the Functioning of the European Union (TFEU), the Member States agree "to strengthen the unity of their economies and to ensure their harmonious development by reducing the differences existing between the various regions". And in Article 121 TFEU the EU also sets the goal of ensuring "sustained convergence of the economic performances of the Member States" through coordination of their economic policies – thus seeking real convergence. In Article 3 of the EU Treaty they also agree to promote economic, social and territorial cohesion and solidarity between the Member States. The legal basis under the Lisbon Treaty for European spending through the Structural, Investment and Cohesion Funds, Article 175 TFEU, also obliges the EU and its Member States to take account of the shared goal of convergence in their national economic policies and in internal market legislation. The EU structural funds are supposed to support the convergence efforts of the Member States and their regions. The decision to create a monetary union led to the inclusion of new indicators of nominal convergence in European primary law in the form of the convergence criteria of the Maastricht Treaty. Under Article 140 TFEU and the Protocol on the convergence criteria, this high level of long-term nominal convergence is the basis for membership of the Eurozone.

Convergence is fundamentally a dynamic concept; convergence within the EMU can certainly vary over time.[2] Economically speaking, convergence of standards of living in the individual Member States is not an absolute precondition for a functioning monetary union. Nor are different levels of social security and welfare state models an obstacle to membership in it.[3] But the EMU requires political stability, which can hardly be achieved without a prospect of convergence in prosperity, standard of living and social protection. To this extent nominal convergence criteria – in the sense of meeting previously defined targets – appear insufficient on their own. Instead, catch-up processes need to be possible both within states and within the EU.

It is no coincidence that the most important steps towards expanding and deepening economic integration through the Single Market and the introduction of the single currency have always been associated with parallel steps to strengthen real convergence within the EU. The rapid rise of the European structural funds since 1988 was one outcome of this process. The economically stronger Member States in the centre of Europe promised the weaker states on the periphery financial aid via the European budget. The unspoken quid pro quo for this transfer was subordination of the periphery under the pressures and imperatives of a hard single currency and the forces of the internal market.[4] The political significance of real convergence for the stability of the internal market and the EMU is thus recognised by all Member States. There is also consensus that real convergence in the EU means social convergence as well as economic.

The sharp economic and social consequences of the crisis have increased pressure to pay clearer attention to the social dimension in the EU and in particular the Eurozone. The latest crisis in particular demonstrated (above all in the Greek example) that lasting stability in the EMU requires not only healthy economic data but also a sound social basis.

In this regard, real convergence always includes welfare state aspects and thus convergence in social and employment matters. Extreme economic and social divergence could otherwise lead to successively growing political differences: Social divergence always also creates political differences. Real convergence in prosperity, on the other hand, implicitly also leads to a convergence of interests and thus facilitates wider integration decisions. Visible and tangible convergence will, moreover, strengthen public support for further integration steps and thus promote identification with the European economic and social model.

The EU's criteria should therefore also include a real convergence of incomes and living conditions in the form of rising incomes and/or falling income differences. Permanent large differences in per-capita income, for example between Slovakia, France and Greece, could otherwise endanger the internal cohesion of the EMU; excessive social and employment divergences would pose a risk to the lasting political stability of the EMU.

In the meantime, additional, far-reaching governance and monitoring instruments have been introduced, in particular an early warning mechanism for avoiding macroeconomic imbalances with new nominal convergence indicators. Under this new procedure, which was introduced in 2011, the Commission measures and evaluates deviations from particular indicators and target corridors. In its communication of 2 October 2013 on Strengthening the Social Dimension of the Economic and Monetary Union, the Commission proposed five employment and social indicators to improve monitoring of the social situation in the scope of the European Semester: 1. unemployment level and changes; 2. NEET rate (young people not in education, employment or training) and youth unemployment rate; 3. real gross disposable income of households; 4. at-risk-of-poverty rate of working age population; and 5. inequalities (S80/S20 ratio). Today these indicators are part of the Excessive Imbalance Procedure and thus elements of the convergence efforts. Moreover, Commission President Jean-Claude Juncker has pointed out the need for future EU assistance and reform programmes to take account of the socio-political impacts in the targeted states.

However, the decisive aspect for assessing economic and social convergence is neither the indicators nor the multitude of scoreboards for measuring progress that have been introduced, but, decisively, analysis and ensuing recommendations for the Member States' economic, budget and social policies. The crucial issue is therefore not the question of the correct convergence indicators, but the targets of the convergence efforts and their evaluation, weighting and ensuing political conclusions.

The jointly agreed social and employment convergence goals of the EU and the Member States are reflected in the European Growth and Jobs Strategy, the so-called Europe 2020 Strategy from spring 2010,[5] under which the EU agreed upon ambitious and far-reaching economic, social, employment, and environmental targets. Alongside economic convergence goals, quantifiable social and employment targets were also defined: The employment rate for 20- to 64-year-olds is to reach 75 per cent by 2020 and social integration promoted by reducing poverty. The number of people threatened by poverty in the EU is to be reduced by 20 million. Besides continuously monitoring the implementation of Europe 2020 targets, the new European Semester creates an additional sophisticated instrument with which the European Commission and the Member States intend to jointly and more closely coordinate their economic and employment policies. The evaluation and monitoring of convergence processes are conducted by the Commission and the Council of Ministers. The European Semester now stands at the centre of the process as the central link between the European and Member States' instruments. Through it, the Commission, in cooperation with the Member States, seeks to turn the conclusions of its observations and analyses of the economic, social and employment policy processes in the EU, the Eurozone and the Member States into political recommendations. The implementation of conclusions and recommendations, in turn, is the task of the Member States – in the so-called National Semester. In order to make this complicated procedure more efficient and focused, the Commission has in the meantime introduced a number of technical modifications to the European Semester. These "small tweaks" involve streamlining the process, improving comparability of national measures, and increasing efficiency. In order to strengthen the transparency and democratic legitimacy of the process, national parliaments have also been integrated more closely. Nevertheless, the European Semester cannot overcome the fundamental weakness of the coordination procedure: While political responsibility for the most important economic, social and employment policy decisions still lies with the Member States, the internal market and the EMU demand ever greater convergence in economic, financial, social and employment policy within the EU and the Eurozone.

ELEMENTS OF A EUROPEAN EMPLOYMENT AND SOCIAL UNION

It is certainly true that the European integration process has always been driven by economic interests and forces since the founding of the European Coal and Steel Community; The great integration projects – the Single Market and the EMU – also have these economic drivers. But the desire to accompany and balance the deepening and expansion of economic integration through social policy is just as old. The European model, it is asserted, must unite economic growth with social cohesion and convergence.

The core problem for the construction of a common European social policy is the lack of congruence between Member States' welfare state models. Just as the *varieties of capitalism*[6] within the EU constrain the options for a European economic policy, so do the various European welfare state models obstruct harmonisation of social policy.[7] Thus, social protection systems still vary considerably between the 28 EU Member States. In particular, the EU's Eastern enlargement of 2004/2007 – with the accession of the less developed economies of Central and Eastern Europe – and the deep cuts in the social welfare systems of the Mediterranean Member States in the course of the economic and debt crisis have greatly expanded the divergence between social and welfare state models in the EU. Differences in levels of pay have grown since the mid-1990s and the arrangements for other wage components (for example holiday pay or bad weather allowance) differ significantly. For example. unemployment benefits in almost all Member States are funded through wage-related contributions, but in Luxembourg exclusively from taxes.

The levels of income-replacement benefits, the duration of entitlement and the minimum period of insurance required for a claim also vary considerably. The duration ranges from open-ended income-replacement benefits in Belgium to a maximum limit of 156 days in Malta and Cyprus. The level of payments ranges from a flat rate of € 7.72 per day in Malta (unrelated to last wage) to 80 per cent of the last gross salary in Luxembourg. The required minimum insurance period ranges from at least two years out of the past three in Slovakia to four months (122 days) insurance membership within the past 2.5 years in France. Similarly, large differences exist with respect to pension systems, in healthcare and nursing services, and the minimum social safety net.[8]

Standardisation of the 28 different systems through Europeanisation therefore remains a tough proposition. True harmonisation through comprehensive European social policy legislation is currently possible only in the fields of occupational safety and working conditions, and in equal opportunities and anti-discrimination. Where the classic fields of social security are concerned – redistributive social policy – the EU's policy space tends to be small. The political consequence to be drawn from this is that expectations placed on the EU's social policy activities should remain realistic. For the foreseeable future, European social policy cannot take on the same tasks as national policies do (or at least should do). Nor will the EU possess the financial resources to construct its own social security systems. And in the near future it is equally unlikely that the economic and social systems of the 28 Member States will converge so closely as to enable comprehensive European harmonisation and regulation.

So a European social policy will be unable to substitute national welfare states for quite some time. But it can and should seek to bring existing national social protection systems closer together. To this end, the EU should define a shared minimum standard of social protection and appropriate levels of basic social benefits. In this way, it can supplement national policies. The goal should be to define a European framework of legally binding minimum conditions. In this connection, for example, a solution needs to be found for the structural problem that Greece's pensions system de facto fills the gap left by the lack of a minimum social safety net.

On 8 March 2016 the Commission presented its first thoughts concerning a minimum social threshold within the EU: A European social pillar. In this document the Commission regards social policy as a core element of the European growth model, and as a central aspect of the EU's economic agenda. The Commission initially restricts its initiative to the Eurogroup, but wishes to keep it open to all other Member States. The social pillar for the Eurozone defines shared principles for three policy fields:

1. Equal opportunities and access to the labour market;
2. Fair working conditions to achieve an adequate and reliable balance of rights and obligations between workers and employers and
3. Adequate and sustainable social protection.

These three areas are in turn divided into 20 sub-areas. Through its initiative the Commission seeks to adapt the EU's social agenda and social legislation to current economic and social trends and to strengthen the European social model as a whole. In view of the challenges of an ageing society, increasing digitalisation of the world of work and increasingly frequent career interruptions, key European principles and common social rights need to be collated to form a shared social policy foundation and guide the social convergence process. In an annex to its Communication, the Commission presents a first draft for such a European pillar for discussion and evaluation in a public consultation. The Commission just published its final proposal for a "European pillar of social rights" on April 26, 2017.

The legal status of this social pillar will be crucial. Non-binding guidance with recommendations for what the shared basic social rights and minimum protection should look like will not be enough. A European social pillar must instead set a Europe-wide minimum level of social protection and thus define the canon of fundamental social services and benefits. Unified structures ensuing from a shared understanding of social security in the EU should consequently include protection against life risks (sickness, invalidity) and ensure an appropriate basic minimum standard of living (unemployment, pensions) as well as convergence of social services (childcare, nursing). Furthermore, such an agreement must include the definition and development of shared indicators for these social services and benefits. The outcome will be a convergence of social policy structures and models of European welfare states without prescribing a full integration or comprehensive harmonisation of national social systems.

This minimum standard of social protection (baseline) should be legally binding in the sense that such a pillar of social rights must apply throughout the Eurozone (ideally the entire internal market) and be backed with national resources – not at identical levels, but with comparable structures and a shared social paradigm. A situation where social differentiation occurs and members of the Eurozone and the EU-27 drift apart – potentially leading to distortions within the common internal market – should be avoided. Only with a structural baseline for social protection across the entire EU can the social objectives formulated in the Lisbon Treaty and the EU's own normative aspirations as expressed in the European Charter of Fundamental Rights actually be fulfilled.

In the shorter term, to make a more concrete start with a European social union, the existing initiatives to fight youth unemployment in the EU (such as Youth on the Move, the European Youth Guarantee and the Youth Employment Initiative) could be brought together in a stand-alone instrument, which should be managed directly by the Commission and provided with more funds from the EU budget. This would mean taking the planning and implementation out of the programmes of the European Social Fund, whose implementation has to date been the sole responsibility of the funded regions. The goal should be to pool these initiatives and the European programmes and projects for reducing youth unemployment while increasing their visibility.

At the same time a further strengthening of the Social Dialogue under Article 155 TFEU should be considered. Through this forum the EU seeks to integrate the social partners – trade unions and employers' organisations – in the process of shaping European social policy. They have been granted extensive consultation rights and may participate actively in the European legislative process. The EU even offers these organisations the possibility to conclude so-called contractual relations or agreements which go beyond mere joint statements. In the form of framework agreements, these serve as the basis for issuing European directives such the 1996 Parental Leave Directive and the 1997 framework agreement on part-time work. If the social partners conclude a joint agreement, the Council can no longer negotiate over the substance of the dossier. The Member States then are left only with the choice of approving or rejecting the agreement. During the 1990s the Social Dialogue was still an instrument through which the social partners were integrated directly into the European legislative process, but it has largely lost this function since the 2000s. Since that point, participation in and preparation of European legislation over and above the purely consultative – in the form of coordination and search for compromise between the social partners – has no longer been possible. The reason for this has not been any lack of willingness to compromise on the part of the partners, but the rejection of their joint proposals by individual Member States. In order to reopen this de facto legislative option for the social partners, a thorough revitalisation of the dialogue should be sought, even if this appears difficult. In any case, the inclusion of the social partners should extend beyond the annual social summits and their advisory role for the Commission – in particular because the EU already possesses a specific advisory body in which the social partners are appropriately represented in the form of the Economic and Social Committee (ESC).

EMPLOYMENT POLICY AND AUTOMATIC STABILISERS IN THE EUROZONE

Imbalances within currency areas are normally balanced out through adaptations in labour markets. For this reason in April 2012 – in the midst of the crisis and against a background of unbearably high unemployment – the European Commission published a broad employment package through which it proposed to create a "real" EU labour market. The goal of the package was to improve the mobility of labour within the EU and remove remaining obstacles to free movement of workers. However, the Commission's instruments of labour market and employment policy are limited, leading it to concentrate primarily on improving coordination and intensifying monitoring of national policies and initiatives. Moreover, measures to improve labour mobility in the European internal market are frequently criticised as promoting undesirable forms of emigration and brain drain.

Against the background of these limited joint employment policy options in the Eurozone, the possibilities for achieving the necessary automatic stabilisation of the Eurozone through a converging European labour market are still small. Continuing differences in the performance of the national economies in the Eurozone intensify the pressure to create new structures and redistribution mechanisms in order to reduce the gap between prosperous strong economies and poorer, less competitive ones. So the EMU should be equipped with a mechanism with which it can transfer funds to those regions and states whose GDP growth lags cyclically behind the rest of it. In regions where the economy threatens to overheat, on the other hand, funds should be encouraged to flow out. A preventive stabilisation instrument should in this regard be capable of balancing out inherent imbalances and asynchronicities in the EMU.

The need for transfers and automatic stabilisers was already raised in the founding phase of the EMU. In the meantime there is now fundamental agreement that EMU requires an automatic stabilising mechanism in order to balance out the imbalances between economies. Like earlier ideas about transfer mechanisms in the Economic and Monetary Union, however, the proposals in circulation today are highly controversial. Firstly, there are doubts as to whether an additional financial instrument within the Eurozone can have a stabilising effect – be it a separate Eurozone budget or a European unemployment insurance system. Secondly, it is criticised that the volume of redistribution required to balance cyclical fluctuations in the Eurozone is simply too large.[9]

In the course of the EU's crisis response, various forms and functions for an additional automatic solidarity and stabilisation instrument for the Eurozone have been discussed as a step towards fiscal union:

1. Fiscal capacity in connection with contractual partnerships: As part of a preventive reform policy, project-specific European financial assistance should be used to create incentives to implement the agreed structural reforms in the Member States of the EMU.
2. EU crisis mechanism *(rainy day funds)*: In the event of crisis and asymmetrical regional shocks, this fund would be employed as a financial instrument for stabilising the Eurozone; in other words, this would entail a conditional redistribution of resources exclusively in the event of crisis.
3. The creation of an additional Eurozone budget in the form of a permanent intergovernmental transfer instrument to cushion economic downturns on the demand side with payments in and transfers out of this budget in accordance with national economic cycles. Such a Eurozone budget should allow cyclical differences to be balanced out and stimulate investment during recession phases redistributing funds similarly to a regional financial equalisation system.
4. A European unemployment insurance system has been proposed as an alternative transfer mechanism, in order to permit social transfers from stronger to poorer Member States of the Eurozone.[10]

The greater the successes of European convergence efforts, the smaller the stability and transfer instruments would have to be. Experience with the convergence criteria of the Maastricht Treaty shows that convergence was greatest in advance of the introduction of the single currency.[11] The prospect of joining EMU and profiting from the advantages of the common currency area facilitated candidates' reform efforts and as such generated successful convergence. In other words, the positive incentives created by the prospect of joining a stability and growth community led to progress on convergence. But as the prospect of further gains and benefits receded, interest in reforms also declined and convergence weakened. Two lessons can be drawn from these experiences:

1. The prospect of membership in a deepened economic, monetary and social union with automatic stabilisers creates strong economic, social and employment incentives for accession candidates, and is capable of strengthening their convergence efforts. This interest in convergence and the great openness towards reforms in advance of accession should be leveraged through clearly defined convergence and/or accession conditions.
2. Openness and enthusiasm for reforms tends to recede after successful qualification. A legally binding procedure for consolidating convergence processes between Member States which makes these more sustainable must therefore be created and adopted before establishment of automatic stabilisation. At the same time a limit on stabilisation and solidarity transfers should be set in advance. Here it would be conceivable to introduce a joint debt management mechanism for restructuring state debt in the individual Member States.

Analyses demonstrate that the stabilisation effects of transfers between EMU Member States are considerably smaller than those of transfers between societies (for example payments directly to citizens) in crisis-affected states.[12] In this connection, there are good arguments for the introduction of a joint unemployment insurance system along the lines of the American model. In the event of an asymmetrical economic shock causing rising unemployment in one member of the Eurozone, its national social system would receive financial support through additional European contributions. Member States with low unemployment would pay more into the joint system.[13] However, in view of the existing differences between national systems, proposals for a European unemployment insurance (for example a EU contribution of limited duration restricted to cyclical unemployment in the event of crisis) would appear very difficult to implement. This solution would probably require a far-reaching harmonisation of national unemployment insurance systems and create a strong *moral hazard* risk (for example in defining structural unemployment).

The stabilisation and transfer mechanism should therefore encompass the following preconditions and prerequisites and tie them together in an overall package:

- Transfers should only be made on the basis of predefined, relatively objective criteria, and should be limited in duration. Financial flows should be based on a new system that permits payments between societies and directly to citizens.
- The mechanism should be managed by the European Commission and funded jointly by all the EMU members; ideally in the form of a new EU tax.
- The transfer mechanism should possess a credible cap. The *no-bailout* vow enshrined in the Maastricht Treaty has lost its credibility. Instead, a

possibility for an orderly debt-restructuring mechanism needs to be created within the EMU, with clearly defined rescheduling arrangements within the framework of the European Stability Mechanism (ESM).

A European short-time working compensation scheme would constitute one conceivable step towards a European unemployment insurance system. Currently, certain EU Member States have various forms of benefit covering partial unemployment, for example for short-time working or seasonal unemployment. Arrangements comparable to the German short-time compensation arrangement, which is paid whenever an economically unavoidable loss of work affects at least one-third of a company's employees, are only to be found in Italy (as wage top-up during a crisis that requires workplace restructuring or transition); in Luxembourg (in the event of cyclical unemployment); in Austria (short-time working support for employers); in France (to avoid redundancies or pay cuts for economic, cyclical or technical reasons); and in Spain and Portugal (in the event of reduced working hours for cyclical, economic or technological reasons, and after natural disasters). In this context, identical or similar approaches with which positive experience has been gained are only to be witnessed in certain Member States. A supplementary new European system could be created for the majority of EMU Member States; modifications to existing systems would be limited. This could also avoid the inevitable doubts, criticisms and resistance that regularly emerge when it is necessary to adapt established national systems.

The criteria for pay-outs would be defined objectively and in advance along with the level and administration of payments. The level of short-time compensation would be calculated in proportion to lost working hours. Disbursement would be subject to review and approval by the European Commission and could be granted for a maximum of six months (assuming the level of employment is kept). National social partners would need to be included in the Commission's decisions on granting European short-time compensation. This could be funded through revenues from an EU-wide corporate tax or levy, which would have to be agreed on the basis of a harmonised taxable base.

The arrangement could also be coordinated with the existing EU Globalisation Fund, which subsidises training for workers who lose their jobs following the closure or relocation of major facilities. Support from the Globalisation Fund is currently approved if there are at least five hundred redundancies (or loss of work for self-employed staff) at a company within a period of four months.[14] The Fund could be used to support qualification and training in the affected companies and branches in connection with the proposed European short-time compensation scheme.

Alongside enhancing the visibility and immediate relevance of the European social union, this Europeanisation and harmonisation of a direct social transfer would also have a potentially stabilising effect on the EMU. Another advantage would be the possibility to tie the disbursement of EU funds to predefined objective criteria that are not subject to political influence or by the Member States or quid pro quo deals, and to limit their duration. Such a European transfer benefit should be associated with a strengthening of the social dialogue at the European and national level.

Notes

1 | High Level Group on Own Resources, Future Financing of the EU (2016): *Final report and recommendations of the High Level Group on Own Resources*. Brussels.
2 | auf dem Brinke, Anna, and Enderlein, Henrik et al. (2015): *What Kind of Convergence Does the Euro Area Need?* Gütersloh and Berlin: Bertelsmann-Stiftung and Jacques Delors-Institut.
3 | Dauderstädt in this volume and Dauderstädt, Michael (2014): *Konvergenz in der Krise: Europas gefährdete Integration*. Berlin: Friedrich-Ebert-Stiftung.
4 | Streeck, Wolfgang, and Elsässer, Lea (2016): Monetary Disunion: 'The Domestic Politics of Euroland', *Journal of European Public Policy*, vol. 23, no. 1, pp. 1–24.
5 | Becker, Peter (2011): Integration ohne Plan – Die neue EU-Wachstumsstrategie 'Europa 2020', *Zeitschrift für Politikwissenschaft*, no. 1, pp. 67–91.
6 | Hall, Peter A., and Soskice, David (2001): *Varieties of Capitalism: The Institutional Foundations of Comparative Advantage*. Oxford: Oxford University Press.
7 | Cf. Esping-Andersen, Gøsta (1990): *The Three Worlds of Welfare Capitalism*. Cambridge; Hacker, Björn (2014): *Konfliktfeld Soziales Europa: Vier Herausforderungen und Chancen zur Gestaltung des europäischen Sozialmodells*. Berlin: Friedrich-Ebert-Stiftung; Platzer, Hans-Wolfgang (2015): Sozialpolitische Integration als Grundbaustein der EU, in: von Alemann, Ulrich et al. (eds.): *Ein soziales Europa ist möglich: Grundlagen und Handlungsoptionen*. Wiesbaden: Springer VS, pp. 25–41.
8 | Detailed insights into the differences between national structures are offered by two databases: Sozialkompass Europa, run by the German Federal Ministry of Labour and Social Affairs (www.sozialkompass. eu) and the European Commission's Mutual Information System on Social Protection (MISSOC) (www.MISSOC.org).
9 | Hishow, Ognian (2014): *Divergenz statt Konvergenz in der Wirtschafts- und Währungsunion? Ein währungstheoretisch begründetes Plädoyer für eine andere Währungsunion*. Berlin: SWP-Studien 2014/S07.
10 | Dullien, Sebastian (2008): *Eine Arbeitslosenversicherung für die Eurozone: Ein Vorschlag zur Stabilisierung divergierender Wirtschaftsentwicklungen in der Europäischen Währungsunion*. Berlin: SWP-Studien 2008/S01.
11 | auf dem Brinke, Anna, and Enderlein, Henrik et al. (2015).
12 | Bargain, Olivier, Dolls, Mathias et al. (2012): *Fiscal Union in Europe? Redistributive and Stabilising Effects of a European Tax-benefit System and Fiscal Equalisation Mechanism*, working paper 12/22, Oxford: Oxford University Centre for Business Taxation.

13 | Cf. Claes, Grégory, Darvas, Zsolt et al. (2014): *Benefits and Drawbacks of European Unemployment Insurance.* Brussels: Bruegel Policy Brief 2014/06; Vetter, Stefan (2014): *Stabilisierung, Solidarität oder Umverteilung? Braucht die Eurozone eine gemeinsame Arbeitslosenversicherung – und wenn ja, wofür?* Frankfurt am Main: Deutsche Bank Research.

14 | In small Member States with small labour markets, group applications from small and medium-sized enterprises would also be a possibility.

11. Plan B – retreat from integration?
Possibilities, risks and costs

Armin Steinbach

INTRODUCTION

Even pro-Europeans should not lose sight of realities. A clear-headed stock-taking reveals disintegration tendencies at various points within the web of European integration. Their origins lie in the EU's multiple troublespots. The economic and financial crisis dominated until 2015, with recurring financial difficulties in individual states leading to the application of a series of conventional and unconventional crisis instruments. With hindsight, the economic and financial crisis can be regarded as one of the more successful cases of crisis management. The bailout packages ultimately fulfilled their purpose of bridge financing. In the meantime, a number of countries, like Ireland and Cyprus, have been able to exit their bailout programmes.[14] But the "permanent crisis" in Greece rumbles on. And it is the persistence of Greek financial problems that is to blame for doubts arising over the very survival of the Euro as a currency. For some time now, "Grexit" has come to be regarded as a plausible scenario across almost all political camps. The Grexit discussion is a surrogate for the idea of enabling countries with financial problems to leave the single currency (at least temporarily). And if one does treat Economic and Monetary Union in this way, as a club one may join and leave again, questions arise as to the economic costs of a temporary exit, the legal feasibility of such a step, and its political repercussions.

The existence of the EU has also come under pressure from another quarter. Driven by the crises that have shaken Europe in recent years and fundamental scepticism over the benefits of EU membership, the "Brexit" referendum raises the very real prospect of British membership ending. In fact, Brexit is only the most concrete example of wider national disenchantment with Europe. Euro-sceptical tones have long become political normality in other countries as well, with the Dutch referendum on the Ukrainian trade deal supplying a prime example. At play here is not only the single currency, but also the irreversibility of EU membership itself. Analytically this raises the question of what economic and political consequences would be associated with leaving the Union – for which the example of Brexit supplies ample pointers.

While the causes of the economic and financial crisis can be traced at least in part to endogenous defects within the EMU, the refugee crisis was an exogenous shock for the EU. Military conflicts in the Middle East have set in motion an unparalleled movement of refugees, which has shown the EU the limits of its capacities. It soon transpired that the European Dublin rules on asylum applications were inadequate to the situation; the result was national unilateralism rather than concerted action at the European level. At the height of the migration and refugee crisis the Schengen Agreement was suspended to allow a temporary reintroduction of border controls within the EU.

Against the backdrop of these multiple crises and associated disintegration tendencies, the following contribution offers an overview of the cost/benefit potentials of particular institutional retrenchment trends; so to speak "Plan B" to "Plan A" outlined in other Chapters in this volume. Relinquishing the idea of an integration process that can move in only one direction allows us to examine the economic and political risks of dismantling the Economic and Monetary Union in the examples of the still-relevant Grexit question, British withdrawal from the EU (Brexit) and the possibility of dissolution of the Schengen Agreement with the reintroduction of border controls.

LEAVING THE EURO – THE GREXIT QUESTION

Grexit has been under discussion for quite some time, with controversy over its political and economic consequences. More recently the urgency of this scenario has rather faded because despite protracted negotiations Greece and its creditors have (at least to date) always succeeded in reaching agreement. Nonetheless, in view of the dubious sustainability of Greece's debt (about which opinions still differ) and the question marks over the permanent role of the International Monetary Fund (IMF), Greek withdrawal from the Eurozone remains a scenario that must be taken seriously.

Opinions about the costs of Grexit inevitably differ in the absence of comparable cases. Given the great uncertainty pertaining to the quantitative effect of Grexit, above all the qualitatively relevant consequences need to be examined. In economic terms, an exit of whatever kind (temporary or permanent) would initially have the advantage of much more rapid price adjustment outside EMU. The price adjustment required to restore competitiveness could occur more quickly through devaluation of the new currency than would be possible within the framework of Economic and Monetary Union – above all through internal devaluation (for example wage cuts) and painful structural reforms.

Calculations show that devaluation would cause an immediate increase in GDP of 17 per cent, with equally positive effects on unemployment and state finances.[2] But this supposed advantage would have massive downsides, too. Foreign debt would spike, casting further doubts over its sustainability. Euro-denominated bonds could no longer be serviced; both private and public creditors would take haircuts. The affected country would lose its access to financial markets; economic collapse would be inevitable, with corresponding consequences for unemployment and social imbalances. In order to alleviate these impacts, the EU would have to supply massive (humanitarian) aid.

As historical experience with debt restructuring shows, restricted access to international capital markets can lead to economic collapse. In some quarters, the repercussions are discussed as manageable, in the context of the introduction of a parallel currency, especially if the new currency is devalued only gradually. For this to be conceivable, there would have to be strict control on capital movement capable of containing the massive capital flight that would ensue. Additionally, the ECB would probably have to make support purchases of the new parallel currency. These steps are associated with great risks and dubious in their efficacy. It is also likely that the Euro would supplant the weak new currency and become the actual means of payment.[3]

It is hard to assess the extent to which Germany and other creditors would be financially liable, and which concrete guarantees would be invoked.[4] Fundamentally, as a major exporter Germany benefits more from the Euro than any other country in the EU. And any reduction in the extent of the currency area reduces the advantages of a single currency in the European market. The following can be said about the costs of successively granted financial assistance: The rescue packages of May 2010 and February 2012 would probably become worthless and the loans granted through the European Stability Mechanism (ESM) would be at risk. And, finally, the TARGET balances that have accrued in the ECB system must be taken into account. The more concrete the threat of Greece leaving, the more quickly the growth of its balances would accelerate. And if it did actually leave, those losses would then be realised – at the German Bundesbank, too. German industry would also be negatively affected, with companies and banks left holding unrecoverable claims against creditors from the crisis country. The impact on national economic climate are not foreseeable, but would be at least significant. A serious quantification of the overall costs appears to all intents and purposes impossible.

Least predictable of all are the potential contagion effects. This hinges on the question of the extent to which the capital markets speculate on the departure of further members of the currency. In the absence of established procedures for a state to leave, the actual process is likely to adopt highly irrational and unpredictable aspects – inflamed by political debates over who should bear the consequential costs and debt write-offs – and could endanger the EU's ability to operate across the board. The process would be accompanied by a political blame game, where Germany as the main creditor would probably come under strong pressure.

Estimates of the economic costs of a Grexit diverge enormously. So any quantitative forecasts need to be treated with caution. The largest influencing factor is likely to be contagion. To that extent, the various Grexit scenarios illustrate the bandwidth of possible economic harm. One can distinguish between the impacts of a simple Grexit and the "GPSI exit scenario", in which Greece, Portugal, Spain and Italy successively leave the Eurozone.[5] In itself, the Grexit scenario involves comparatively small growth effects for Europe and the global economy. The total GDP loss in the forty-two countries that account for more than 90 per cent of global GDP would amount to € 674 billion by 2020. But geographically, the effects would vary widely. In Greece, cumulative GDP losses by 2020 would amount to 94 per cent of 2013 GDP, but in Germany and the United States just 2.9 and 0.9 per cent, respectively. France, Portugal and Bulgaria would be affected relatively greatly, with cumulative GDP losses of about 8 per cent in each case.

The contrasting GPSI exit scenario illustrates the potential contagion effects: If all four vulnerable countries were to leave, a global recession would ensue. France would be hit especially hard on account of exposure of its banks. Here cumulative GDP loss by 2020 would reach 154 per cent of 2013 GDP. Italy's cumulative GDP loss of about 75 per cent of 2013 GDP would be a little higher than Germany's (69 per cent). The figure for the United States would be almost 25 per cent and for China about 49 per cent. While such calculations are based on numerous assumptions and thus lie in the realm of speculation, they certainly demonstrate that only a clinically isolated Grexit would avoid significant harm to the other Eurozone countries. But in reality the interconnectedness of economies and financial markets means that isolating Greece is an unlikely proposition.[6]

Regardless of the economic consequences, the legal situation for a country seeking to leave the Euro is far from clear because the European Treaties provide no explicit legal basis for such.[7] Here, Regulation (EC) No 974/98 on the introduction of the Euro, under which the Euro replaced the Greek drachma at a fixed exchange rate, is of crucial importance. This meant the loss of unrestricted monetary sovereignty. A legal amendment would be required to end application of Regulation 974/98 to Greece. The only possible legal basis for such an "exit regulation" amendment would be Article 140 (3) TFEU – adopted unanimously without the involvement of the European Parliament.[8]

But the discussion does not end with a temporary exit by one country. Across the political spectrum the demand for a dissolution of the Euro, a return to national currencies and flexible exchange rates is no longer taboo. For the sake of argument, one can approach the debate from different angles. Wolfgang Streeck, for example, sees the root of the problem in the "market-expanding rationalisation project" of the single currency.[9] To him, the road to political union is a path straight to "unitary-Jacobin" statehood. At the same time, he sees strengthening of the national aspect as enhancing the nation *(Staatsvolk)* as the source of legitimacy. In economic terms, Streeck (and others such as Martin Höpner[10]) equate this with a dismantling of EMU. The line of argument is plausible: In a very heterogeneous economic space, standard economic policies cannot do justice to the different national "varieties of capitalism". Salvation is sought in flexible exchange rates, restored adaptability and competitiveness (see also the contribution by Hacker and Koch in this volume). The pre-Euro epoch of the European Monetary System, which sought convergence of inflation, interest and exchange rates around largely non-binding targets, and was backed up by market interventions, could serve as a historical model.

What has been skepticism over the adequacy of uniform solutions for economically and politically diverse states has become a far-reaching demand for competition and the demonisation of any form of (even temporary) financial transfer by the right-wing populist Alternative for Germany (AfD), heavily influenced by its founding father Bernd Lucke (who, however, left the party in the meanwhile). The dogmatic starting point of this position is the ordoliberal school with its insistence on responsibility and liability and the idea of decentralised competition at the level of states. Two arguments must be cited against both opponents of transfers – notoriously concerned about the supposed good of the taxpayer – and the proponents of dismantling the currency entirely: Certainty of the economic achievements of the Economic and Monetary Union and uncertainty over the risks of dismantling it. Eventually, all Euro members (and not just Germany as a major exporter) profit to this day from the trademarks of the single currency: Economies of scale in an internal market with a single currency, reduced transaction costs in cross-border trade, and enhanced transparency. These advantages must be balanced against the risk of economic instability. A return to national currencies – as in the case of Grexit – will probably involve not only disruption through the reintroduction of old or new currencies, but in the medium term also see a return of the curse of currency speculation. The weaknesses of the loose EMS system were brutally exposed in the 1990s. Any reopening of the currency market channel is likely to worsen the vulnerability of weak ex-Euro countries rather than improving their competitiveness. The risks of a dismantling of the single currency are certainly not foreseeable, the potentials uncertain. "Plan A" described in preceding Chapter is better equipped to solve the undeniable problems of asymmetrical macro-economic developments (see the Chapters by Jeromin Zettelmeyer and Daniela Schwarzer in this volume).

LEAVING THE EU – THE BREXIT EXAMPLE

Slogans like a "multi-speed Europe" and "variable geometry" are bandied about today. They reflect more than ideas about focussing on deepening integration between a limited number of states pursuing economic and fiscal union. At the latest since the Brexit referendum, these catchwords are also associated with the idea of retreating from the level of integration already achieved. Here the upcoming British withdrawal from the EU is only one symbol of a Europe pulling in different directions, in which crises have accelerated centrifugal forces. And this is by no means restricted to the idea of crisis-stricken countries leaving. Alongside the prominent example of the United Kingdom, the course of the financial crisis has witnessed a revival of populist nationalist currents in a series of countries. Concretely, for example Ireland, the Netherlands and Cyprus are being discussed as the next to go after Brexit.[11]

Economic consequences of Brexit

The economic impact of Brexit, as an example for others possibly considering leaving the EU, are outlined in the following. Of course, quantitative forecasts about the effects of the United Kingdom withdrawing from the EU are by necessity laden with uncertainty, especially as this involves predicting impacts on international trade.[12] Where there is no uncertainty, however, is the fact that the United Kingdom is closely bound up with the EU. More than 50 per cent of the United Kingdom's exports go to EU Member States and more than 50 per cent of its imports originate in the EU. So in qualitative terms there seems to be no doubt that trade integration will decline, both with the EU and with the global economy.

Opinions diverge as to whether Brexit will ultimately be positive for the United Kingdom because of possible savings. Declining integration in the global economy is likely to have a dampening effect on British economic growth. On the other side of the ledger, such welfare losses may be counterbalanced by ending contributions to the EU budget. Concretely, various analyses of the pros and cons of EU membership arrive at different conclusions. A study by the Eurosceptic think tank Open Europe, for example, asserts that the best case for British economic growth would be plus 1.6 per cent by 2030, the worst case minus 2.2 per cent. Other estimates put the range between plus 0.6 per cent and minus 0.8 per cent.[13]

The starting point in any quantitative analysis using simulation modelling is the robustness of assumptions. In the case of a country leaving the EU, scenarios can be developed to reflect differences in the extent to which trade relations with the EU are maintained. This certainly applies to the status of the EU's fundamental freedoms as the basis for unhindered movement of goods, services and workers. Another relevant question arises in relation to third states: Whether and to what extent the EU's trade agreements are modified or invalidated. This is also the point where trade relations with the global economy as a whole are affected. Three scenarios can be identified:[14] First a Brexit that leaves the United Kingdom in a comparable situation with Norway or Switzerland (soft Brexit), in which trade relations continue without tariffs (but with non-tariff trade barriers). In a second scenario, the United Kingdom applies protective tariffs to EU trade at levels comparable to those with the United States. And in a third scenario the country becomes isolated, with all the effects of scenario two plus the loss of all advantages from existing trade agreements. According to calculations by ifo-Institut, the balance for the United Kingdom is negative in all three scenarios – even after the saving of the billions paid into the EU budget is taken into account. Even in a soft Brexit (first scenario) the net losses would be 0.1 per cent of GDP. The losses increase with the degree of economic isolation, and are exacerbated by dynamic effects such as the decline in productivity growth due to lower pressure of competition. In the third scenario, British real per-capita GDP in 2030 could be up to 14 per cent below the baseline scenario of remaining in the EU.[15]

It must also be remembered that different sectors would be affected to different degrees. The consequences for trade-intensive sectors, especially chemicals, engineering and car-making, are regarded as especially grave because their value chains are international. Beyond this, disadvantageous consequences are seen in a decline in cross-border trade having a negative effect on productivity because it lessens the pressure on businesses to increase their competitiveness through investment and innovation.

Brexit will also be economically disadvantageous for the EU, even if to a smaller extent than for the United Kingdom. For Germany declining trade is estimated to reduce real per-capita GDP by 0.1 to 0.3 per cent by 2030. Here too, the impact varies according to the sectoral vulnerability of value chains. For the EU-27 as a whole, the fall in real per-capita GDP caused by a reduction in trade with the United Kingdom is put at between 0.1 per cent for a soft Brexit scenario and almost 0.4 per cent in the event of isolation.[16]

All these calculations differ depending on the study and the underlying assumptions. But quantitatively speaking, these studies also fail to include further significant variables that might have both economic and political consequences. One significant channel for possible harm is uncertainty over future developments. Especially for economic actors, this leads to a high degree of planning insecurity, which creates considerable investment risks. The financial markets' very first reactions to the referendum clearly demonstrated the worries of business. Uncertainty about the country's status after its decision to leave, future relations with the EU, the legal basis for trade relations and the repercussions for trade agreements with non-EU states would all, over a period lasting potentially several years, harm the investment climate – above all in the United Kingdom.

The legal framework for Brexit

What do the European Treaties say about withdrawal? The modalities for the exit process laid out in Article 50 TEU make one thing quite clear: A rapid departure is not to be expected. Moreover, a series of political obstacles are likely to create a stony path. To begin the process the British government must notify the European Council of its intention to leave – a step which was taken in March 2017.

Then the European Council must adopt "guidelines" on the withdrawal to serve as the basis for an exit agreement between the EU and the United Kingdom – this happened in April 2017. The twist here is that while the United Kingdom is not at the table to negotiate the guidelines, all the other Member States must agree to them unanimously.[17] Up until and including the adoption of the guidelines, the Member States have acted unanimously, which is astonishing given the heterogeneity of interests involved. It remains to be seen whether this unanimity remains firm once it becomes clearer that certain exit deals favour some Member States more than others.

All parties involved also face pressure due to the *sunset clause*, which stipulates that if no agreement is reached, the withdrawal comes into effect automatically two years after formal notification. The danger of a *"Braccident"* with devastating economic consequences is acute if the parties fail to reach an agreement. The deadline can be extended, but this requires unanimity in the Council and British agreement.

Following the adoption of the guidelines, the Council is to negotiate a bilateral exit agreement with the United Kingdom, whose approval only requires a qualified majority in the Council (20 of the 27 remaining states representing at least 65 per cent of the EU's population). This constitutes a further reason why unanimity on the guidelines in the European Council in the absence of – at least visible – tactical games and veto threats was somewhat surprising.

Political implementation of Brexit

The actual economic costs of Brexit will depend heavily on the outcome of the talks. What is certain is that there is more than one path for a country leaving the EU. Various arrangements are conceivable, in which both political and economic attachment to the European integration objective can be preserved. Here the EU faces a tricky balancing act. Because preserving the internal market is of great importance to the continental European economies, they will want to maintain close ties with an important country like the United Kingdom. But conceding too favourable conditions would open the door for other countries seeking to leave to seek a similarly good deal. Various models would be conceivable: One would be to base the relationship on the EU's association agreements with Switzerland, Iceland, Liechtenstein and Norway. If the other EEA states were agreeable, it would also appear possible for the United Kingdom to join the European Economic Area.

It lies in the interests of all parties involved for the almost universally accepted historic and economic heart of the integration project – the internal market – to continue to be pursued in one or form. Given that participation in the internal market presupposes a right to participate in decisions concerning the regulations involved, associate membership with selective participation in decisions of the Council of Ministers would be one possible solution. That would leave the United Kingdom in a privileged position compared to the existing relationships with Switzerland and Norway. These could for their part serve as a point of reference for ensuring that the United Kingdom's economic relations with the EU remained as liberal as possible after it leaves.

Politically, therefore, a soft Brexit is probably the most likely option. This could take the form of agreeing an associated status taking into consideration that the United Kingdom has been a long-standing member of the EU and has to date adopted the *acquis communautaire*. In the best case, some form of soft Brexit, it should be assumed that alongside integration in the European Customs Union, extensive preservation of the economic fundamental freedoms will be agreed (although with reservations on the British side). Such an "internal market light" would be one means to cushion the economic impacts of Brexit.

Both sides will conduct the withdrawal talks with the objective of minimising the economic harm described above. But in order to avoid domino effects, the EU faces pressure to send a message that other EU members seeking to leave cannot expect overly generous concessions. The British example will undoubtedly expose the growing heterogeneity of enthusiasm for integration across the EU. And it will consolidate the situation of differentiated integration within the EU. Other EU-sceptical governments will join the nationalist bandwagon, and may attempt to withdraw from the EU in areas of national importance. To that extent, differentiated integration will be more the rule than the exception.

In the exit negotiations on the basis of Article 50 TEU, the British position is likely to be moderated by the fact that leaving the EU is associated with a loss of influence. This first of all has consequences for the United Kingdom, which relinquishes all influence over the fate of the EU. Considering that all the EU's economic policy decisions will continue to have external effects on the United Kingdom, giving up its seat on the European Council is disadvantageous. With respect to the associated changes in the balance of power between EU institutions, the loss of a free-trade heavyweight will boost protectionist interests within the EU.

Finally, the potential political contagion effects remain a central factor of uncertainty. If the United Kingdom takes the path of economic and political independence, this could accelerate centrifugal political forces in an already fragile Europe. Populist nationalist currents would be boosted and other states could be tempted to follow the British example – or at least demand greater independence within the EU. The bottom line for Brexit is: Even if strict isolation does not appear desirable to either side, the process will inevitably lead to economic losses (both in the United Kingdom and in the EU) and create considerable and largely unforeseeable political risks. If a country leaves the EU, this also expands the basis for an even stronger differentiation of the EU's relations with non-members. There obviously needs to be a clear graduation among non-members. The fact that decades of accepting the EU's *acquis communautaire* will leave "ex-EU states" closer than other associated non–member states needs to be reflected both in the closeness of economic relations and in the institutional setup.

Dismantling Schengen

Aside from economic crisis, the recent movements of refugees have revealed another problem facing the EU. Appeals for "European solidarity" and fair burden-sharing went unheard in the face of national egotisms and unilateralism. Right-wing populist parties have made gains, undermining the willingness of many EU states to accept refugees. The refugee crisis upended the Dublin Rules, leading to uncontrollable movements of refugees. In response, several states reintroduced national border controls and thus called into question the Schengen Agreement. Although strictly speaking temporary border controls are permitted under Schengen, the EU's inability to agree upon a collective line to tackle the refugee crisis encouraged discussion as to the desirability of greater national leeway in managing refugee flows, and thus also in establishing national border controls.

Consistently pursuing the idea of greater national sovereignty over border controls would call into question the continued existence of the Schengen Agreement, which came into force in 1995 and now includes 26 states. It provides for the abolition of passport controls at internal Schengen borders. The Schengen rules also provide for standardisation of entry and residence regulations and the issuing of single visas for the Schengen area as a whole.

What cost abandoning Schengen?

A series of empirical studies examine the economic effect of the Schengen Agreement. Dane Davis and Thomas Gift estimate that membership in Schengen increased bilateral trade by 10 to 15 per cent between 1980 and 2011.[18] Conversely, considerable friction is forecast in the event of Schengen collapsing. According to calculations by Vincent Aussilloux and Boris Le Hir, border controls would reduce trade between the Schengen countries by 10 to 20 per cent.[19]

Perhaps the most comprehensive analysis of impacts is that prepared by Prognos.[20] Calculations of the costs of reintroducing border controls must first define the type and scope of costs involved. Concretely, the reintroduction of border controls means that travel documents and often also vehicles need to be checked when a person crosses a border. This would result in long waiting times for HGV drivers, commuters and tourists. Decentralised production processes depending on just-in-time deliveries would suffer, as would value chains relying on deliveries from different EU states. This would influence the structure of value chains and indirectly also companies' location decisions and price competitiveness.

The starting point for economic cost calculations is the degree of obstruction to cross-border trade. At the level of businesses this would increase transaction and personnel costs, hamper just-in-time production systems and potentially require expanded warehousing. At the macro-economic level, relevant import costs would rise because of the greater time required for border crossings, which can be expressed in tariff equivalents.[21] Aussilloux and Le Hir put the rise in cost of goods at 3 per cent, while other studies of tariff equivalents put the figure between 1.4 and 1.7 per cent.[22] As with quantifications of economic costs of a country leaving the Euro or the EU, the forecasts depend heavily on their assumptions and vary with the frequency and efficiency of border controls and the adaptability of commercial logistics.

According to Prognos, economic costs can be estimated as follows: In a conservative scenario (border controls in the Schengen area increase import prices in intra-European trade by 1 per cent), the German economy would grow on average by 0.03 percentage points less annually through 2025 compared to a scenario of open borders. Cumulated over ten years, the costs would amount to € 77 billion. In a worse scenario (border controls in the Schengen area increase import prices in intra-European trade by 3 per cent) the average GDP loss for Germany would be 0.08 per cent, which would amount to € 235 billion in total lost GDP growth by 2025. The costs to other Western European countries would be of a similar order of magnitude. On average the annual loss would be 0.04, respectively 0.12 percentage points compared to the situation with open borders. So at first glance the economic costs of dismantling Schengen do not appear to be horrendous. This, however, fails to take account of macro-economically relevant costs of restrictions on daily commuting. For workers, these can be classed as loss of time which could otherwise be used for more productive purposes.

Political repercussions of a Schengen collapse

The political repercussions of a termination of the Schengen Agreement are likely to be more weighty than the economic. First of all, these would include security aspects: Security-relevant data that has to date been shared across the Schengen area would in future have to be exchanged at the bilateral level. This would hamper the fight against human trafficking, drug crime, organised crime and international terrorism. Judicial cooperation would also be affected.

As in the exit scenarios discussed above, the real explosiveness of abandoning Schengen would likely lie in its political ramifications. Retrenching integration in one of its core areas, border controls, would mark a watershed in EU history. It would be tantamount to admitting that the Member States of the EU are no longer willing or able to overcome their national egotisms for the sake of coordinated action at the EU level. After waves of economic and financial crisis and unresolved controversies over recurring bailouts and rescue packages always ended with agreements, reintroduction of national border controls would send a message that the EU is incapable of reaching agreement in certain fields. A suspension of Schengen would obviously set a poor example for other areas of the integration process.

SUMMARY

"Plan B" would involve the European integration process taking turns that are less desirable from the political and economic perspective. It outlines paths that result from a continuing dynamic of disintegration. Their roots are found in the various crises of recent years, which call into question parts of the previously untouchable *acquis communautaire*. Concretely, this concerns the stability of membership in EMU and the question of whether it should enable a member to leave – and thus operate as a club with members joining and leaving. In practice this is realistically likely to apply only to Greece. Economically the risks of leaving are unforeseeable. Despite rapidly assumed gains in competitiveness, the impact analysis for the affected country is fatal because of inevitable default and economic collapse. The uncontrollable contagion effects for other countries are liable to be devastating. The costs for the other Euro states would also be enormous.

Dissolution of the single currency would go another big step further. The apparent benefits (better adjustment of national economies, regained competitiveness, greater legitimacy of national state regulation) are likely to be cancelled out in practice by the crisis-susceptibility of such a "European Bretton Woods" system, as illustrated by experience with the pre-Euro EMS. Metaphorically speaking, unwinding the Economic and Monetary Union is likely to be like trying to squeeze toothpaste back into the tube.

In economic terms the negative impact of Brexit will be considerably smaller than that of an uncontrolled withdrawal from the Euro. All Brexit scenarios project negative effects, but these are in their nature and extent considerably smaller than in the case of a country leaving the Euro. The abolition of Schengen and the reintroduction of border controls also causes costs to be incurred, but these remain within reason.

While disintegration with EMU is likely to involve considerably greater economic costs than a non-Euro member leaving the EU or the abolition of Schengen, the political repercussions of all three developments would be negative in all respects. A Grexit would prove that the Eurozone's *governance* has failed in both fiscal and monetary terms. A Brexit could encourage other countries where anti-European forces are also gaining ground. Similarly the abolition of Schengen would shake one of the central pillars (and taboos) of European understanding of integration. These are all pessimistic paths that would best be avoided – and with the Brexit referendum we have already embarked upon one of them.

Notes

[1] | Häberle, Peter (2015): Fünf Krisen im EU-Europa – Weltweite Implikationen, Möglichkeiten und Grenzen der Verfassungstheorie für Europa, *Archiv des Völkerrechts*, vol. 53, no. 4, pp. 409–423.
[2] | Rudolf, Markus (2012): *Die Kosten eines Euro-Zerfalls für Europa sind hoch*, https://www.whu.edu/fakultaet-forschung/finance-accounting-group/finanzwirtschaft/aktuelles/aktuelles-einzelansicht/article/die-kosten-eines-euro-zerfalls-fuereuropa-sind-hoch (last accessed 14/07/2016).
[3] | Fratzscher, Marcel, Fuest, Clemens et al. (2013): Ein Plädoyer für den Euro, *Süddeutsche Zeitung* (1 June 2013), www.sueddeutsche.de/wirtschaft/plaedoyer-fuerden-euro-top-oekonomen-attackieren-alternative-fuer-deutschland-1.1685686 (last accessed 03/07/2016).
[4] | ifo Institut (2015): Möglicher Verlust des deutschen Staates bei einem Staatskonkurs Griechenlands (6 January 2015); https://www.cesifo-group.de/ifoHome/presse/Presse mitteilungen/Pressemitteilungen-Archiv/2015/Q1/press 20150106_Griechenland/ main/0/text_files/file0/document/GRexit_Haftung_Deutschlands.pdf (last accessed 03/07/2016).

5 | Bertelsmann Stiftung (2012): *Wirtschaftliche Folgen eines Euro-Austritts der südeuropäischen Mitgliedsstaaten*, Policy Brief 2012/06, 2012.
6 | Bertelsmann Stiftung (2012).
7 | Herrmann, Christoph (2015): Auf der Suche nach dem Ariadnefaden: von den rechtlichen Schwierigkeiten von Grexit und Graccident, VerfBlog (16 March 2015), http://verfassungsblog.de/auf-der-suche-nach-dem-ariadnefaden-von-den-rechtlichen-schwierigkeiten-von-grexit-und-graccident/ (accessed 3 July 2016).
8 | Herrmann, Christoph (2015).
9 | Streeck, Wolfgang (2012): Gekaufte Zeit – Die vertagte Krise des demokratischen Kapitalismus, Frankfurter Adorno-Vorlesung 2012
10 | Höpner, Martin (2015): Man hätte den Euro niemals einführen dürfen, *Zeit* (online) (7 August 2015); www.zeit.de/wirtschaft/2015-08/euro-waehrungsunion-kriseeuropa (last accessed 03/07/2016).
11 | Global Counsel (2015): *Brexit: The Impact on the UK and the EU* (June 2015); https://www.global-counsel.co.uk/sites/default/files/special-reports/downloads/Global %20Counsel_Impact_of_Brexit.pdf (last accessed 05/07/2016).
12 | See for example Bertelsmann Stiftung (2015): *Brexit – Mögliche wirtschaftliche Folgen eines britischen EU-Austritts*, Policy Brief 2015/05, https://www.bertelsmann-stiftung.de/de/publikationen/publikation/did/policy-brief-201505-brbrexit-moegliche-wirtschaftliche-folgen-eines-britischen-eu-austrit-1/ (last accessed 05/07/2016).
13 | Persson, Mats et al. (2015): *What if ...? The Consequences, Challenges and Opportunities Facing Britain Outside EU*, Open Europe Report 3/2015, London et al., http://openeurope.org.uk/intelligence/britain-and-the-eu/what-if-there-were-abrexit/ (last accessed 05/07/2016).
14 | Bertelsmann Stiftung (2015).
15 | Bertelsmann Stiftung (2015).
16 | Bertelsmann Stiftung (2015).
17 | Thiele, Alexander (2016): Der Austritt aus der EU – Hintergründe und rechtliche Rahmenbedingungen eines 'Brexit', *Europarecht*, no. 3, 2016.
18 | Davis, Dane, and Gift, Thomas (2014): The Positive Effects of the Schengen Agreement on European Trade, *World Economy* 37 (11), pp. 1541–1557.
19 | Aussilloux, Vincent, and Le Hir, Boris (2016): *The Economic Cost of Rolling Back Schengen*, Analytical Note 39, Paris: France Stratégie, www.strategie.gouv.fr/sites/strategie.gouv.fr/files/atoms/files/the_economic_cost_of_rolling_back_schengen_0.pdf (last accessed 06/07/2016).
20 | Prognos (2016): *Abkehr vom Schengen-Abkommen: Kurzstudie* (15 February 2016), www.prognos.com/uploads/tx_atwpubdb/20160215_Prognos_Kurzstudie_-_Abkehr_vom_Schengen-Abkommen__002_.pdf (last accessed 06/07/2016).
21 | Aussilloux and Le Hir (2016); Prognos (2016).
22 | Prognos (2016).

12. Three scenarios for the Eurozone – and conclusions

Alexander Schellinger and Philipp Steinberg

The Brexit vote has shaken the European Union to its core, coming after a series of earnest crises regarding the Euro, refugee flows and the war in Ukraine. In this volume we address the future of the Eurozone and thus that of the EU. We hope to invigorate the debate by presenting proposals for the reforms needed in order to rectify the deficits. What we want to emphasise above all is the political, economic and social conditions of the Eurozone. Only if we understand their relationship is there a chance for progress, for conceptual analyses and prescriptive policy recommendations.

THREE SCENARIOS

We can identify three fundamental scenarios for the future development of the Eurozone.

Scenario 1: Incremental change

This is the most likely course, limited to relatively small, incremental change to the architecture of the Eurozone (and the EU). Even after the Brexit referendum this scenario does not include a window of opportunity for fundamental reforms. The heterogeneity of interests across Europe and a widespread Euroscepticism preclude Treaty amendments. More substantial reforms towards a "fiscal union" of the kind discussed in this volume cannot be implemented.

In Chapter 2 Christian Deck analyses the conflicts of interest between the largest Member States, and, in particular, also between the European and national levels. Mark Schieritz (Chapter 5) and Björn Hacker and Cédric M. Koch (Chapter 6) demonstrate how the German position on Europe is structurally tied to economic beliefs and interests. Due to the particular governance framework and the specific constellation of actors there is no real momentum to carry through structural modifications to the Eurozone of the kind proposed in this volume, in particular by Peter Becker (Chapter 10), Henrik Enderlein (Chapter 3), Daniela Schwarzer (Chapter 9) and Jeromin Zettelmeyer (Chapter 8). Nevertheless, even in this scenario it is conceivable for shifts to occur that partially implement or at least prepare the ground for some of the reforms proposed in this volume. That is what we now address in this section.

The bottom line in this scenario is most likely for the Eurozone countries to agree that the Eurozone and the EU need to keep their promise of prosperity and revive their economic dynamism. Henrik Enderlein and Michael Dauderstädt convincingly outline the dangers associated with the persistent economic and social divergence that has created a "social catastrophe" in southern Europe (see Chapter 4). So the Eurozone must reaffirm its promise of prosperity and back it up with concrete action. Equitable prosperity uniting economic growth with solidarity is the basis for political stability and European cohesion. This scenario of incremental change is most likely to produce progress on developing the Single Market (in particular, the digital single market), on freedom of services and on product market reforms. Even here resistance is strong, especially concerning services and product markets. But the advantage of these areas is that the tried and tested Community method can be applied (legislation proposed by the Commission and adopted by the European Parliament and the Council), the required qualified majorities are plausible and no Treaty amendments would be required. Especially in the areas of product markets and developing the internal market for services there is still great potential to enable economic growth. Investment capability could also be strengthened, building on the European Fund for Strategic Investments. It would be conceivable for a central investment framework to be established combining new growth impulses with more determined modernisation investments in the trans-European transport and energy networks, in creating a European gigabit network, in training for a digital economy, in fighting youth unemployment, and in risk capital and start-up financing.

It would also be conceivable to continue to reform the Stability and Growth Pact without altering the fundamental parameters of its present iteration. These are specified in a protocol to the Treaty on the Functioning of the European Union and as such possess the character of primary law. Any modification would thus require unanimity. The debt restructuring instrument that Jeromin Zettelmeyer regards as a vital part of comprehensive reform would therefore, however, be problematic, as its introduction would require unanimity. That said, options below the threshold of Treaty amendments are conceivable here too.[1] Already today all new government bonds come with so-called collective action clauses that force all creditors to take losses in debt restructuring (subject to a specified qualified majority). The introduction of a Eurozone budget with new own resources would require a Treaty amendment.

But a reallocation of existing resources is thinkable under this scenario nonetheless. In principle this could be accomplished without a Treaty amendment, given that reallocation of funds between (existing) budget lines within the headings and across the various years of the Multiannual Financial Framework is an established EU budgetary technique. The preconditions are merely that scope exists and the ceiling is not exceeded. It would also be possible to create a new budget line – again without a Treaty amendment – as the keystone of a fiscal policy. In this case, however, it remains unclear how this new budget line would be funded: If existing EU-own resources were used – in the absence of specific own resources for the Eurozone – this would amount to non-Euro Member States participating in funding the new budget line, which is unlikely to be politically communicable. On the other hand, we see no reason why a mechanism could not be established whereby the Euro Member States relinquish funds from other budget lines that have already been assigned to them (but not yet spent) in order to fund the new budget line (again, only within the limits of the existing budget ceiling). Amending the Own Resources Decision could also create new own resources to fund a Eurozone budget. But this would be associated with procedural obstacles almost as great as those for a Treaty amendment, as it would require an unanimous decision by the Council and all Euro Member States would have to ratify such in accordance with their respective constitutions. Additionally, EU-own resources being raised only by Eurozone countries and used only for purposes of the Eurozone would also be a new departure.

The existing provisions of the European Treaties are insufficient to permit the introduction of a separate Eurozone budget. Neither the EU's responsibility for economic and monetary policy nor that for internal market harmonisation apply in this case. Recourse to the flexibility clause is not legally justifiable for such a far-reaching budget measure. One legally solid route to creating a fiscal capacity in the form of a Eurozone budget is therefore to introduce a new power similar to the arrangements for the structural funds. The inter-governmental mechanism could be used to create a fund stocked by contributions from the participating states (analogously to the structures of the European Stability Mechanism). But this would require a Treaty between the participating (Euro) states and would thus have the same practical implications as a Treaty amendment.

Even if the scenario of incremental change can be regarded as the most likely, it is still associated with considerable risks. It remains doubtful whether it can prevent a creeping dissolution process, while it is unlikely to create adequate safeguards to respond to any further outbreak of crisis. Large economic and social divergences in the Eurozone and the refugee crisis demand solutions that strengthen responsiveness at the Eurozone level. But in this scenario the Community is too weak to make any effective contribution, while the Europe of national governments is blocking each other (see Chapter 2 by Christian Beck).

In many quarters the crisis responses of recent years have been perceived as setting north against south, Greek against German, while the refugee crisis has created a new rift between eastern and western Europe. The decades of broad public confidence in Europe (and in partners' national governments) appears to have largely evaporated.

In this context, European consensus is coming under increasing pressure from the right-wing populists who are enjoying considerable growth in support almost everywhere in Europe – as was confirmed by the British referendum. It is questionable whether and how incremental reforms can resolve the Eurozone's problems quickly and effectively enough to rein in this right-wing populism, as the new political forces are stepping up the pressure on established parties by proposing national solutions and demanding the end of the Economic and Monetary Union and the Single Market. By promoting a renationalisation of the political debate, they are making it increasingly difficult for established forces to argue for collective solutions. If the Eurozone's responsiveness remains as weak as it has been to date and unexpected crises occur – such as the departure of a Member State or a new round of the refugee or currency crisis – there is a danger that incremental change will lead not to gradual improvement but instead function as an accelerator in a grand dissolution process. Yet – as we have outlined – even in this scenario there are possibilities to take steps in the right direction.

Scenario 2: Extensive reforms towards fiscal union

This scenario could include elements of incremental improvement but also implements further-reaching reforms that are widely discussed under the heading "fiscal union". It starts from a need to reform the Eurozone that can no longer be addressed incrementally, but requires steps towards closer fiscal integration. Especially the lack of macroeconomic instruments at Eurozone level is pinpointed here (see Chapter 8 by Henrik Enderlein and Jeromin Zettelmeyer). Possible solutions would include a Eurozone budget, bolder reform of the economic policy framework, debt restructuring regimes and measures to strengthen social cohesion (see Chapter 10 by Peter Becker), which could to some extent also have an economically stabilising effect (for example the European short-time work allowance scheme). Institutional innovations like a Eurozone finance minister would also be put into practice (see Chapter 9 by Daniela Schwarzer).

Many regard this extensive reform scenario as unlikely because it would require Treaty amendments at a time when further integration appears impossible in light of observable disintegration tendencies. In this context referendums would be unacceptable and doomed to failure, as the Brexit referendum left no doubt. These arguments cannot be dismissed out of hand. But if we do nothing but bend to that which is expedient without discussing what is politically and economically sensible, there is no chance of the necessary changes coming about. The extensive reform scenario will only be feasible if it can be shown that it places the citizens of Europe – rather than abstract institutional debates – at its heart and that it is about "improving" rather than "deepening". There is a chance of this succeeding when one recalls that Eurozone GDP in 2016 was still only marginally higher than in 2008, that unemployment is still unacceptably high in most Member States and that Eurozone growth – outside a handful of Member States like Germany – is still weak. Moreover, social inequality has increased in almost all Member States (including Germany) constituting an economic as well as social problem (see Chapter 4 by Michael Dauderstädt).

The reform scenario will only come about if its added value for the individual is visible and if such an assertive political coalition can form in Germany and together with actors from other Member States. This scenario can only be communicated in Germany if there are no new institutionalised transfers permanently redistributing resources away from Germany and a few other states. We believe that the proposals in this volume pass that test. But it is just as important to recognise that Germany cannot isolate itself for long from developments in the other Euro states and the Community as a whole.

Scenario 3: Dismantling the Eurozone

The Eurozone's ability to address problems is regarded as inadequate in many quarters. Consequently, actors on the left and right also bring a dismantling scenario into play (see the Chapters by Armin Steinbach and by Björn Hacker and Cédric M. Koch). The problems identified here are similar to those in the other two scenarios, but greater weight is given to the loss of national macroeconomic policy instruments with the advent of EMU. Proponents of dismantling question whether the Eurozone has any problem-solving capacity at all. If the political, economic and social framework means that problems cannot be rectified through measures at the level of the Eurozone, the obvious consequence is to dismantle. Opinions diverge concerning the details, but the idea is that dismantling will restore political and economic agency. Against this scenario, it is argued that the promise of going back to an idyll of national sovereignty is an illusion. National unilateralism and national autonomy are impossible in an increasingly globalised world. Currency devaluation, as a central argument of the proponents of dismantling both left and right, will help only briefly, if at all (see Chapter 11). In the longer term, entering this dead end will mean not gaining sovereignty, but in all probability losing it. We believe these arguments to be credible. That is why we wish – in the form of this volume – to present an alternative to Eurosceptic positions and offer solutions for an internationalised and globalised world. Scenarios 1 and 2 are complementary: Closer fiscal integration can also follow incremental improvements. But neither will be possible if the advocates of Scenario 3 come out on top.

Conclusions

In the end we are left with a question: Why do we want to develop the Eurozone as an integral component of the EU? European integration is not an end in itself, even if the functional necessity is obvious in certain respects. For example, one can explain why a monetary union can only function with a banking union and a stability mechanism, but that does not explain why European integration is necessary in the first place. Nor can normative objectives, such as post-national utopias (in the positive sense), supply satisfactory answers. And certainly not in a time where the nation-state remains the most important political frame of reference for many people. The answer to the "why" of European integration can only be a political one.

After two world wars and the subsequent Cold War, peace has always been a central motivator. But such convictions fade from generation to generation. And they remain weak, even if current developments in Ukraine and Russia demonstrate that they are anything but "history".

By far the most powerful and significant processes of change in our time are economic in nature. These forces burst into view in the global economic and financial crisis. Triggered by global financial markets, the unfolding crisis paid no heed to national borders, affecting all spheres of life. At no other point in recent decades has the unbridled force of markets gone astray been felt as tangibly as in those years. Numerous legal, political and social corrective mechanisms painstakingly established over many decades either failed or had already been abolished. Today the welfare state in many crisis countries is still groaning under the consequences. The great challenge for politics – and for economic and social actors too – is to develop national economic models under and also against the international pressure of the capital markets.[2] An answer to the question "Why Europe?" can only be given relative to this greatest challenge of our time, which is often so hastily labelled "globalisation". The role of the EU and, in particular, the Eurozone in this process is anything but unambiguous. In its contemporary form it is both agent and moderator of capitalist development under the liberal market economy model. It simultaneously promotes and undermines institutions of the social market. Especially through the crisis policies in Southern Europe it has massively eroded social production systems and has for years (for example, through internal market legislation) permanently altered national systems – sometimes but not always for the better.

Yet the new political frame of the Eurozone has also made it possible for national economic models to preserve and even develop their specificities and has generated positive growth impulses. The possibility for specific economic models to survive is demonstrated not least by the success of Germany's social market economy. It is one of the ironies of capitalism that the "German model" – whose demise had been taken for granted – has rebounded with almost shocking vigour from the global economic and financial crisis.[3] Ironic because in a system where global financial markets exert enormous pressure of convergence on all economic actors this specific form of market economy appears to prove that there can be different varieties of capitalism. Certain essential traits of this model have survived the deep transformations of the capitalist system since the 1970s,[4] even if "Deutschland AG" is no more. In fact, this system has flourished not only against but also with this capitalist dynamic. All this is of great political significance, with many of the institutions that make up this model opening up new spaces for progressive economic policy. That means economic policy that far transcends the supply/demand dichotomy, resists excessively liberalised labour markets and excessive income differentials on the Anglo-Saxon model (even in the digital age), and finds economic as well as social reasons for democratic workplace co-determination, trade union organisation, vocational training systems and so on.

The "coordinated market economy", as it is referred to in *Varieties of Capitalism*,[5] is generally shaped by national institutions such as its financing systems, social partnership, and cooperation networks between enterprises and the training system. The global success of this social production system rests on the comparative advantages of these national institutions, but also on the ongoing political embedding enabled by European integration and specifically the Eurozone. The Eurozone and the EU have long since become part of this model, and certainly not only as external (exogenous) pressures or for the size of their markets. The European dimension is an essential component of the financing system, of business collaboration, of value creation, etc. In central areas the embedding of the European market and the Economic and Monetary Union is well advanced even if aspects such as forms of workplace co-determination and social partnership are still comparatively unimportant at the European level. This Europeanisation of economic and social institutions is difficult to undo. It represents in equal parts a chance and a danger for economic development continuing on a socially equitable and productive path.

The fact that the different production models can also produce different and directly conflicting national interests is observed nowhere more clearly than in the Eurozone, with the coordinated and export-driven model of the north and the demand-driven economies of the south.[6] EMU intensifies reciprocal dependencies between its members, but does not diminish the partly systemic conflicts of interest. However, not every historically rooted institution is economically efficient and not every conflict of interest is unbridgeable. Europe can only truly profit from the diversity of its political economies (which by global comparison are not in fact really so different) if differences are perceived, if the advantages of other models are adapted and integrated. That applies to all countries alike.

On the one hand this means that national diversity in the production systems of the Member States of the EU and, in particular, of the Eurozone needs to be better protected and promoted. This includes minimum social standards and a fiscal union that generates greater economic leeway for creating growth and employment for the Eurozone and its Member States. On the other hand, it demands a reform process in the Member States (coordinated at the European level) comprising necessary structural reforms – in particular in public administration, in streamlining the tax system and tax administration, in reforming product markets and in improving conditions for private investors. This is a political task whose concrete content is defined at the national level – but whose framework must be located at the level of the Community. Only then is a sustainable Eurozone possible and only then will "social Europe" have a future.

Notes

[1] See Zettelmeyer, Jeromin (2016): A Sovereign Debt Restructuring Mechanism for the Euro Area?, in: Rehn, Olli/Zettelmeyer, Jeromin (eds.): Global Fiscal Systems: From Crisis to Sustainability, World Economic Forum, May, pp. 24–29.
[2] Abelshauser, Werner (2011): Deutsche Wirtschaftsgeschichte von 1945 bis zur Gegenwart. Munich: C. H. Beck.
[3] Unger, Brigitte (2015): The German Model: Seen by Its Neighbours. London: SE Publishing.
[4] Streeck, Wolfgang (2013): Gekaufte Zeit: Die vertagte Krise des demokratischen Kapitalismus: Frankfurter Adorno-Vorlesungen 2012. Berlin: Suhrkamp.
[5] Hall, Peter A./Soskice, David (2001) (eds.): Varieties of Capitalism: The Institutional Foundations of Comparative Advantage. Oxford: Oxford University Press.
[6] Iversen, Torben/Soskice, David et al. (2016): The Eurozone and Political Economic Institutions, Annual Review of Political Science, vol. 19, pp. 163–185.

Authors

Christian Beck, born 1981, is head of office for MEP Sven Giegold since 2014. He studied politics in Berlin and Delhi and served as member of the executive board of the Young European Federalists and spokesperson for the Berlin state working group on Europe of Alliance 90/The Greens. He has previously been a researcher in the German Bundestag.

Dr. Peter Becker, born 1963, is a researcher in the EU/Europe Research Division at Stiftung Wissenschaft und Politik in Berlin since 2004. He has previously been deputy head of the Europe department at the State Chancellery of the state of Thuringia in Erfurt and researcher at the Institut für Europäische Politik. He studied politics and modern history at the University of Bonn and gained his doctorate from the University of Trier.

Dr. Michael Dauderstädt, born 1947, is managing director of the publishing house J.H.W. Dietz. He served in various functions at the Friedrich-Ebert-Stiftung from 1980 until 2013, latterly as director of the division of economic and social policy. He studied mathematics, economics and international development in Aachen, Paris and Berlin.

Prof. Dr. Henrik Enderlein, born 1974, is director of the Jacques Delors Institute in Berlin and Vice-President and Professor of Political Economy at the Hertie School of Governance. He studied in Paris and New York, gained his doctorate at the Max-Planck-Institut für Gesellschaftsforschung in Cologne and worked as an economist at the European Central Bank. He has been visiting professor at Harvard University and Duke University. He is a member of the advisory board of the German Stability Council.

Prof. Dr. Björn Hacker, born 1980, has been Professor of Economic Policy at the Hochschule für Technik und Wirtschaft Berlin since 2014. He gained his doctorate on the European social model and worked for five years at Friedrich Ebert-Stiftung.

Cédric M. Koch, born 1991, is a PhD candidate at the Berlin School for Transnational Studies (BTS) at the Free University and the Social Science Research Centre (WZB) in Berlin. Before that, he has been working since 2015 at the Faculty of Economics and Law at the Hochschule für Technik und Wirtschaft Berlin. He studied international political economy and served as an advisor to Deutsche Gesellschaft für Internationale Zusammenarbeit.

Prof. Dr. Franz C. Mayer, born 1968, holds the Chair of Public Law, European Law, Public International Law, Comparative Law, and Law and Politics at the University of Bielefeld. He represented the German Bundestag at the Federal Constitutional Court in hearings on the Lisbon Treaty (2008/2009) and on aid for Greece and the Euro rescue package (2010/2011). He is also a member of the Glienicker Group and serves as an expert in parliamentary hearings on the Euro crisis.

Dr. Alexander Schellinger, born 1985, has been personal assistant to the chair of the board of Techniker Krankenkasse in Hamburg since September 2016. Previously he served as policy analyst on European economic and social policy at Friedrich-Ebert-Stiftung in Berlin and at the Federal Ministry of Labour and Social Affairs. He studied politics and economics at Columbia University in New York and the London School of Economics and gained his doctorate at the University of Bremen.

Mark Schieritz, born 1974, is economics correspondent of the German weekly *Die Zeit*. He studied at the University of Freiburg and the London School of Economics and has received numerous awards for his reporting on the Euro crisis.

Dr. Daniela Schwarzer, born 1973, is Director of the research institute of the Deutsche Gesellschaft für Auswärtige Politik (DGAP). Previously she was research director on the Board of the German Marshall Fund. She is Senior Research Professor at SAIS, Johns Hopkins University, and previously worked at Stiftung Wissenschaft und Politik and Financial Times Deutschland.

Dr. Armin Steinbach, born 1978, lawyer and economist, is Associate Member of Nuffield College (Oxford University), Senior Research Fellow at the Max-Planck-Institut für Gemeinschaftsgüter in Bonn and Jean Monnet Fellow at the European University Institute in Florence, Italy. Previously he was legal officer at the World Trade Organisation in Geneva, lawyer for Cleary Gottlieb Steen & Hamilton in Brussels and policy analyst at the Federal Ministry of Economic Affairs and Energy.

Dr. Philipp Steinberg, born 1974, has been Director General of the economic policy department at the Federal Ministry of Economic Affairs and Energy since September 2016. Previously he was head of the Minister's Office and the subdivision for political planning. After completing his doctorate in European economic law he worked as a lawyer at a large practice and joined the civil service in the Europe department of the Federal Ministry of Finance. He studied law, taxation and political economy in Berlin, Münster and Paris.

Dr. Jeromin Zettelmeyer, born 1964, is Senior Fellow at the Peterson Institute for International Economics and was previously head of the Department of Economic Policy at the Federal Ministry of Economic Affairs and Energy. After gaining his doctorate at the Massachusetts Institute of Technology in 1990 he worked for the International Monetary Fund, largely in the research department. From 2008 to early 2014 he was Director of Research and Deputy Chief Economist at the European Bank for Reconstruction and Development.

Social Sciences and Cultural Studies

Carlo Bordoni
Interregnum
Beyond Liquid Modernity

2016, 136 p., pb.
19,99 € (DE), 978-3-8376-3515-7
E-Book
PDF: 17,99 € (DE), ISBN 978-3-8394-3515-1
EPUB: 17,99 € (DE), ISBN 978-3-7328-3515-7

Maik Fielitz, Laura Lotte Laloire (eds.)
Trouble on the Far Right
Contemporary Right-Wing Strategies and Practices in Europe

2016, 208 p., pb.
19,99 € (DE), 978-3-8376-3720-5
E-Book
PDF: 17,99 € (DE), ISBN 978-3-8394-3720-9
EPUB: 17,99 € (DE), ISBN 978-3-7328-3720-5

Gundolf S. Freyermuth
Games | Game Design | Game Studies
An Introduction
(With Contributions by André Czauderna, Nathalie Pozzi and Eric Zimmerman)

2015, 296 p., pb.
19,99 € (DE), 978-3-8376-2983-5
E-Book
PDF: 17,99 € (DE), ISBN 978-3-8394-2983-9

All print, e-book and open access versions of the titles in our list are available in our online shop www.transcript-verlag.de/en!

Social Sciences and Cultural Studies

Suzi Mirgani
Target Markets – International Terrorism Meets Global Capitalism in the Mall

2016, 198 p., pb.
29,99 € (DE), 978-3-8376-3352-8
E-Book: available as free open access publication
ISBN 978-3-8394-3352-2

Ramón Reichert, Annika Richterich, Pablo Abend, Mathias Fuchs, Karin Wenz (eds.)
Digital Culture & Society
Vol. 1, Issue 1 – Digital Material/ism

2015, 242 p., pb.
29,99 € (DE), 978-3-8376-3153-1
E-Book
PDF: 29,99 € (DE), ISBN 978-3-8394-3153-5

Ramón Reichert, Annika Richterich, Pablo Abend, Mathias Fuchs, Karin Wenz (eds.)
Digital Culture & Society (DCS)
Vol. 2, Issue 2/2016 – Politics of Big Data

2016, 154 p., pb.
29,99 € (DE), 978-3-8376-3211-8
E-Book
PDF: 29,99 € (DE), ISBN 978-3-8394-3211-2

All print, e-book and open access versions of the titles in our list are available in our online shop www.transcript-verlag.de/en!